Louis and Brigitte Bell
4/2/69

THE WIDENING GYRE

Turning and turning in the widening gyre
The falcon cannot hear the falconer . . .

W. B. YEATS, *The Second Coming*

THE WIDENING GYRE

Crisis and Mastery in Modern Literature
by JOSEPH FRANK

INDIANA UNIVERSITY PRESS
BLOOMINGTON & LONDON

Copyright © 1963 by Rutgers, The State University
First Midland Book edition 1968 by arrangement with
Rutgers University Press
All rights reserved
No part of this book may be reproduced or utilized in any form or by any means, electronic or mechanical, including photocopying and recording, or by any information storage and retrieval system, without permission in writing from the publisher. The Association of American University Presses Resolution on Permissions constitutes the only exception to this prohibition.

Library of Congress catalog card number: 68-27360

Manufactured in the United States of America

Permission to quote has been granted by the following periodicals in which these essays first appeared:

The Sewanee Review: "Spatial Form in Modern Literature," Volume LIII, Number 2 (Spring, 1945), Number 3 (Summer, 1945), Number 4 (Autumn, 1945); "Malraux's Metaphysics of Art," Volume LXX, Number 4 (Autumn, 1962); "Lionel Trilling and the Conservative Imagination," Volume LXIV, Number 2 (Spring, 1956).

The Hudson Review: "Malraux: The Image of Man," Volume XIV, Number 1 (Spring, 1961); "Romanticism and Reality in Robert Penn Warren," Volume IV, Number 2 (Summer, 1951).

The Chicago Review: "Reaction as Progress: Thomas Mann's *Dr. Faustus*," Volume 15, Number 2 (Autumn, 1961).

The Minnesota Review: "The Achievement of John Peale Bishop," Volume II, Number 3 (Spring, 1962).

Partisan Review: "Ideas of Order," Volume XXII, Number 2 (Spring, 1956).

For Guiguite, with love

Foreword

This collection of essays is long overdue. Yet had it appeared as recently as five years ago, it would not have been as good as it is. At least four of the leading essays—"Spatial Form" and the essays on Mann, John Peale Bishop, and Malraux—have been rewritten and enlarged. What has actually been long overdue is the general recognition of the critical stature of Joseph Frank. This can no longer be delayed. The earlier versions of the essays have been scattered in a large number of periodicals that have supposedly been the strongholds of the New Criticism, the opponents of which have ignored Mr. Frank because there has been nothing in his essays which they could elect to attack—perhaps nothing, or very little, that they could take the time to try to understand. For Mr. Frank is not a New Critic (whatever that may be); he is a philosophical critic with an international point of view; and he is his own man. I take it that he is the most original critical mind to appear in America since the Second World War. But he first appeared during that War. His second published essay, "Spatial Form in Modern Literature," in a shorter version, came out in *The Sewanee Review* in 1945, when Mr. Frank was in his middle twenties.

In this brief Foreword I wish to dwell a little upon the importance of this essay. The groundwork of the essay is an immense knowledge of European philosophy from Descartes, Locke, and Lessing to the modern Germans, particularly Worringer, of whom he says:

> One German writer in particular exercised a strong influence on Hulme and through Hulme, by way of Eliot, probably on the whole of modern English criticism. This writer is Wilhelm Worringer, the author of the important book, *Abstraction and Empathy;* and it is in Worringer that we shall find the key to our own problem of spatial form. . . . The problem that Worringer sets out to solve is why, throughout the history of the plastic arts, there has been a continual alternation between naturalistic and non-naturalistic styles.

What Mr. Frank calls spatial form the late T. E. Hulme called "classicism," the opposite of "romanticism," and by placing his campaign for non-naturalistic art in this eighteenth-century framework, Hulme failed to see that non-naturalism *in literature* led to spatial form, the plastic effect of the instantaneous aesthetic experience, of which literature, or the arts of temporal sequence, had formerly been considered incapable. This insight represents an advance upon Worringer, and is similar to the theory of Sir Herbert Read, who, himself a "disciple" of Worringer, has justified abstract expressionism in the plastic arts and organicism in literature with an argument similar to Mr. Frank's: both the plastic and the verbal object arrest the naturalistic flux of experience at an instant of time that, having neither temporal antecedents nor temporal consequences, exists only in space.

As theory, both Frank's and Read's philosophy would be neither here nor there; that is to say, a literary theory is no better than what it can illuminate. I have elsewhere discussed Sir Herbert's doctrine of poetic organicism. The influence of Worringer upon Mr. Frank is undoubtedly important; yet more important is his empirical citation of *actual* spatial techniques in modern literature. A careful reading of the essay will surely demonstrate that the perception of spatial form preceded the theory of spatial form; and it is this direct perception, applied to almost every leading writer from Flaubert to T. S. Eliot, which makes Mr. Frank a literary critic first, and second a philosopher. The most difficult task of the philosophical aesthetician has always been to keep the art-object in sight and to prevent its disappearing into the cloud of theory. The aesthetician uses literature; the critic uses aesthetics. This is Mr. Frank's special contribution to contemporary criticism.

But to put it so is only to indicate the stance of the critic, not the astonishing versatility of the performance. The fine essays on Malraux and Ortega y Gasset are aesthetic criticism at its best: they expose the basic theories of the authors and the latent contradictions, and are thus sallies into the history of ideas which fall a little short of literary criticism or criticism of the plastic arts. (Mr. Frank's interest in the plastic arts seems to have been the result of his theory of spatial form in literature: it did not, I believe, instigate that interest.) In this book there are, in addition to "Spatial Form," at least two critical masterpieces. The essay on the later work of R. P. Blackmur, who in spite of his linguistic self-indulgence remains the most profound and searching

American critic of his generation—this essay is also the best statement that I know of the aims of the critical generation known as the New Critics. If one task of criticism is to make available a fine, neglected writer, Mr. Frank has performed that task brilliantly in the essay on John Peale Bishop. With other writers under Mr. Frank's scrutiny previous criticism gave him much to go on. With Bishop he had very little: he had to start from scratch. I say this in spite of the fact that Mr. Edmund Wilson, Mr. Blackmur, and myself have over a number of years written about Bishop; but I see now that none of the three of us knew anything about him beyond random insights. Bishop was my close friend and I thought I knew his work if anybody did. I will have to read it again and through Mr. Frank's eyes for the first time; and likewise the work of Blackmur, Trilling, and Warren. I know no other way to end this Foreword than to end on a commonplace: Joseph Frank has the disquieting gift of going to the heart of whatever matter he undertakes to expound.

Allen Tate

Preface

The following essays represent a selection from articles and reviews published over the past decade and a half. Some remain substantially as they were printed, with what I hope are improvements both in style and through the addition of supplementary material. Others embody a total reworking of old themes because, on rereading the original versions, I felt they were no longer adequate to my present grasp of the subject.

For the benefit of those who may find my choice of title arbitrary or puzzling, I might explain that the image it evokes seems to me to picture one of the crucial dilemmas of modern culture. It is a dilemma to which I return constantly in the course of these essays—the dilemma of a culture whose creations more and more tend to deny or negate some essential aspect of the human agency at their source and to escape from its control. Whether through a preference for the mythical imagination, the dehumanization of art, or the depreciation and renunciation of spirit, the same dialectic may be observed at work all through modern culture. The falcon cannot hear the falconer—or, at least, the voice of the latter becomes fainter and fainter all the time.

I discovered that the writers and books that had aroused my deepest interest were those in which this dialectic received its most wide-ranging and self-conscious expression; and that I had, without quite being aware of it myself, been drawn time and again to deal with this issue wherever I could detect it in contemporary literature. Hence the title occurred to me as a way of expressing the unifying link that, with the benefit of hindsight, I could now see ran through the disparate subjects on which I had written.

For personal encouragement, criticism, and intellectual stimulation, I should like to express my thanks to H. B. Parkes, Allen Tate, David Baumgardt, R. P. Blackmur, Francis Fergusson, R. W. B. Lewis, Ralph Ross, and Charles H. Foster.

I am also indebted to John Marshall of the Rockefeller Foundation, John U. Nef, David Grene, Peter H. von Blanckenhagen, Otto von Simson, and Edward Shils of the Committee on Social Thought of the University of Chicago, E. B. O. Borgerhoff and the Christian Gauss Seminars in Criticism at Princeton University, the Guggenheim Foundation, and the National Institute of Arts and Letters. All these persons and organizations provided either an opportunity for travel and study, or an incentive to reflection whose results have gone into one or another of these essays. I am very grateful for their support, and I hope they will find this collection not unworthy of their expectations.

The Research Council of the Graduate School of the University of Minnesota generously gave me a grant to help meet the expenses of preparing the manuscript of this volume for publication.

J. F.
New Brunswick, N. J.
1963

Contents

1 Spatial Form in Modern Literature

I. Introduction

"Lessing's *Laocoön*," André Gide once remarked, "is one of those books it is good to reiterate or contradict every thirty years." [1] Despite this excellent advice, neither of these attitudes toward *Laocoön* has been adopted by modern writers. Lessing's attempt to define the limits of literature and the plastic arts has become a dead issue; it is neither reiterated nor contradicted but simply neglected. Lessing, to be sure, occupies an honorable place in the history of criticism and aesthetics. But while his work is invariably referred to with respect, it can hardly be said to have exercised any fecundating influence on modern aesthetic thinking.* This was comprehensible enough in the nineteenth century, with its overriding passion for historicism; but it is not so easy to understand at present when so many writers on aesthetic problems are occupied with questions of form. To a historian of literature or the plastic arts, Lessing's effort to define the unalterable laws of these mediums may well have seemed quixotic. Modern critics, however, no longer overawed by the bugbear of historical method, have begun to take up again the problems he tried to solve.

Lessing's own solution to these problems seems at first glance to have little relation to modern concerns. The literary school against which the arguments of *Laocoön* were directed—the school of pictorial poetry—has long since ceased to interest the modern sensibility. Many of Lessing's conclusions grew out of a now antiquated archaeology, whose discoveries, to make matters worse, he knew mainly at second hand. But it was precisely his attempt to rise above history, to define the unalterable laws of aesthetic perception rather than to attack or defend any particular school, that gives his work the perennial freshness to which André Gide alluded. The validity of his theories does not depend on their relationship to the literary movements of his time, or on the extent of his firsthand acquaintanceship with the art works of antiquity. It is thus always possible to consider them apart from these circumstances and to use them in the analysis of later developments.

In *Laocoön* Lessing fuses two distinct currents of thought,

---

* This statement is less true now than it was approximately twenty years ago when first written. Recent years have seen a notable increase in studies concerned with the space- and time-aspects of literature and art. In part, as Wellek and Warren have remarked, this is attributable to the growing influence of Existentialist philosophy. For further references, see R. Wellek and A. Warren, *Theory of Literature* (New York: Harvest, Harcourt, Brace, 1956), p. 264.

both of great importance in the cultural history of his time. The archaeological researches of his contemporary Winckelmann had stimulated a passionate interest in Greek culture among the Germans. Lessing went back to Homer, Aristotle, and the Greek tragedians, and, using his firsthand knowledge, attacked the distorted critical theories (supposedly based on classical authority) that had filtered into France through Italian commentators and had then taken hold in Germany.

At the same time Locke and the empirical school of English philosophy had given a new impulse to aesthetic speculation. For Locke tried to solve the problem of knowledge by breaking down complex ideas into simple elements of sensation and then examining the operations of the mind to see how these sensations were combined to form ideas. This method was soon taken over by aestheticians, whose focus of interest shifted from external prescriptions for beauty to an analysis of aesthetic perception; and writers like Shaftesbury, Hogarth, Hutcheson, and Burke concerned themselves with the precise character and combination of impressions that gave aesthetic pleasure to the sensibility.

Lessing's friend and critical ally Mendelssohn popularized this method of dealing with aesthetic problems in Germany; and Lessing himself was a close student of all the works of this school. As a result, *Laocoön* stands at the confluence of these intellectual currents. Lessing analyzes the laws of aesthetic perception; shows how they prescribe necessary limitations to literature and the plastic arts; and then demonstrates how Greek writers and painters, especially his cherished Homer, created masterpieces in obedience to these laws.

Lessing's argument starts from the simple observation that literature and the plastic arts, working through different sensuous mediums, must differ in the fundamental laws governing their creation. "If it is true," Lessing wrote in *Laocoön*, "that painting and poetry in their imitations make use of entirely different means or symbols—the first, namely, of form and color in space, the second of articulated sounds in time—if these symbols indisputably require a suitable relation to the thing symbolized, then it is clear that symbols arranged in juxtaposition can only express subjects of which the wholes or parts exist in juxtaposition; while consecutive symbols can only express subjects of which the wholes or parts are themselves consecutive."

Lessing did not originate this formulation, which has a long and complicated history; but he was the first to use it systematically as an instrument of critical analysis. Form in the plastic arts, according to Lessing, is necessarily spatial because the visible aspect of objects can best be presented juxtaposed in an instant of time. Literature, on the other hand, makes use of language, composed of a succession of words proceeding through time; and it follows that literary form, to harmonize with the essential quality of its medium, must be based primarily on some form of narrative sequence.

Lessing used this argument to attack two artistic genres highly popular in his day: pictorial poetry and allegorical painting. The pictorial poet tried to paint with words; the allegorical painter to tell a story in visible images. Both were doomed to fail because their aims were in contradiction to the fundamental properties of their mediums. No matter how accurate and vivid a verbal description might be, Lessing argued, it could not give the unified impression of a visible object. No matter how skillfully figures might be chosen and arranged, a painting or a piece of sculpture could not successfully set forth the various stages of an action.

As Lessing develops his argument, he attempts to prove that the Greeks, with an unfailing sense of aesthetic propriety, respected the limits imposed on different art mediums by the conditions of human perception. The importance of Lessing's distinction, however, does not depend on these ramifications of his argument, nor even on his specific critical judgments. Various critics have quarreled with one or another of these judgments and have thought this sufficient to undermine Lessing's position; but such a notion is based on a misunderstanding of *Laocoön*'s importance in the history of aesthetic theory. It is quite possible to use Lessing's insights solely as instruments of analysis, without proceeding to judge the value of individual works by how closely they adhere to the norms he laid down; and unless this is done, as a matter of fact, the real meaning of *Laocoön* cannot be understood. For what Lessing offered was not a new set of norms but a new approach to aesthetic form.

The conception of aesthetic form inherited by the eighteenth century from the Renaissance was purely external. Greek and Roman literature—or what was known of it—was presumed to have reached perfection, and later writers could do little better than imitate its example. A horde of commentators and critics had deduced certain rules from the classical masterpieces (rules like the Aristotelian unities, of which Aristotle had never heard), and modern writers were warned to obey these rules if they wished to appeal to a cultivated public. Gradually, these rules became an immutable mold into which the material of a literary work had to be poured: the form of a work was nothing but the technical arrangement dictated by the rules. Such a superficial and mechanical notion of aesthetic form, however, led to serious perversions of taste—Shakespeare was considered a barbarian even by so sophisticated a writer as Voltaire, and, in translating Homer, Pope found it necessary to do a good deal of editing. Lessing's point of view, breaking sharply with this external conception of form, marks the road for aesthetic speculation to follow in the future.

For Lessing, as we have seen, aesthetic form is not an external arrangement provided by a set of traditional rules. Rather, it is the relation between the sensuous nature of the art medium and the conditions of human perception. The "natural man" of the eighteenth century was not to be bound by traditional political forms but was to create them in accordance with his own nature. Similarly, art was to create its own forms out of itself rather than accept them ready-made from the practice of the past; and criticism, instead of prescribing rules for art, was to explore the necessary laws by which art governs itself.

No longer was aesthetic form confused with mere externals of technique or felt as a strait jacket into which the artist, willy-nilly, had to force his creative ideas. Form issued spontaneously from the organization of the art work as it presented itself to perception. Time and space were the two extremes defining the limits of literature and the plastic arts in their relation to sensuous perception; and, following Lessing's example, it is possible to trace the evolution of art forms by their oscillations between these two poles.

The purpose of the present essay is to apply Lessing's method to modern literature—to trace the evolution of form in modern poetry and, more particularly, in the novel. For modern literature, as exemplified by such writers as T. S. Eliot, Ezra Pound, Marcel Proust, and James Joyce, is moving in the direction of spatial form; and this tendency receives an original development in

Djuna Barnes's remarkable book *Nightwood*. All these writers ideally intend the reader to apprehend their work spatially, in a moment of time, rather than as a sequence. And since changes in aesthetic form always involve major changes in the sensibility of a particular cultural period, an effort will be made to outline the spiritual attitudes that have led to the predominance of spatial form.

II. Modern Poetry

Modern Anglo-American poetry received its initial impetus from the Imagist movement of the years directly preceding and following the First World War. Imagism was important not so much for any actual poetry written by Imagist poets—no one knew quite what an Imagist poet was—but rather because it opened the way for later developments by its clean break with sentimental Victorian verbiage. The critical writings of Ezra Pound, the leading theoretician of Imagism, are an astonishing farrago of acute aesthetic perceptions thrown in among a series of boyishly naughty remarks whose chief purpose is to *épater le bourgeois*. But Pound's definition of the image, perhaps the keenest of his perceptions, is of fundamental importance for any discussion of modern literary form.

"An 'Image,'" Pound wrote, "is that which presents an intellectual and emotional complex in an instant of time." The implications of this definition should be noted: an image is defined not as a pictorial reproduction but as a unification of disparate ideas and emotions into a complex presented spatially in an instant of time. Such a complex does not proceed discursively, in unison with the laws of language, but strikes the reader's sensibility with an instantaneous impact. Pound stresses this aspect by adding, in the next paragraph, that only the *instantaneous* presentation of such complexes gives "that sense of sudden liberation; that sense of freedom from time limits and space limits; that sense of sudden growth, which we experience in the presence of the greatest works of art." [2]

At the very outset, therefore, modern poetry advocates a poetic method in direct contradiction to Lessing's analysis of language. And if we compare Pound's definition of the image with Eliot's description of the psychology of the poetic process, we can see clearly how profoundly this conception has influenced our modern idea of the nature of poetry. For Eliot, the distinctive quality of a poetic sensibility is its capacity to form new wholes, to fuse seemingly disparate experiences into an organic unity. The ordinary man, Eliot writes, "falls in love, or reads Spinoza, and these two experiences have nothing to do with each other, or with the noise of the typewriter or the smell of cooking; in the mind of the poet these experiences are always forming new wholes." [3] Pound had attempted to define the image in terms of its aesthetic attributes; Eliot, in this passage, is describing its psychological origin; but the result in a poem would be the same in both cases.

Such a view of the nature of poetry immediately gave rise to numerous problems. How was more than one image to be included in a poem? If the chief value of an image was its capacity to present an intellectual and emotional complex simultaneously, linking images in a sequence would clearly destroy most of their efficacy. Or was the poem itself one vast image, whose individual components were to be apprehended as a unity? But then it would be necessary to undermine the inherent consecutiveness of language, frustrating the reader's normal expectation of a sequence and forcing him to perceive the elements of the poem as juxtaposed in space rather than unrolling in time.

This is precisely what Eliot and Pound attempted in their major works. Both poets, in their earlier work, had still retained some elements of conventional structure. Their poems were looked upon as daring and revolutionary chiefly because of technical matters, like the loosening of metrical pattern and the handling of subjects ordinarily considered nonpoetic. Perhaps this is less true of Eliot than of Pound, especially the Eliot of the more complex early works like *Prufrock, Gerontion* and *Portrait of a Lady;* but even here, although the sections of the poem are not governed by syntactical logic, the skeleton of an implied narrative structure is always present. The reader of *Prufrock* is swept up in a narrative movement from the very first lines:

> Let us go then, you and I,
> When the evening . . .

And the reader, accompanying Prufrock, finally arrives at their mutual destination:

> In the room the women come and go
> Talking of Michelangelo.

At this point the poem becomes a series of more or less isolated fragments, each stating some aspect of Prufrock's emotional dilemma. But the fragments are now localized and focused on a specific set of circumstances, and the reader can organize them by referring to the implied situation. The same method is employed in *Portrait of a Lady,* while in *Gerontion* the reader is specifically told that he has been reading the "thoughts of a dry brain in a dry season"—the stream of consciousness of "an old man in a dry month, being read to by a boy, waiting for the rain." In both poems there is a perceptible framework around which the seemingly disconnected passages of the poem can be organized.

This was one reason why Pound's *Mauberley* and Eliot's early work were first regarded, not as forerunners of a new poetic form, but as latter-day *vers de société*—witty, disillusioned, with a somewhat brittle charm, but lacking that quality of "high seriousness" which Matthew Arnold had brandished as the touchstone of poetic excellence. These poems were considered unusual mainly because *vers de société* had long fallen out of fashion, but there was little difficulty in accepting them as an entertaining departure from the grand style of the nineteenth century.

In the *Cantos* and *The Waste Land,* however, it should have been clear that a radical transformation was taking place in aesthetic structure; but this transformation has been touched on only peripherally by modern critics. R. P. Blackmur comes closest to the central problem while analyzing what he calls Pound's "anecdotal" method. The special form of the *Cantos,* Blackmur explains, "is that of the anecdote begun in one place, taken up in one or more other places, and finished, if at all, in still another. This deliberate disconnectedness, this art of a thing continually alluding to itself, continually breaking off short, is the method by which the *Cantos* tie themselves together. So soon as the reader's mind is concerted with the material of the poem, Mr. Pound deliberately disconcerts it, either by introducing fresh and disjunct material or by reverting to old and, apparently, equally disjunct material." [4]

Blackmur's remarks apply equally well to *The Waste Land,* where syntactical sequence is given up for a structure depending on the perception of relationships between disconnected word-groups. To be properly understood, these word-groups must be juxtaposed with one another and perceived simultaneously. Only when this is done can they be adequately grasped; for, while they follow one another in time, their meaning does not depend on this temporal relationship. The one difficulty of these poems, which no amount of textual exegesis can wholly overcome, is the internal conflict between the time-logic of language and the space-logic implicit in the modern conception of the nature of poetry.

Aesthetic form in modern poetry, then, is based on a space-logic that demands a complete reorientation in the reader's attitude toward language. Since the primary reference of any word-group is to something inside the poem itself, language in modern poetry is really reflexive. The meaning-relationship is completed only by the simultaneous perception in space of word-groups that have no comprehensible relation to each other when read consecutively in time. Instead of the instinctive and immediate reference of words and word-groups to the objects or events they symbolize and the construction of meaning from the sequence of these references, modern poetry asks its readers to suspend the process of individual reference temporarily until the entire pattern of internal references can be apprehended as a unity.

It would not be difficult to trace this conception of poetic form back to Mallarmé's ambition to create a language of "absence" rather than of presence—a language in which words negated their objects instead of designating them; [5] nor should one overlook the evident formal analogies between *The Waste Land* and the *Cantos* and Mallarmé's *Un Coup de Dés*. Mallarmé, indeed, dislocated the temporality of language far more radically than either Eliot or Pound has ever done; and his experience with *Un Coup de Dés* showed that this ambition of modern poetry has a necessary limit. If pursued with Mallarmé's relentlessness, it culminates in the self-negation of language and the creation of a hybrid pictographic "poem" that can only be considered a fascinating historical curiosity. Nonetheless, this conception of aesthetic form, which may be formulated as the principle of reflexive reference, has left its traces on all of modern poetry. And the principle of reflexive reference is the link connecting the aesthetic development of modern poetry with similar experiments in the modern novel.

III. Flaubert and Joyce

For a study of aesthetic form in the modern novel, Flaubert's famous county fair scene in *Madame Bovary* is a convenient point of departure. This scene has been justly praised for its mordant caricature of bourgeois pomposity, its portrayal—unusually sympathetic for Flaubert—of the bewildered old servant, and its burlesque of the pseudo-romantic rhetoric by which Rodolphe woos the sentimental Emma. At present, however, it is enough to notice the method by which Flaubert handles the scene—a method we might as well call cinematographic since this analogy comes immediately to mind.

As Flaubert sets the scene, there is action going on simultaneously at three levels; and the physical position of each level is a fair index to its spiritual significance. On the lowest plane, there is the surging, jostling mob in the street, mingling with the livestock brought to the exhibitions. Raised slightly above the street by a platform are the speechmaking officials, bombastically reeling off platitudes to the attentive multitudes. And on the highest level of all, from a window overlooking the spectacle, Rodolphe and Emma are watching the proceedings and carrying on their amorous conversation in phrases as stilted as those regaling the crowds. Albert Thibaudet has compared this scene to the medieval mystery play, in which various related actions occur simultaneously on different stage levels; [6] but this acute comparison refers to Flaubert's intention rather than to his method. *"Everything should sound simultaneously,"* Flaubert later wrote, in commenting on this scene; "one should hear the bellowing of cattle, the whispering of the lovers, and the rhetoric of the officials all at the same time." [7]

But since language proceeds in time, it is impossible to approach this simultaneity of perception except by breaking up temporal sequence. And this is exactly what Flaubert does. He dissolves sequence by cutting back and forth between the various levels of action in a slowly rising crescendo until—at the climax of the scene—Rodolphe's Chateaubriandesque phrases are read at almost the same moment as the names of prize winners for raising the best pigs. Flaubert takes care to underline this satiric similarity by exposition as well as by juxtaposition—as if afraid the reflexive relations of the two actions might not be grasped: "From magnetism, by slow degrees, Rodolphe had arrived at affinities, and while M. le Président was citing Cincinnatus at his plow, Diocletian planting his cabbages and the emperors of China ushering in the new year with sowing-festivals, the young man was explaining to the young woman that these irresistible attractions sprang from some anterior existence."

This scene illustrates, on a small scale, what we mean by the spatialization of form in a novel. For the duration of the scene, at least, the time-flow of the narrative is halted; attention is fixed on the interplay of relationships within the immobilized time-area. These relationships are juxtaposed independently of the progress of the narrative, and the full significance of the scene is given only by the reflexive relations among the units of meaning. In Flaubert's scene, however, the unit of meaning is not, as in modern poetry, a word-group or a fragment of an anecdote; it is the totality of each level of action taken as an integer. The unit is so large that each integer can be read with an illusion of complete understanding, yet with a total unawareness of what Thibaudet calls the "dialectic of platitude" interweaving all levels and finally linking them together with devastating irony.

In other words, the adoption of spatial form in Pound and Eliot resulted in the disappearance of coherent sequence after a few lines; but the novel, with its larger unit of meaning, can preserve coherent sequence within the unit of meaning and break up only the time-flow of narrative. Because of this difference readers of modern poetry are practically forced to read reflexively to get any literal sense, while readers of a novel like *Nightwood,* for example, are led to expect narrative sequence by the deceptive normality of language sequence within the unit of meaning. But this does not affect the parallel between aesthetic form in modern poetry and the form of Flaubert's scene. Both can be properly understood only when their units of meaning are apprehended reflexively in an instant of time.

Flaubert's scene, although interesting in itself, is of minor importance to his novel as a whole and is skillfully blended back into the main narrative structure after fulfilling its satiric function. But Flaubert's method was taken over by James Joyce and applied on a gigantic scale in the composition of *Ulysses.* Joyce composed his novel of a vast number of references and cross references that relate to each other independently of the time sequence of the narrative. These references must be connected by the reader and viewed as a whole before the book fits together into any meaningful pattern. Ultimately, if we are to believe Stuart Gilbert, these systems of reference form a complete picture of practically everything under the sun, from the stages of man's life and the organs of the human body to the colors of the spectrum; but these structures are far more important for Joyce, as Harry Levin has remarked, than they could ever possibly be for the reader.[8] And while students of Joyce, fascinated by his erudition, have usually applied themselves to exegesis, our problem is to inquire into the perceptual form of his novel.

Joyce's most obvious intention in *Ulysses* is to give the reader a picture of Dublin seen as a whole—to re-create the sights and sounds, the people and places, of a typical Dublin day, much as Flaubert had re-created his *comice agricole*. And like Flaubert, Joyce aimed at attaining the same unified impact, the same sense of simultaneous activity occurring in different places. As a matter of fact, Joyce frequently makes use of the same method as Flaubert (cutting back and forth between different actions occurring at the same time) and he usually does so to obtain the same ironic effect. But Joyce faced the additional problem of creating this impression of simultaneity for the life of a whole teeming city, and of maintaining it—or rather of strengthening it—through hundreds of pages that must be read as a sequence. To meet this problem Joyce was forced to go far beyond what Flaubert had done. Flaubert had still maintained a clear-cut narrative line except in the county fair scene; but Joyce breaks up his narrative and transforms the very structure of his novel into an instrument of his aesthetic intention.

Joyce conceived *Ulysses* as a modern epic. And in the epic, as Stephen Dedalus tells us in *The Portrait of the Artist as a Young Man,* "the personality of the artist, at first sight a cry or a cadence and then a fluid and lambent narrative, finally refines itself out of existence, impersonalizes itself, so to speak . . . the artist, like the God of creation, remains within or beyond or above his handiwork, invisible, refined out of existence, indifferent, paring his finger-nails." The epic is thus synonymous for Joyce with the complete self-effacement of the author; and with his usual uncompromising rigor Joyce carries this implication further than anyone had previously dared.

For Joyce assumes—what is obviously not true—that all his readers are Dubliners, intimately acquainted with Dublin life and the personal history of his characters. This allows him to refrain from giving any direct information about his characters and thus betraying the presence of an omniscient author. What Joyce does, instead, is to present the elements of his narrative—the relations between Stephen and his family, between Bloom and his wife, between Stephen and Bloom and the Dedalus family—in fragments, as they are thrown out unexplained in the course of casual conversation or as they lie embedded in the various strata of symbolic reference. The same is true of all the allusions to Dublin life and history, and to the external events of the twenty-four hours during which the novel takes place. All the factual background summarized for the reader in an ordinary novel must here be reconstructed from fragments, sometimes hundreds of pages apart, scattered through the book. As a result, the reader is forced to read *Ulysses* in exactly the same manner as he reads modern poetry, that is, by continually fitting fragments together and keeping allusions in mind until, by reflexive reference, he can link them to their complements.

Joyce desired in this way to build up in the reader's mind a sense of Dublin as a totality, including all the relations of the characters to one another and all the events that enter their consciousness. The reader is intended to acquire this sense as he progresses through the novel, connecting allusions and references spatially and gradually becoming aware of the pattern of relationships. At the conclusion it might almost be said that Joyce literally wanted the reader to become a Dubliner. For this is what Joyce demands: that the reader have at hand the same instinctive knowledge of Dublin life, the same sense of Dublin as a huge, surrounding organism, that the Dubliner possesses as a birthright. It is this birthright that, at any one moment of time, gives the native a knowledge of Dublin's past and present as a whole; and it is only such knowledge that would enable the reader, like the characters, to place all the references in their proper context. This, it should be realized, is the equivalent of saying that Joyce cannot be read—he can only be reread. A knowledge of the whole is essential to an understanding of any part; but unless one is a Dubliner such knowledge can be obtained only after the book has been read, when all the references are fitted into their proper places and grasped as a unity. The burdens placed on the reader by this method of composition may well seem insuperable. But the fact remains that Joyce, in his unbelievably laborious fragmentation of narrative structure, proceeded on the assumption that a unified spatial apprehension of his work would ultimately be possible.

IV. Proust

In a far more subtle manner than in either Joyce or Flaubert, the same principle of composition is at work in Marcel Proust. Since Proust himself tells us that his novel will have imprinted on it "a form which usually remains invisible, the form of Time," it may seem strange to speak of Proust in connection with spatial form. He has almost invariably been considered the novelist of time par excellence—the literary interpreter of that Bergsonian "real time" intuited by the sensibility, as distinguished from the abstract, chronological time of the conceptual intelligence. To stop at this point, however, is to miss what Proust himself considered the deepest significance of his work.

Oppressed and obsessed by a sense of the ineluctability of time and the evanescence of human life, Proust was suddenly, he tells us, visited by certain quasi-mystical experiences (described in detail in the last volume of his book, *Le Temps Retrouvé*). These experiences provided him with a spiritual technique for transcending time, and thus enabled him to escape time's domination. Proust believed that these transcendent, extratemporal moments contained a clue to the ultimate nature of reality; and he wished to translate these moments to the level of aesthetic form by writing a novel. But no ordinary narrative, which tried to convey their meaning indirectly through exposition and description, could really do them justice. For Proust desired, through the medium of his novel, to communicate to the reader the full impact of these moments as he had felt them himself.

To define the method by which this is accomplished, we must first understand clearly the precise nature of the Proustian revelation. Each such experience was marked by a feeling that "the permanent essence of things, usually concealed, is set free and our true self, which had long seemed dead but was not dead in other ways, awakes, takes on fresh life as it receives the celestial nourishment brought to it." This celestial nourishment consists of some sound, or odor, or other sensory stimulus, "sensed anew, simultaneously in the present and the past."

But why should these moments seem so overwhelmingly

valuable that Proust calls them celestial? Because, Proust observes, imagination ordinarily can operate only on the past; the material presented to imagination thus lacks any sensuous immediacy. At certain moments, however, the physical sensations of the past came flooding back to fuse with the present; and Proust believed that in these moments he grasped a reality "real without being of the present moment, ideal but not abstract." Only in these moments did he attain his most cherished ambition—"to seize, isolate, immobilize for the duration of a lightning flash" what otherwise he could not apprehend, "namely: a fragment of time in its pure state." For a person experiencing this moment, Proust adds, the word "death" no longer has meaning. "Situated outside the scope of time, what could he fear from the future?"

The significance of this experience, though obscurely hinted at throughout the book, is made explicit only in the concluding pages, which describe the final appearance of the narrator at the reception of the Princesse de Guermantes. And the narrator decides to dedicate the remainder of his life to re-creating these experiences in a work of art. This work will differ essentially from all others because, at its root, will be a vision of reality refracted through an extratemporal perspective. This decision, however, should not be confused with the Renaissance view of art as the guarantor of immortality, nor with the late nineteenth-century cult of art for art's sake (though Proust has obvious affinities with both traditions, and particularly with the latter). It was not the creation of a work of art per se that filled Proust with a sense of fulfilling a prophetic mission; it was the creation of a work of art that should stand as a monument to his *personal* conquest of time. His own novel was to be at once the vehicle through which he conveyed his vision and the *concrete experience* of that vision expressed in a form that compelled the world (the reader) to re-experience its exact effect on Proust's own sensibility.

The prototype of this method, like the analysis of the revelatory moment, appears during the reception at the Princesse de Guermantes'. The narrator has spent years in a sanatorium and has lost touch almost completely with the fashionable world of the earlier volumes; now he comes out of his seclusion to attend the reception. Accordingly, he finds himself bewildered by the changes in social position, and the even more striking changes in character and personality, among his former friends. No doubt these pages paint a striking picture of the invasion of French society by the upper bourgeoisie, and the gradual breakdown of all social and moral standards caused by the First World War; but, as the narrator takes great pains to tell us, this is far from being the most important theme of this section of the book. Much more crucial is that, almost with the force of a blow, these changes jolt the narrator into a consciousness of the passage of time. He tries painfully to recognize old friends under the masks that, he feels, the years have welded to them. And when a young man addresses him respectfully instead of familiarly, he realizes suddenly that, without being aware of it, he too has assumed a mask—the mask of an elderly gentleman. The narrator now begins to understand that in order to become conscious of time it has been necessary for him to absent himself from his accustomed environment (in other words, from the stream of time acting on that environment) and then to plunge back into the stream again after a lapse of years. In so doing he finds himself presented with two images—the world as he had formerly known it and the world, transformed by time, that he now sees before him. When these two images become juxtaposed, the narrator discovers that the passage of time may suddenly be experienced through its visible effects.

Habit is a universal soporific, which ordinarily conceals the passage of time from those who have gone their accustomed ways. At any one moment of time the changes are so minute as to be imperceptible. "Other people," Proust writes, "never cease to change places in relation to ourselves. In the imperceptible, but eternal march of the world, we regard them as motionless in a moment of vision, too short for us to perceive the motion that is sweeping them on. But we have only to select in our memory two pictures taken of them at different moments, close enough together however for them not to have altered in themselves—perceptibly, that is to say—and the difference between the two pictures is a measure of the displacement that they have undergone in relation to us." By comparing these two images in a moment of time, the passage of time can be experienced concretely through the impact of its visible effects on the sensibility. And this discovery provides the narrator with a method that, in T. S. Eliot's phrase, is an "objective correlative" to the visionary apprehension of the fragment of "pure time" intuited in the revelatory moment.

When the narrator discovers this method of communicating his experience of the revelatory moment, he decides, as we have already observed, to incorporate it in a novel. But the novel the narrator undertakes to write has just been finished by the reader; and its form is controlled by the method that he has outlined in its concluding pages. In other words, the reader is substituted for the narrator and is placed by the author throughout the book in the same position as that occupied by the narrator before his own experience at the reception of the Princesse de Guermantes. This is done by the discontinuous presentation of character—a simple device which nonetheless is the clue to the form of Proust's vast structure.

Every reader soon notices that Proust does not follow any of his characters continuously through the whole course of his novel. Instead, they appear and reappear in various stages of their lives. Hundreds of pages sometimes go by between the time they are last seen and the time they reappear; and when they do turn up again, the passage of time has invariably changed them in some decisive way. Rather than being submerged in the stream of time and intuiting a character progressively, in a continuous line of development, the reader is confronted with various snapshots of the characters "motionless in a moment of vision" taken at different stages in their lives; and in juxtaposing these images he experiences the effects of the passage of time exactly as the narrator had done. As Proust has promised, therefore, he does stamp his novel indelibly with the form of time; but we are now in a position to understand exactly what he meant by this engagement.

To experience the passage of time, Proust had learned, it was necessary to rise above it and to grasp both past and present simultaneously in a moment of what he called "pure time." But "pure time," obviously, is not time at all—it is perception in a moment of time, that is to say, space. And, by the discontinuous presentation of character Proust forces the reader to juxtapose disparate images spatially, in a moment of time, so that the experience of time's passage is communicated directly to his sensibility. Ramon Fernandez has acutely stressed this point in some remarks on Proust and Bergson. "Much attention has been given to the importance of time in Proust's work," he writes, "but perhaps it has not been sufficiently noted that he gives time the value and characteristics of space . . . in affirming that the different parts of time reciprocally exclude and remain external to each other." And he adds that, while Proust's method of making contact with his *durée* is quite Bergsonian (that is, springing from the interpenetration of the past with the present), "the reactions of his intelligence on his sensibility, which determine the trajectory of his work, would orient him rather toward a *spatialisation* of time and memory." [9]

There is a striking analogy here between Proust's method and that of his beloved Impressionist painters; but this analogy goes far deeper than the usual comments about the "impressionism" of Proust's style. The Impressionist painters juxtaposed pure tones on the canvas, instead of mixing them on the palette, in order to leave the blending of colors to the eye of the spectator. Similarly, Proust gives us what might be called pure views of his characters—views of them "motionless in a moment of vision" in various phases of their lives—and allows the sensibility of the reader to fuse these views into a unity. Each view must be apprehended by the reader as a unit; and Proust's purpose is achieved only when these units of meaning are referred to each other reflexively in a moment of time. As with Joyce and the modern poets, spatial form is also the structural scaffolding of Proust's labyrinthine masterpiece.

V. *Djuna Barnes: Nightwood*

The name of Djuna Barnes first became known to those readers who followed, with any care, the stream of pamphlets, books, magazines, and anthologies that poured forth to enlighten America in the feverish days of literary expatriation. Miss Barnes, it is true, must always have remained a somewhat enigmatic figure even to the most attentive reader. Born in New York State, she spent most of her time in England and France; and the glimpses one catches of her in the memoirs of the period are brief and unrevealing. She appears in *The Dial* from time to time with a drawing or a poem; she crops up now and again in some anthology of advance-guard writers—the usual agglomeration of people who are later to become famous or to sink into the melancholy oblivion of frustrated promise. Before the publication of *Nightwood,* indeed, one might have been inclined to place her name in the latter group. For while she had a book of short stories and an earlier novel to her credit, neither prepares one for the maturity of achievement so conspicuous in every line of this work.

Of the fantastical quality of her imagination; of the gift for imagery that, as T. S. Eliot has said in his preface to *Nightwood,* gives one a sense of horror and doom akin to Elizabethan tragedy; of the epigrammatic incisiveness of her phrasing and her penchant, also akin to the Elizabethans, for dealing with the more scabrous manifestations of human fallibility—of all these there is evidence in *Ryder,* Miss Barnes's first novel. But all this might well have resulted only in a momentary flare-up of capricious brilliance, whose radiance would have been as dazzling as it was insubstantial. *Ryder,* it must be confessed, is an anomalous creation from any point of view. Although Miss Barnes's unusual qualities gradually emerge from its kaleidoscope of moods and styles, these qualities are still, so to speak, held in solution or at best placed in the service of a literary *jeu d'esprit.* Only in *Nightwood* do they finally crystallize into a definitive and comprehensible pattern.

Many critics—not least among them T. S. Eliot—have paid tribute to *Nightwood*'s compelling intensity, its head-and-shoulders superiority, simply as a stylistic phenomenon, to most of the works that currently pass for literature. But *Nightwood*'s reputation is similar, in many respects, to that of *The Waste Land* in 1922—it is known as a collection of striking passages, some of breath-taking poetic quality, appealing chiefly to connoisseurs of somewhat gamy literary items. Such a reputation, it need hardly be remarked, is not conducive to intelligent appreciation or understanding. Thanks to a good many critics, we have become able to approach *The Waste Land* as a work of art rather than as a battleground for opposing poetic theories or as a curious piece of literary esoterica. It is time that we began to approach *Nightwood* in the same way.

Before dealing with *Nightwood* in detail, however, we must make certain broad distinctions between it and the novels already considered. While the structural principle of *Nightwood* is the same as of *Ulysses* and *A la recherche du temps perdu*—spatial form, obtained by means of reflexive reference—there are marked differences in technique that will be obvious to every reader. Taking an analogy from another art, we can say that these differences are similar to those between the work of Cézanne and the compositions of a later and more abstract painter like Braque. What characterizes the work of Cézanne, above all, is the tension between two conflicting but deeply rooted tendencies. On the one hand, there is the struggle to attain aesthetic form—conceived of by Cézanne as a self-enclosed unity of form-and-color harmonies—and, on the other, the desire to create this form through the recognizable depiction of natural objects. Later artists took over only Cézanne's preoccupation with formal harmonies, omitting natural objects altogether or presenting them in some distorted manner.

Like Cézanne, Proust and Joyce accept the naturalistic principle, presenting their characters in terms of those commonplace details, those descriptions of circumstance and environment, that we have come to regard as verisimilar. Their experiments with the novel form, it is true, were inspired by a desire to conform more closely to the experience of consciousness; but while the principle of verisimilitude was shifted from the external to the internal, it was far from being abandoned. At the same time, these writers intended to control the abundance of verisimilar detail reflected through consciousness by the unity of spatial apprehension. But in *Nightwood,* as in the work of Braque, the Fauves or the Cubists, the naturalistic principle has lost its dominance. We are asked only to accept the work of art as an autonomous structure giving us an individual vision of reality; and the question of the relation of this vision to an extra-artistic "objective" world has ceased to have any fundamental importance.

To illustrate the transition that takes place in *Nightwood,* we may examine an interesting passage from Proust where the process can be caught at a rudimentary level. In describing Robert de Saint-Loup, an important character in the early sections of the novel, the narrator tells us that he could see concealed "beneath a courtier's smile his warrior's thirst for action—when I examined him I could see how closely the vigorous structure of his triangular face must have been modelled on that of his ancestors' faces, a face devised rather for an ardent bowman than for a delicate student. Beneath his fine skin the bold construction, the feudal architecture were apparent. His head made one think of those old dungeon keeps on which the disused battlements are still to be seen, although inside they have been converted into libraries."

By the time the reader comes across this passage he has already learned a considerable number of facts about Saint-Loup. The latter, he knows, is a member of the Guermantes family, one of the oldest and most aristocratic in the French nobility and still the acknowledged leaders of Parisian society. Unlike their feudal ancestors, however, the Guermantes have no real influence over the internal affairs of France under the Third Republic. Moreover, Saint-Loup is by way of being a family black sheep. Seemingly uninterested in social success, a devoted student of Nietzsche and Proudhon, he was "imbued with the most profound contempt for his caste." Knowing these facts from earlier sections of the novel, the reader accepts the passage quoted above simply as a trenchant summation of Saint-Loup's character. But so precisely do the images in this passage apply to everything the reader has learned about Saint-Loup, so exactly do they communicate the central impression of his personality, that it would be possible to derive a total knowledge of his character solely from the images without attaching them to a set of external social and historical details.

Images of this kind are commoner in poetry than in prose—more particularly, since we are speaking of character description, in dramatic poetry. In Shakespeare and the Elizabethans, descriptions of characters are not "realistic" as we understand the word today. They are not a collection of circumstantial details whose bare conglomeration is assumed to convey a personality. The dramatic poet, rather, defined both physical and psychological aspects of character at one stroke, in an image or a series of images. Here is Antony, for example, as Shakespeare presents him in the opening scene of *Antony and Cleopatra:*

> Nay, but this dotage of our general's
> O'erflows the measure: those his goodly eyes
> That o'er the files and musters of the war
> Have glow'd like plated Mars, now bend, now turn,
> The office and devotion of their view
> Upon a tawny front: his captain's heart,
> Which in the scuffles of great fights hath burst
> The buckles on his breast, reneges all temper,
> And is become the bellows and the fan
> To cool a gipsy's lust.

And then, to complete the picture, Antony is contemptuously called the "triple pillar of the world transform'd into a strumpet's fool."

Or, to take a more modern example, from a poet strongly influenced by the Elizabethans, here is the twentieth-century Everyman:

> He, the young man carbuncular, arrives,
> A small house agent's clerk, with one bold stare,
> One of the low on whom assurance sits
> As a silk hat on a Bradford millionaire.

As Ramon Fernandez has remarked of similar character descriptions in the work of George Meredith, images of this kind analyze without dissociating. They describe character but at the same time hold fast to the unity of personality, without splintering it to fragments in trying to seize the secret of its integration.[10]

Writing of this order—charged with symbolic overtones—pierces through the cumbrous mass of naturalistic detail to express the essence of character in an image; it is the antithesis to the reigning convention in the novel.

Ordinary novels, as T. S. Eliot justly observes, "obtain what reality they have largely from an accurate rendering of the noises that human beings currently make in their daily simple needs of communication; and what part of a novel is not composed of these noises consists of a prose which is no more alive than that of a competent newspaper writer or government official." Miss Barnes abandons any pretensions to this kind of verisimilitude, just as modern painters have abandoned any attempt at naturalistic representation; and the result is a world as strange to the reader, at first sight, as the world of Cubism was to its first spectators. Since the selection of detail in *Nightwood* is governed not by the logic of verisimilitude but by the demands of the décor necessary to enhance the symbolic significance of the characters, the novel has baffled even its most fascinated admirers. Let us attack the mystery by applying our method of reflexive reference, instead of approaching the book, as most of its readers have done, in terms of a coherent temporal pattern of narrative.

Since *Nightwood* lacks a narrative structure in the ordinary sense, it cannot be reduced to any sequence of action for purposes of explanation. One can, if one chooses, follow the narrator in Proust through the various stages of his social career; one can, with some difficulty, follow Leopold Bloom's epic journey through Dublin; but no such reduction is possible in *Nightwood*. As Dr. O'Connor remarks to Nora Flood, with his desperate gaiety: "I have a narrative, but you will be put to it to find it." Strictly speaking, the doctor is wrong—he has a static situation, not a narrative, and no matter how hard the reader looks he will find only the various facets of this situation explored from different angles. The eight chapters of *Nightwood* are like searchlights, probing the darkness each from a different direction yet ultimately illuminating the same entanglement of the human spirit.

In the first four chapters we are introduced to each of the important persons—Felix Volkbein, Nora Flood, Robin Vote, Jenny Petherbridge, and Dr. O'Connor. The next three chapters are, for the most part, long monologues by the doctor, through which the developments of the earlier chapters begin to take on meaning. The last chapter, only a few pages long, has the effect of a coda, giving us what we have already come to feel is the only possible termination. And these chapters are knit together, not by the progress of any action—either narrative action or, as in a stream-of-consciousness novel, the flow of experience—but by the continual reference and cross reference of images and symbols that must be referred to each other spatially throughout the time-act of reading.

At first sight, Dr. O'Connor's brilliant and fantastic monologues seem to dominate the book and overshadow the other characters; but the central figure—the figure around which the situation revolves—is in reality Robin Vote. This creation—it is impossible to call her a character, since character implies humanity and she has not yet attained the level of the human—is one of the most remarkable figures in contemporary literature. We meet her first when the doctor, sitting and drinking with Felix Volkbein in a Paris bar, is summoned by a bellboy from a nearby hotel to look after a lady who has fainted and cannot be awakened. "The perfume that her body exhaled," Miss Barnes writes of Robin,

> was of the quality of that earth-flesh, fungi, which smells of captured dampness and yet is so dry, overcast with the odor of oil of amber, which is an inner malady of the sea, making her seem as if she had invaded a sleep incautious and entire. Her flesh was the texture of plant life, and beneath it one sensed

a frame, broad, porous and sleep-worn, as if sleep were a decay fishing her beneath the visible surface. About her head there was an effulgence as of phosphorus growing about the circumference of a body of water—as if her life lay through her in ungainly luminous deteriorations—the troubling structure of the born somnambule, who lives in two worlds—meet of child and desperado.

Taken by itself, this description is likely to prove more confusing than enlightening; but a few pages later another attempt is made to explain Robin's significance:

Sometimes one meets a woman who is beast turning human. Such a person's every movement will reduce to an image of a forgotten experience; a mirage of an eternal wedding cast on the racial memory; as insupportable a joy as would be the vision of an eland coming down an aisle of trees, chapleted with orange blossoms and bridal veil, a hoof raised in the economy of fear, stepping in the trepidation of flesh that will become a myth.

It is significant that we first meet Robin—*la somnambule,* the sleepwalker—when she is being awakened; before that moment we have no knowledge of her life. Her life might be said to begin with that moment, and the act of awakening to be the act of birth.

From these descriptions we begin to realize that Robin symbolizes a state of existence which is before, rather than beyond, good and evil. She is both innocent and depraved —meet of child and desperado—precisely because she has not reached the human state where moral values become relevant. Lacking responsibility of any kind, abandoning herself to wayward and perverse passions, she yet has the innocence and purity of a child. (Nora tells the doctor in the seventh chapter that Robin played "with her toys, trains, and animals and cars to wind up, and dolls and marbles and toy soldiers.") Gliding through life like a sleepwalker, living in a dream from which she has not awakened—for awakening would imply a consciousness of moral value—Robin is at once completely egotistical and yet lacking in a sense of her own identity.

"And why does Robin feel innocent?" Dr. O'Connor asks, when Nora, Robin's lover, comes to him with her agonizing questions. "Every bed she leaves, without caring, fills her heart with peace and happiness. . . . She knows she is innocent because she can't do anything in relation to anyone but herself." But at the same time the doctor tells Felix, Robin's erstwhile husband, that Robin had written from America saying, "Remember me." "Probably," he remarks, "because she has difficulty in remembering herself." By taking these passages together, we can understand what the doctor means when he says that "Robin was outside the 'human type'—a wild thing caught in a woman's skin, monstrously alone, monstrously vain."

The situation of the novel, then, revolves around this extraordinary creature. Robin, Felix eagerly confides to the doctor, "always seemed to be looking for someone to tell her that she was innocent. . . . There are some people who must get permission to live, and if the Baronin [Robin] finds no one to give her that permission, she will make an innocence for herself; a fearful sort of primitive innocence." To be conscious of one's innocence, of course, implies a consciousness of moral value that, we have seen, Robin does not possess. If Robin could have found someone to tell her that she was innocent, she would have found someone who had raised her to the level of the human—someone who had given her "permission to live" as a human being, not merely to exist as an amorphous mass of moral possibility.

Once this fundamental problem is grasped, much of

what we read in the rest of *Nightwood* becomes considerably clearer. At the beginning of the book we are introduced to Felix Volkbein, a Viennese half-Jew with a somewhat questionable title. What Miss Barnes says of Felix immediately gives him the same type of symbolic stature that Robin possesses:

> What had formed Felix from the date of his birth to his coming to thirty was unknown to the world, for the step of the wandering Jew is in every son. No matter where and when you meet him you feel that he has come from . . . some secret land that he has been nourished on but cannot inherit, for the Jew seems to be everywhere from nowhere. When Felix's name was mentioned, three or more persons would swear to having seen him the week before in three different countries simultaneously.

Combined with this aspect of Felix is a curious "obsession for what he termed 'Old Europe': aristocracy, nobility, royalty. . . . He felt that the great past might mend a little if he bowed low enough, if he succumbed and gave homage." Immediately after seeing Robin, Felix confesses to the doctor that he "wished a son who would feel as he felt about the 'great past.'" "To pay homage to our past," he says, "is the only gesture that also includes the future." He pays court to Robin and, since her "life held no volition for refusal," they marry. Felix, then, makes the first effort to shape Robin, to give her permission to live by informing her with his own sense of moral values. He does so because he senses, almost instinctively, that with Robin "anything can be done."

Felix fails with Robin, just as do the others who try to provide her with a moral framework. But what exactly does Felix's failure imply? In other words, what is the sense of values that proves inadequate to lifting Robin to the level of the human? Because Felix is so astonishingly individual a creation, despite the broader significance of his role in the novel, this is a particularly difficult question to answer. Some clue may be found if we remind ourselves of another Wandering Jew in modern fiction, Leopold Bloom. Seeking for a character to typify *l'homme moyen sensuel,* not only of our own time but through all history, Joyce chose the figure of a Wandering Jew vainly trying to integrate himself into a culture to which he is essentially alien. And this predicament of the Jew is merely a magnification of the predicament of modern man himself, bewildered and homeless in a mechanical wilderness of his own creation. If Felix is viewed in this light, we may understand his dubious title, his abject reverence for the great tradition of the past, and his frantic desire to assimilate this tradition to himself, as so many examples of a basic need to feel at home in some cultural framework.

Until his meeting with Robin, Felix's relationship to what he considered the great traditions of the European past had been completely negative. The first chapter of the novel, dominated by Felix, is appropriately entitled "Bow Down"—for this phrase defines Felix's attitude toward the great tradition, even toward its trivial and unworthy modern representatives. "In restaurants he bowed slightly to anyone who looked as if he might be 'someone,' making the bow so imperceptible that the surprised person might think he was merely adjusting his stomach." The doctor links this blind, unthinking worship of the aristocratic traditions of the past with the attitude of the masses in general toward an aristocracy they have falsely deified; and he lights up in a flash the symbolic meaning of Felix's obsession.

"Nobility, very well, but what is it?" The Baron started to answer him, but the doctor held up his hand. "Wait a minute! I know—the few that the many have lied about well and long enough to make them deathless." Felix is in the position of the masses, the common men, desperately lying to themselves about an inherited sense of values which they know only by its external trappings. But by marrying Robin, the doctor realizes, Felix is staking his existence on the belief that these traditional values still have vitality—that they will succeed in shaping the primeval chaos of Robin into order. (On Felix's first visit to court Robin he carries two volumes on the life of the Bourbons.) Knowing that Felix's attempt is doomed to failure, the doctor makes an effort to warn him: "The last muscle of aristocracy is madness—remember that"— the doctor leaned forward—"the last child born to aristocracy is sometimes an idiot. . . . So I say beware! In the king's bed is always found, just before it becomes a museum piece, the droppings of the black sheep."

Robin does bear Felix a sickly, stunted, prematurely aged, possibly feeble-minded child—the droppings of the black sheep. And, after unwillingly conceiving the child "amid loud and frantic cries of affirmation and despair," Robin leaves Felix. The child had meant for Felix the creative reaffirmation of the great European aristocratic tradition; but Robin's flight reveals that this tradition is impotent. It contains nothing for the future except the wistful and precocious senility of Guido, Felix's child.

The next character to enter the lists with Robin is Nora Flood, who comes perhaps closest of all to giving Robin "permission to live." Nora, as a symbolic figure, is given meaning on a number of levels; but the title of the third chapter, "Night Watch," expresses the essence of her spiritual attitude. We are told that she keeps "a 'paupers' salon for poets, radicals, beggars, artists, and people in love; for Catholics, Protestants, Brahmins, dabblers in black magic and medicine"—this last, of course, being an allusion to the doctor. Nora was "by temperament an early Christian; she believed the word"; this meant that she "robbed herself for everyone. . . . Wandering people the world over found her profitable in that she could be sold for a price forever, for she carried her betrayal money in her own pocket."

It is significant that Nora is described in images of the American West: "Looking at her, foreigners remembered stories they had heard of covered wagons; animals going down to drink; children's heads, just as far as the eyes, looking in fright out of small windows, where in the dark another race crouched in ambush." These images, Nora's paupers' salon, and her early Christian temperament all represent different crystallizations of the same spiritual attitude. Among the determinants of this attitude are a belief in the innate goodness of man (or at least in his capacity for moral improvement), a belief in progress, and an indiscriminate approbation of all forms of ethical and intellectual unconventionality—in short, the complete antithesis to the world of values represented by Felix. Irving Babbitt would have called Nora a hopeless Rousseauist, and he would have been right.

Characteristically, while Felix was drawn to Robin because he wished to use her, Nora is drawn to her through pity. The scene in which Nora meets Robin is important not only for what it reveals of their relationship, but also because there is a passage that confirms our interpretation of Robin. Both Robin and Nora are watching a circus performance when,

> . . . As one powerful lioness came to the turn of the bars, exactly opposite the girl [Robin], she turned her furious great head with its yellow eyes afire and went down, her paws thrust through the bars and, as she regarded the girl, as

if a river were falling behind impassable heat, her eyes flowed in tears that never reached the surface.

Being neither animal nor human, Robin evokes pity from both species. Nora, intuitively understanding Robin's perturbation at the lioness's stare, takes her by the hand and leads her outside. And, although strangers until that moment, Robin is soon telling Nora "her wish for a home, as if she were afraid she would be lost again, as if she were aware, without conscious knowledge, that she belonged to Nora, and that if Nora did not make it permanent by her own strength, she would forget." What Robin would forget was where she belonged, her own identity, given to her at least for a while by the strength of Nora's love and pity.

Nora's failure with Robin is already foreshadowed in the first description of Nora as having "the face of all people who love the people—a face that would be evil when she found out that to love without criticism is to be betrayed." While Felix had deliberately tried to shape Robin, Nora simply envelops her in an all-embracing love that, because of Nora's belief in natural goodness, has no room for praise or blame. "In court," we read, Nora "would have been impossible; no one would have been hanged, reproached or forgiven because no one would have been accused." With a creature like Robin, the result was inevitable. Nora's self-sacrificing devotion does succeed for a time in giving Robin a sense of identity. Robin's unconditional acceptance by Nora, exactly as she is, eases the tension between the animal and the human that is tearing Robin's life apart; but in the end Nora is not able to give Robin "permission to live" any more than Felix could. Most of the third chapter of the novel is given over to an analysis of this slow estrangement between Robin and Nora, an estrangement all the more torturous because, while desired by neither, it is recognized as inevitable by both.

Yet the quality of Robin's relationship with Nora shows how much more closely Nora came to success than Felix. With Felix Robin had been passive, almost disinterested, in conformity with her somnambulistic nature. Although her life was a frenzy of activity, she never really acted in more than an animal sense; Robin's acts were always reactions to obscure impulses whose meaning she did not understand. With Nora, however, there are moments when Robin realizes the terror of their inevitable separation; and in these moments, clinging to Nora like a child, Robin becomes almost human because her terror reveals an implicit moral choice.

> Yet sometimes, going about the house, in passing each other, they would fall into an agonized embrace, looking into each other's face, their two heads in their four hands, so strained together that the space that divided them seemed to be thrusting them apart. Sometimes in these moments of insurmountable grief Robin would make some movement, use a peculiar turn of phrase not habitual to her, innocent of the betrayal, by which Nora was informed that Robin had come from a world to which she would return. To keep her (in Robin there was this tragic longing to be kept, knowing herself astray) Nora knew now that there was no way but death.

As usual, the appropriate comment on this situation is made by the doctor, seeing Nora out roaming the streets at night in search of Robin. " 'There goes the dismantled— Love has fallen off her wall. A religious woman,' he thought to himself, 'without the joy and safety of the Catholic faith, which at a pinch covers up the spots on the wall when the family portraits take a slide; take that safety from a woman,' he said to himself, quickening his steps to follow her, 'and love gets loose and into the rafters. She sees her everywhere,' he added, glancing at Nora as she passed into the dark. 'Out looking for what she's afraid to find—Robin. There goes the mother of mischief, running about, trying to get the world home.'" Robin, it should be noticed, is identified with "the world"—which may mean that the world is really no better off than she is—and Nora's failure with Robin, or rather her derangement over this failure, is attributed to her lack of the Catholic faith.

The doctor does not say that the Catholic faith would have allowed Nora to control Robin by giving her a framework of moral values, but he does say that, if Nora had been a Catholic, the eccentricities of Robin's nature would not have plunged her into an abyss of self-torture and suffering. It is Nora's faith in natural goodness, her uncritical acceptance of Robin because of this faith, that has caused her to suffer. The doctor implies that as a Catholic she would have been able to rationalize Robin's nature in terms of the Catholic understanding of sin and evil; and while this would not have prevented the evil, it would certainly have eased the disillusionment and suffering. As we shall see later, this passage is crucial to an understanding of the book as a whole.

Nora realizes that Robin is lost to her when, at dawn, she looks out the window and sees another woman "her arms about Robin's neck, her body pressed to Robin's, her legs slackened in the hang of the embrace." This other woman, Jenny Petherbridge, is the only person in the novel without a trace of tragic grandeur—and this is not surprising, for she is depicted as the essence of mediocrity, the incarnation of the second-hand and the second-rate.

Chapter four, in which she makes her main appearance, is appropriately entitled "The Squatter." For her life is a continual infringement on the rights of other people, an infringement that becomes permanent merely by the power of persistence. "Her walls, her cupboards, her bureaux, were teeming with second-hand dealings with life. It takes a bold and authentic robber to get first-hand plunder. Someone else's marriage ring was on her finger; the photograph taken of Robin for Nora sat upon her table."

Jenny, again, is the only person in the novel who might be called bourgeois; and there is more than a touch of the *nouveau riche* in her ostentation and her lavishness with money. Wanting to possess anything that had importance, "she appropriated the most passionate love that she knew, Nora's for Robin." Jenny's relationship to Robin differs from those of Felix and Nora, for she has no intuition of Robin's pathetic moral emptiness; nor does she seize on Robin as a teeming chaos of vitality through which to realize her own values. She simply appropriates Robin as another acquisition to her collection of objects that other people have valued. Staking her claim to Robin immediately after Nora, Jenny's main function in the novel seems that of underlining the hopelessness of Robin's plight. To fall from Nora to Jenny—to exchange the moral world of one for the moral world of the other—is only too convincing a proof that Robin has still failed to acquire any standards of value.

At the conclusion of the fourth chapter, when we learn that Robin and Jenny have sailed for America, the novel definitely shifts its focus. Until this point Robin has been its center both spiritually and actually; but Robin now drops out of sight—though she is talked about at great length—and does not appear directly again until the brief concluding episode.

The next three chapters are completely dominated by the doctor, "Dr. Matthew-Mighty-grain-of-salt-Dante-O'Connor," whose dialogues with Felix and Nora—or rather his monologues, prompted by their questions—make up the bulk of these pages. The doctor serves as commentator on the events of the novel, if events they can be called; and as T. S. Eliot says of Tiresias in *The Waste Land,* what he sees, in fact, is the substance of the novel.

This comparison can bear closer application. There is an evident—and probably not accidental—similarity between the two figures. Like the man-woman Tiresias, symbol of universal experience, the doctor has homosexual inclinations; like Tiresias he has "fore-suffered all" by apparently being immortal (he claims to have a "prehistoric memory," and is always talking as if he had existed in other historical periods). Like Tiresias again, who "walked among the lowest of the dead," the doctor is father confessor to the creatures of the night world who inhabit the novel as well as being an inhabitant of that world himself. And in his role of commentator, the doctor "perceived the scene, and foretold the rest." For these reasons, Nora comes to him with the burning question—the title of the fifth chapter— "Watchman, What of the Night?"

It is impossible to give any exact idea of the doctor's monologues except by quoting them at length; and that would unduly prolong an already protracted analysis. But to find anything approaching their combination of ironic wit and religious humility, their emotional subtlety and profound human simplicity, their pathos, their terror, and their sophisticated self-consciousness, one has to go back to the religious sonnets of John Donne. It is these monologues that prove the main attraction of the novel at first reading, and their magnetic power has, no doubt, contributed to the misconception that *Nightwood* is only a collection of magnificent fragments. Moreover, since the doctor always speaks about himself *sub specie aeternitatis,* it is difficult at first to grasp the relations between his monologues and the central theme of the novel.

T. S. Eliot notes in his preface that he could place the doctor in proper focus only after a number of readings; and this is likely to be the experience of other readers as well. But as Eliot rightly emphasizes, the book cannot be understood unless the doctor is seen as part of the whole pattern, rather than as an overwhelming individual creation who throws the others into the background by the magnitude of his understanding and the depth of his insight. Now that the pattern has been sketched, we can safely approach the doctor a little more closely and explain his individual spiritual attitude. It is this attitude that, in the end, dominates the book and gives it a final focus.

"Man," the doctor tells Felix, "was born damned and innocent from the start, and wretchedly—as he must—on those two themes—whistles his tune." Robin, it will be remembered, was described as both child and desperado, that is, both damned and innocent; and since the doctor generalizes her spiritual predicament, we can infer that he views the condition of the other characters—and of himself—as in essentials no different. The doctor, who calls himself "the god of darkness," is a good illustration of his own statement. He is damned by his excess of the knowledge of evil, which condemns him to a living death. "You know what none of us know until we have died," Nora tells him. "You were dead in the beginning." But beyond the doctor's knowledge, beyond his twisted bitterness, is the pathos of abused innocence. "No matter what I may be doing," he cries, "in my heart is the wish for children and knitting. God, I never asked better than to boil some good man's potatoes and toss up a child for him every nine months by the calendar." And after the striking Tiny O'Toole episode, in which the doctor reveals all his saint-like simplicity (his attitude toward animals is reminiscent of St. Francis of Assisi) Nora says: "Sometimes I don't know why I talk to you. You're so like a child; then again I know well enough."

Because of his knowledge of man's nature, the doctor realizes that he himself, and the other people in the novel, differ from Robin only in degree; they are all involved to some extent in her desperate dualism, and in the end their doom is equally inescapable. "We are but skin about a wind," he says, "with muscles clenched against mortality. . . . Life, the permission to know death." Come to ask the "god of darkness" about that fabulous night-creature Robin, Nora draws the only possible conclusion from the doctor's harangues: "I'll never understand her—I'll always be miserable—just like this?" To which the doctor responds by one of his tirades that seems to be about nothing in particular, and yet turns out to be about everything.

The essential quality in the doctor that grows upon the reader is the practical futility of his knowledge, his own hopelessness and helplessness. In the early chapters he turns up occasionally, exhibiting an insight into the other people that they themselves do not possess and seeming to stand outside their dilemmas. But as the doctor comes to the foreground, we find this impression completely erroneous. He talks because he knows there is nothing else to do—and because to stop talking would be to think, and to think would be unbearable.

> "Look here," said the doctor. "Do you know what has made me the greatest liar this side of the moon, telling my stories to people like you to take the mortal agony out of their guts . . . to stop them from . . . staring over their knuckles with misery which they are trying to keep off, saying, 'Say some-

thing, Doctor, for the love of God!' And me talking away like mad. Well, that, and nothing else, has made me the liar I am."

And in another place he sums it up succinctly: "I talk too much because I have been made so miserable by what you're keeping hushed."

Still, the doctor cannot always maintain this role; he cannot always drown his own agony in a flood of talk for the benefit of others. And so, his own tension exacerbated by Nora's increasing hysteria, he bursts forth:

"Do you think, for Christ's sweet sake, that I am so happy that you should cry down my neck? Do you think there is no lament in this world, but your own? . . . A broken heart have you! [he says scornfully, a few sentences later] "I have falling arches, flying dandruff, a floating kidney, shattered nerves and a broken heart! . . . Am I going forward screaming that it hurts . . . or holding my guts as if they were a coil of knives . . . ? Do I wail to the mountains of the trouble I have had in the valley, or to every stone of the way it broke my bones, or of every life, how it went down into my belly and built a nest to hatch me my death there?"

It is on this note that we take leave of the doctor, cursing "the people in my life who have made my life miserable, coming to me to learn of degradation and the night."

But, although the doctor as an individual ends on a note of complete negation, this is not his final judgment on the total pattern of the novel—it is only his final verdict on himself. His attitude toward Robin and the people surrounding her is somewhat more complex. We have already indicated the nature of this complexity by quoting the doctor's remark, when he sees Nora wandering through the streets in search of Robin, that she was a religious woman "without the joy and safety of the Catholic faith, which at a pinch covers up the spots on the wall when the family portraits take a slide." There may be nothing to do about Robin's situation—man's attempts to achieve a truly human existence have always ended in failure; but there is at least the consolation of what the doctor calls "the girl that you love so much that she can lie to you"—the Catholic Church. Discussing the confessional with Felix, the doctor describes it as the place where, although a person may lack genuine contrition, "mischief unravels and the fine high hand of Heaven proffers the skein again, combed and forgiven."

It would be unwise to bear down too heavily on this point and make the doctor's attitude more positive than it actually is. His Catholicism, although deeply rooted in his emotional nature, can offer consolation but not hope; and even its consolation is a puny thing compared to the realities of the human situation as the doctor knows it. "I, as good a Catholic as they make," he tells Nora, "have embraced every confection of hope, and yet I know well, for all our outcry and struggle, we shall be for the next generation not the massive dung fallen from the dinosaur, but the little speck left of the humming-bird."

If the doctor derives any consolation from his Catholicism, it is the consolation of Pascal contemplating the wretchedness and insignificance of man rather than that of Thomas Aquinas admiring an orderly and rational moral universe. "Be humble like the dust, as God intended, and crawl," he advises Nora, "and finally you'll crawl to the end of the gutter and not be missed and not much remembered." What the doctor would like to attain is the spiritual attitude that T. S. Eliot prays for in *Ash Wednesday:*

> Teach us to care and not to care
> Teach us to sit still.

The doctor cannot reach this state because he is too deeply involved in the sufferings of others ("I was doing well enough," he says to Nora, "until you came and kicked my stone over, and out I came, all moss and eyes"), but he recognizes it as the only attitude offering some measure of inner peace.

Since the doctor is not the center of the pattern in *Nightwood,* the novel cannot end merely with his last appearance. We know Robin's fate from his monologues, but we have not had it presented to us dramatically; all we know is that Robin has gone to America with Jenny. The brief last chapter fills this gap and furnishes, with the inevitability of great tragedy, the only possible conclusion.

Robin soon leaves Jenny in America, and, impelled by some animal instinct, makes her way to where Nora lives. Without Nora's knowledge she lives in the woods of Nora's estate—we are not told how, and it is of no importance— sleeping in a decaying chapel belonging to Nora's family. One night Nora's watchdog scents Robin, and Nora, hearing the dog bark, follows him to investigate. Entering the chapel, she is witness to this strange and horrible scene between Robin and the dog:

> Sliding down she [Robin] went . . . until her head swung against his [the dog's]; on all fours now, dragging her knees. The veins stood out in her neck, swelled in her arms, and wide and throbbing rose up on her fingers as she moved forward. . . . Then she began to bark also, crawling after him— barking in a fit of laughter, obscene and touching. The dog began to cry then . . . and she grinning and crying with him; crying in shorter and shorter spaces, moving head to head, until she gave up, lying out, her hands beside her, her face turned and weeping; and the dog too gave up then, his eyes bloodshot, his head flat along her knees.

What this indicates, clearly, is that Robin has abandoned her efforts to rise to the human and is returning to the animal state; the somnambule is re-entering her age-old sleep.

So ends this amazing book, which combines the simple majesty of a medieval morality play with the verbal subtlety and refinement of a Symbolist poem. This exposition, of course, has barely skimmed its surface; there are ramifications of the various characters that need a detailed exegesis far beyond the scope of my intention. But, limited as it is, the discussion should have proved one point. *Nightwood* does have a pattern—a pattern arising from the spatial interweaving of images and phrases independently of any time-sequence of narrative action. And, as in *The Waste Land,* the reader is simply bewildered if he assumes that, because language proceeds in time, *Nightwood* must be perceived as a narrative structure. We can now understand why T. S. Eliot wrote that "*Nightwood* will appeal primarily to readers of poetry," and that "it is so good a novel that only sensibilities trained on poetry can wholly appreciate it." Since the unit of meaning in *Nightwood* is usually a phrase or sequence of phrases—at most a long paragraph—it carries the evolution of spatial form in the novel forward to a point where it is practically indistinguishable from modern poetry.

VI. The Parallel with the Plastic Arts

All the works so far considered are thus structurally similar in their employment of spatial form. And the question naturally arises of how to account for this surprising unanimity. But to answer this question satisfactorily, we must first widen the bounds of our analysis and consider the more general problem of the relation of art forms to the cultural climates in which they are created. This latter issue has attracted the attention of students of the arts at least since the time of Herder and Winckelmann; and Hegel, in his *Vorlesungen über die Aesthetik,* gave a masterly analysis of various art styles as sensuous objectifications of diverse *Weltanschauungen.*

Stimulated by this intellectual heritage, and by the vast increase in historical knowledge accumulated during the nineteenth century, a group of German and Austrian art scholars and critics concentrated on the problem of form in the plastic arts. In a series of works published during the first quarter of the present century, they defined various categories of form in the plastic arts, traced in detail the shift from one form to another, and attempted to account for these changes of form by changes in the general cultural ambience.[11] T. E. Hulme, one of the few writers in English to have seriously concerned himself with the problem of form in literature, turned to this group for guidance; and we can do no better than to follow his example.

One German writer in particular exercised a strong influence on Hulme and through Hulme, by way of Eliot, probably on the whole of modern English criticism. This writer is Wilhelm Worringer, the author of the important book, *Abstraction and Empathy* (subtitled *A Contribution to the Psychology of Style*);[12] and it is in Worringer that we shall find the key to the problem of spatial form. Worringer's book appeared in 1908 as its author's doctoral dissertation, but despite this academic provenance it quickly went through numerous editions.

This fact proves—as Worringer himself notes in his third edition—that his subject was not merely academic but touched on problems vital to the modern sensibility. Moreover, as Worringer further remarks, while he and other scholars were rescuing and re-evaluating neglected non-naturalistic styles, creative artists at the very same moment were turning to these styles for inspiration. Worringer's book is impeccably scholastic, confining itself strictly to the past and excluding all but the briefest references to the art of his contemporaries; but it is nonetheless of the utmost relevance for modern art. And this relevance, along with Worringer's unusually expressive and incisive style, gives the book its noticeable quality of intellectual excitement and discovery—a quality that it retains even at the present time, when most of its ideas have become part of the standard jargon of art criticism.

The problem that Worringer sets out to solve is why, throughout the history of the plastic arts, there has been a continual alternation between naturalistic and non-naturalistic styles. Periods of naturalism have included the classical age of Greek art, the Italian Renaissance, and the art of Western Europe to the end of the nineteenth century. In these eras the artist strives to represent the objective, three-dimensional world of "natural" vision and to reproduce with loving accuracy the processes and forms of organic nature (among which man is included). Periods of non-naturalism include most of primitive art, Egyptian monumental sculpture, Byzantine art, Romanesque sculpture, the dominant art styles of the twentieth century. In these eras the artist abandons the projection of space entirely and returns to the plane, reduces organic nature to linear-geometric forms, and frequently eliminates all traces of organicism in favor of pure lines, forms, and colors. To be sure, there are vast differences between the styles of various periods thrown together in these rough categories; but the basic similarities between the works in one category and their basic opposition, taken as a group, to all the styles in the other category are no less striking and instructive. Worringer argues that we have here a fundamental polarity between two distinct types of creation in the plastic arts. And, most important of all, neither can be set up as the norm to which the other must adhere.

From the Renaissance to the close of the nineteenth century it was customary to accept one of these styles—naturalism—as an absolute standard. All other styles were regarded as barbarous aberrations, whose cause could only be ignorance and lack of skill; it was inconceivable that artists should have violated the canons of naturalism except as the result of a low level of cultural development. Franz Wickhoff, a well-known Austrian art historian of the old school, called non-naturalistic art the "charming, childlike stammering of stylization." [13] This was the dominant opinion at the time Worringer's book was written, although the hegemony of naturalism had already begun to lose its power over the artists themselves; and Worringer applies himself to the task of dethroning naturalism as an absolute and eternal aesthetic standard.

To do so, Worringer employs the concept of *Kunstwollen,* or will-to-art, which had been developed in the extremely influential writings of another Austrian scholar, Alois Riegl. Riegl had argued that the impulse to creation in the plastic arts was not primarily an urge toward the imitation of the organic world. Instead, he postulated what he called an absolute will-to-art, or better still, will-to-form. This absolute will-to-form is the element common to all activity in the plastic arts, but it cannot be identified with any particular style. All styles, as a matter of fact, express this will-to-form in diverse fashions throughout the course of history. The importance of this idea is that it shifts the center of gravity in the study of style away from mechanical causation (the state of technical artistic knowledge at the time the style flourished) to a causality based on human will, feeling, and response. "The stylistic peculiarities of past epochs," Worringer writes, "are, therefore, not to be explained by lack of ability, but by a differently directed volition." [14] Non-naturalism cannot be explained as a grotesquely unsuccessful attempt to reproduce natural appearances; nor should it be judged as if it were attempting to compete with naturalism on the latter's own terms. Both types of art were created to satisfy differing spiritual needs, and can only be understood if we examine the climates of feeling responsible for the predominance of one or the other at different times.

The heart of Worringer's book consists in his discussion of the spiritual conditions which impel the will-to-art to move in the direction of either naturalism or its opposite. Naturalism, Worringer points out, always has been created by cultures that have achieved an equilibrium between man and the cosmos. Like the Greeks of the classical period, man feels himself at one with organic nature; or, like modern man from the Renaissance to the close of the nineteenth century, he is convinced of his ability to dominate and control natural forces. In both these periods man has a relationship of confidence and intimacy with a world in which he feels at home; and he creates a naturalistic art that delights in reproducing the forms and appearances of the organic world. Worringer warns us, however, not to confuse this delight in the organic with a mere impulse toward imitation. Such imitation is a by-product of naturalism, not its cause. What we enjoy is not the imitation per se but our heightened sense of active harmony with the organic crystallized in the creation or apprehension of a naturalistic work of art.

On the other hand, when the relationship between man and the cosmos is one of disharmony and disequilibrium, we find that nonorganic, linear-geometric styles are always produced. To primitive peoples, for example, the external world is an incomprehensible chaos, a meaningless or terrifying confusion of occurrences and sensations; hence they would hardly take pleasure in depicting this world in their art. Living as they do in a universe of fear, the representation of its features would merely intensify their sense of anguish. Accordingly, their will-to-art goes in the opposite direction: it reduces the appearances of the natural world to linear-geometric forms. Such forms have the stability, the harmony, and the sense of order that primitive man cannot find in the flux of phenomena as—to use a phrase of Hart Crane's—they "plunge in silence by."

At a higher level of cultural development, non-naturalistic styles like Byzantine and Romanesque are produced during periods dominated by a religion that rejects the natural world as a realm of evil and imperfection. Instead of depicting the profuse vitality of nature with all its temptations, the will-to-art turns toward spiritualization; it eliminates mass and corporeality and tries to approximate the eternal, ethereal tranquillity of otherworldly existence. In both instances—the primitive and the transcendental—the will-to-art, in response to the prevalent climate of feeling, diverges from naturalism to create aesthetic forms that will satisfy the spiritual needs of their creators. Such forms are always characterized by an emphasis on linear-geometric patterns, on the disappearance of modeling and the attempt to capture the illusion of space, on the dominance of the plane in all types of plastic art.

VII. The Meaning of Spatial Form

The relevance of Worringer's views to modern developments in the plastic arts hardly requires any elaborate commentary. If there is one theme that dominates the history of modern culture since the last quarter of the nineteenth century, it is precisely that of insecurity, instability, the feeling of loss of control over the meaning and purpose of life amidst the continuing triumphs of science and technics. Artists are always the most sensitive barometers of cultural change; and it is hardly surprising that the stylistic evolution of modern art, when viewed as a whole, should reveal the effects of this spiritual crisis. But, as T. E. Hulme was one of the first to realize, aesthetic form in modern literature could be expected to undergo a similar change in response to the same climate of feeling; and Hulme's most interesting essay, *Romanticism and Classicism,* is an attempt to define this change as it affects literary form.

Regrettably, Hulme's notion of aesthetic form in literature was not very clearly worked out, and he mistakenly identified his own problem with the attack on Romanticism made by French neoclassic critics like Charles Maurras and Pierre Lasserre. These writers, who also exercised a strong influence on Irving Babbitt, had bitterly criticized the French Romantics on every conceivable ground; but what most impressed Hulme was their violent denunciation of Romantic subjectivity, their rejection of the unrestrained emotionalism that the Romantics sometimes fobbed off as literature. In reading Worringer, Hulme had remarked that non-naturalistic styles suppressed the organic, which could also mean the personal and the subjective; and this, he thought, gave him the clue to the new and corresponding style in modern literature.

Accordingly, he announced that the new style in literature would also be impersonal and objective, or at least would not be "like pouring a pot of treacle over the dinner table." It would have a "dry hardness," the hardness of

Pope and Horace, as against "the sloppiness which doesn't consider that a poem is a poem unless it is moaning or whining about something or other." "I prophesy," Hulme concludes, "that a period of dry, hard, classical verse is coming." [15]

From Hulme's own poetry we know that he was thinking of something resembling Imagism rather than the later influence of Donne and the Metaphysicals. Moreover, while his prophecy may seem to have struck remarkably close to home, his adoption of the time-honored classic-romantic antithesis could only confuse the issue. Hulme's great merit lies in having been among the first to realize that literary form would undergo a change similar to changes in the plastic arts; but he failed to define this literary form with any exactitude. Let us go back to Worringer, and, by combining his ideas with those of Lessing, see if we can take up where Hulme's happy but fragmentary intuitions left off.

Since literature is a time-art, we shall take our point of departure from Worringer's discussion of the disappearance of depth (and hence of the world in which time occurs) in non-naturalistic styles. "It is precisely space," writes Worringer, "which, filled with atmospheric air, linking things together and destroying their individual closedness, gives things their temporal value and draws them into the cosmic interplay of phenomena." [16] Depth, the projection of three-dimensional space, gives objects a time-value because it places them in the real world in which events occur. Now time is the very condition of that flux and change from which, as we have seen, man wishes to escape when he is in a relation of disequilibrium with the cosmos; hence non-naturalistic styles shun the dimension of depth and prefer the plane. If we look only at the medium of the plastic arts, it is, then, absolutely spatial when compared with literature. But if we look at the relation of form and content, it is thus possible to speak of the plastic arts as being more or less spatial in the course of their history. Paradoxically, this means that the plastic arts have been most spatial when they did not represent the space dimension and least spatial when they did.

In a non-naturalistic style, then, the inherent spatiality of the plastic arts is accentuated by the effort to remove all traces of time-value. And since modern art is non-naturalistic, we can say that it is moving in the direction of increased spatiality. The significance of spatial form in modern literature now becomes clear; it is the exact complement in literature, on the level of aesthetic form, to the developments that have taken place in the plastic arts. Spatial form is the development that Hulme was looking for but did not know how to find. In both artistic mediums, one naturally spatial and the other naturally temporal, the evolution of aesthetic form in the twentieth century has been absolutely identical. For if the plastic arts from the Renaissance onward attempted to compete with literature by perfecting the means of narrative representation, then contemporary literature is now striving to rival the spatial apprehension of the plastic arts in a moment of time. Both contemporary art and literature have, each in its own way, attempted to overcome the time elements involved in their structures.

In a purely formal sense, therefore, we have demonstrated the complete congruity of aesthetic form in modern art with the form of modern literature. Thus we have laid bare what Worringer would call the "psychological" roots of spatial form in modern literature. But for a true psychology of style, as Worringer remarks in his *Form in Gothic,* the "formal value" must be shown "to be an accurate expression of the inner value, in such a way that duality of form and content ceases to exist." [17] Hence we must still discuss the relation between spatial form and the content of modern literature, and make some effort to resolve the duality to which Worringer refers.

In the case of Proust, we have already shown that his use of spatial form arose from an attempt to communicate the extratemporal quality of his revelatory moments. Ernst Robert Curtius, at the conclusion of one of the best studies of Proust, has rightly called him a Platonist; for his ultimate value, like that of Plato, was an existence wrenched free from all submission to the flux of the temporal.[18] Proust, as we have seen, was fully alive to the philosophic implications of his own work; and by explaining these implications for us in his analysis of the revelatory moment, Proust himself indicated the relationship between form and content in his great novel.

With the other writers, however, the problem is more complex. Proust had been primarily concerned with a private and personal experience whose extension to other lives was only implicit; but Pound, Eliot, and Joyce all move out beyond the personal into the wider reaches of history—all deal, in one way or another, with the clash of historical perspectives induced by the identification of modern figures and events with various historical or mythological prototypes. This is quite clear in the *Cantos, The Waste Land,* and in *Ulysses,* where the chief source of meaning is the sense of ironic dissimilarity and yet of profound human continuity between the modern protagonists and their long-dead (or only imaginary) exemplars. A similar palimpsest effect is found in *Nightwood,* where Dr. O'Connor is continually drawing on his "prehistoric memory" for images and metaphors, weaving in the past with the present and identifying the two; and where, even apart from his monologues, the characters are seen in terms of images that depict them as historical embodiments of certain permanent and ahistorical human attitudes.

Allen Tate, in his penetrating essay on the *Cantos,* writes that Ezra Pound's "powerful juxtapositions of the ancient, the Renaissance, and the modern worlds reduce all three elements to an unhistorical miscellany, timeless and without origin." [19] This is called "the peculiarly modern quality of Mr. Pound"; but it is also the "peculiarly modern quality" of all the works we have been considering. They all maintain a continual juxtaposition between aspects of the past and the present so that both are fused in one comprehensive view. Both Tiresias and Dr. O'Connor are focuses of consciousness precisely because they transcend historical limits and encompass all times; the same is true of the unspecified voice intoning the *Cantos.* Leopold Bloom and the other major characters in *Ulysses* are projected in the same fashion; but Joyce, true to the traditions of literary naturalism, refuses to make even the central figure of Bloom more than the *unconscious* bearer of his own immortality.

By this juxtaposition of past and present, as Allen Tate realized, history becomes ahistorical. Time is no longer felt as an objective, causal progression with clearly marked-out differences between periods; now it has become a continuum in which distinctions between past and present are wiped out. And here we have a striking parallel with the plastic arts. Just as the dimension of depth has vanished from the sphere of visual creation, so the dimension of historical depth has vanished from the content of the major works of modern literature. Past and present are apprehended spatially, locked in a timeless unity that, while it may accentuate surface differences, eliminates any feeling of sequence by the very act of juxtaposition. Ever since the Renaissance, modern man has cultivated both the objective visual imagination (the ability to portray space) and the objective historical imagination (the ability to apprehend chronological time); both have now been abandoned.

What has occurred, at least so far as literature is concerned, may be described as the transformation of the historical imagination into myth—an imagination for which historical time does not exist, and which sees the actions and events of a particular time only as the bodying forth of eternal prototypes. The historian of religion, Mircea Eliade, has recently noted in modern thought "a resistance to history, a revolt against historical *time,* an attempt to restore this historical time, freighted as it is with human experience, to a place in the time that is cosmic, cyclical, and infinite. In any case," he adds, "it is worth noting that the work of two of the most significant writers of our day— T. S. Eliot and James Joyce—is saturated with nostalgia for the myth of eternal repetition and, in the last analysis, for the abolition of time." [20] These observations from another discipline confirm the view that modern literature has been engaged in transmuting the time world of history into the timeless world of myth. And it is this timeless world of myth, forming the common content of modern literature, that finds its appropriate aesthetic expression in spatial form.*

---

* A reader who wishes another perspective on the key issues raised in this essay can find a fair and cogent refutation of my position in Walter Sutton's article, "The Literary Image and the Reader," *Journal of Aesthetics and Art Criticism,* XVI, 1 (1957–1958), 112–123.

Mr. Sutton's objections, however, seem to me to be based on a misunderstanding. His major argument is that, since reading is a time-act, the achievement of spatial form is really a physical impossibility. I could not agree more. But this has not stopped modern writers from working out techniques to achieve the impossible—as much as possible.

NOTES

1. SPATIAL FORM IN MODERN LITERATURE

1. André Gide, *Prétextes* (Paris: Gallimard, 1913), p. 42.

2. Ezra Pound, *Make It New* (London: Faber and Faber, 1934), p. 336.

3. T. S. Eliot, *Selected Essays* (New York: Harcourt, Brace), p. 247.

4. R. P. Blackmur, *The Double Agent* (New York: Arrow Editions, 1935), p. 49.

5. Maurice Blanchot, "Le Mythe de Mallarmé," *La Part du Feu* (Paris: Gallimard, 1949).

6. Albert Thibaudet, *Gustave Flaubert* (Paris: Gallimard, 1935), p. 105.

7. Gustave Flaubert, "Correspondence," Vol. III (1852–1854), p. 75, *Oeuvres Complètes* (Paris: Louis Conard, 1947).

8. Stuart Gilbert, *James Joyce's Ulysses* (New York: Alfred Knopf, 1952); Harry Levin, *James Joyce* (Norfolk, Conn.: New Directions, 1941), p. 75.

9. Ramon Fernandez, *Messages* (New York: Harcourt, Brace, 1927), p. 210.

10. *Ibid.,* p. 158.

11. The best résumé of this movement may be found in Walter

Passarge, *Die Philosophie der Kunstgeschichte in der Gegenwart* (Berlin: Junker and Dunnhaupt, 1930). A penetrating summary is given by Meyer Schapiro in his article "Style," in *Aesthetics Today,* ed. Morris Philipson (New York: Meridian, 1961), pp. 81–113.

12. New York: International Universities Press, 1953.

13. *Ibid.,* p. 44.

14. *Ibid.,* p. 9.

15. T. E. Hulme, *Speculations* (New York: Harvest, Harcourt, Brace, N. Y.), pp. 113–140.

16. *Abstraction and Empathy,* p. 38.

17. Wilhelm Worringer, *Form in Gothic* (London: G. P. Putnam Sons, 1927), p. 7.

18. Ernst Robert Curtius, *Französischer Geist im XX. Jahrhundert* (Bern: A. Francke, 1952), p. 352.

19. Allen Tate, *The Man of Letters in the Modern World* (New York: Meridian, 1955), p. 262.

20. Mircea Eliade, *The Myth of the Eternal Return* (New York: Bollingen, 1954), p. 153.

2 Malraux's Metaphysics of Art

—For David Baumgardt.

There can be little doubt that the succession of André Malraux's works on art—first *The Psychology of Art,* then *The Voices of Silence* and, more recently, the first volume of *The Metamorphosis of the Gods*—are among the most impressive books published in the present century. Nowhere else in modern art criticism can we find so magnificent a style (which combines the sumptuousness of Chateaubriand with the nervous intensity of Pascal) allied to so vast a knowledge of cultural, religious, and artistic history. One would have to go back to Hegel,

Taine, and Nietzsche on the Continent, or to Ruskin and Walter Pater in England, to find anything comparable to Malraux in scope and grandeur. And if a primary task of art criticism is to translate the affective aura of the visual arts into the medium of language, then Malraux certainly takes his place in the very first rank.

The implications of Malraux's books, however, extend far beyond the limited area of art criticism, or even of the wider discipline of aesthetics. Malraux uses art to argue a metaphysical thesis which touches on the deepest dilemmas of modern culture and has implications both for a philosophy of history and for what the Germans call philosophical anthropology—that is, a philosophy of human culture that attempts to found and define an image of man. And, while everyone has paid some tribute to Malraux's coruscating style, his epigrammatic flair, and his aesthetic sensibility, there has been little effort to analyze and evaluate these larger aspects of his work.

Indeed, there has been a growing tendency to discount them altogether and to regard Malraux as a gifted dilettante, whose stimulating but somewhat frenetic and disorganized *aperçus* do not add up to anything that could be called a unified argument. Moreover, the art historians have had little trouble picking holes in his documentation (as scholars have done with every major work of speculative synthesis since the rise of positivism). And this has contributed to the prevalent impression that Malraux's works on art are more the utterances of an immensely talented personality than a serious contribution to their announced subjects.

Is Malraux really nothing more than a "charlatan of genius" (as Irving Babbitt once called Spengler, in the heyday of the latter's glory), a dazzling spellbinder whose blinding eloquence conceals an ultimate emptiness of thought? Or has he something more positive to offer? Answers to this question swing from the supercilious sniping of the scholars to the totally uncritical enthusiasm of Malraux's admirers; and neither of these alternatives is very enlightening. To be sure, such extreme reactions are certainly encouraged by the haughty peremptoriness of Malraux's prose and his maddening penchant for alluding to ideas in preference to expounding them; but this is all the more reason for trying to hold one's balance. Accordingly, we shall endeavor to grasp his thought as soberly and precisely as possible, for only in this way shall we ever be able to criticize or to praise it with any relevance. And since Malraux's ideas are developed most lucidly and systematically in *The Voices of Silence,* we shall focus our analysis on this central work of his trilogy.

I. The Imaginary Museum

The first book of *The Voices of Silence* is called "Le Musée imaginaire," which for some unknown reason, in Stuart Gilbert's translation, emerges as "The Museum Without Walls." [1] One might gather from this that Malraux was talking about some open-air exhibition; but by "the imaginary museum" Malraux is of course referring to the photographic processes which have made available—first for the scholar, now for the public at large—the immense kaleidoscope of world art. No visual memory could ever have contained the impressions of so many forms, themes, and particularly colors, scattered everywhere on the face of the globe. Photography has thus transformed the relation of modern man to his past, so far as that past is crystallized and preserved in architecture, sculpture, painting, and the whole gamut of minor arts which, as a result of enlargement and isolation of detail, can now be studied with greater accuracy than ever before. But this transformation is qualitative as well as quantitative. For the possibility of seeing all the works of a great artist or the greatest works of a single style *as a whole* gives us a new sense of the common quality in each, and of the manner in which a tradition of forms persists, evolves, and mutates.*

Technology, then, furnishes a necessary condition for the existence of the imaginary museum. But, contrary to the popular view, photography is not by any means the "cause" of its creation. To understand what this cause is, from Malraux's point of view, we must first highlight a central aspect of his whole approach to art. Like Hegel and Nietzsche, but in opposition to the dominating tradition of modern aesthetics, Malraux views art primarily in a religious or metaphysical perspective. Differences in style reflect differences in metaphysical *Weltanschauungen;* and Malraux constantly employs a fundamental dichotomy derived from Worringer's categories of immanence and transcendence. "An art that favors the earth," Malraux writes, "finds its greatest strength in its harmony with man; an art of the world of eternity and destiny, in its disharmony with the human." †

* Malraux's notion of the importance of the imaginary museum has been much misunderstood. Claude-Edmonde Magny, in a perceptive but malicious article obviously inspired by political antipathy, once accused Malraux of wishing to turn world art into a "Buchenwald" where nothing would be left but lifeless photographs. See Claude-Edmonde Magny, "Malraux le fascinateur," *Esprit,* 16 (October, 1948), 525. It is regrettable that Etienne Gilson should recently have added the weight of his name to this invidious charge in his *Painting and Reality* (New York: Meridian, 1959), p. 379. To an impartial reader such attacks seem completely beside the point. Malraux is not advocating a program but trying to explore the implications of a *fact* of contemporary culture. Rather than praising or decrying its existence, he wishes to understand its significance.

† For a more detailed discussion of Worringer's ideas, see pp. 50–54.

The first type of art gives us the anthropomorphism of the Greco-Roman style, with its continuation in Western art from the Renaissance to the mid-nineteenth century; the second, all the non-naturalistic styles ranging from the primitivism of Africa and the South Sea Islands to the sophisticated and elegant deformations of Egyptian, Byzantine, and Romanesque art. Each style reflects one or another type of communal response to the ultimate problem of *la condition humaine;* and for the greater part of the history of mankind "art" in the modern sense was unknown because it had not yet been separated from cult and ritual.

Only when art became a self-contained and autonomous activity was any museum possible at all; hence one cause of the imaginary museum is nothing less than the "real" museum itself. And so far as modern culture is concerned, the idea of art as a *specific* value arose in the Italian Renaissance.[2] But this idea was linked with the revived prestige of the Greco-Roman style, and with the realm of what Malraux calls "poetry" or "fiction," i.e., a repertory of mythological and symbolic imagery through which the artist projected his vision. Hence the Renaissance idea of art, in its rejection of Gothic and Byzantine, clearly lacked universality. And while the world of "poetry" it conjured up was no more "realistic" than the idealized humanity of Greek sculpture, the search for verisimilitude in the Renaissance paved the way for the fatal identification of art with illusion and the imitation of natural appearance. Moreover, the art of the Renaissance was still in the service of religion. And even when this bond became looser and more secularized, as it did very quickly, art remained in the service of the state. Whether a painter glorified God or dignified the power of the ruling monarch, the importance of his art still derived from what it portrayed.

"Until the nineteenth century, a work of art was essentially a representation of something real or imaginary, which conditioned its existence qua work of art."

The real museum emerged on the scene only in the eighteenth century, when art finally became detached from any religious or cultural extra-aesthetic value. "For this concept [i.e., art] to come into being," Malraux notes acutely, "works of art needed to be isolated from their functions. What common link existed between a 'Venus' that *was* Venus, a crucifix that *was* Christ crucified, and a bust? But three 'statues' could be linked together." The creation of the real museum reflected this process of metamorphosis by which crucifixes, altarpieces, commemorations of great events, and symbols of power all became "works of art." But the real museum still imposed certain limits on this metamorphosis—limits determined by the hegemony of the Renaissance tradition. So long as this tradition reigned unchallenged, the very notion of a work of art was synonymous with the creation of a semblance of reality. Nor was the real museum broadened in scope when it began, in the second quarter of the nineteenth century, to include Byzantine, Romanesque, and Egyptian art. For these styles were considered curios of historical interest, not rivals to the masterpieces of the Renaissance canon.

This situation continued until the rise of modern art, which reflected the artist's growing awareness of his change of status. Such awareness, indeed, had betrayed itself a good while before modern art properly so called arrived on the scene (Malraux dates modern art from the first important exhibitions of Manet). Delacroix, Constable, and Corot, for example, all showed a distinct preference for the sketch over the "finished" picture—or at least for certain of their sketches, which were clearly not conceived merely as the preliminary stage of a larger work. These sketches allowed the painter "oblivious of the spectator and indifferent to the 'realism' of the picture [to reduce] a perceived or imagined scene to its purely pictorial content: an aggregate of patches, colors, and movements." Beginning with Manet, this dominance of the "purely pictorial" became the rule rather than the exception; modern art discarded the whole realm of "fiction" or "subject matter," which had ceased to have any real meaning with art's loss of function. Malraux thus defines modern art—in a sentence that has already become classic—as "the annexation of forms by means of an inner pattern or schema, which may or may not take the shape of objects, but of which, in any case, figures and objects are no more than the expression."

By rediscovering the power of art to transform the world independently of verisimilitude or representation, modern art became the chief architect of the imaginary museum. For the stylizations of the moderns showed that past nonnaturalistic styles had also created "works of art" and were not simply examples of cultural inferiority or deficient craftsmanship. No longer was it taken for granted, as it had been in the seventeenth and early eighteenth centuries, "that the Gothic sculptor aimed at making a classical statue, [and] that, if he failed to do so, it was because he could not." The latter half of the nineteenth century, guided by the experience of modern art, instituted a revision of all a priori theories of aesthetics based on accepting one or another school of post-Renaissance painting as a norm. For when confronted with Byzantine, Romanesque, Gothic, and Egyptian art, "idealized faces, realistic faces, Raphael, Rembrandt, and Velásquez were all grouped together in one collective style, and against this the 'accents' of the newly found arts were calling for a totally new conception of art." This new conception ceased to equate "style" with the Greek or Renaissance tradition and art with the creation of illusion or the search for "beauty."

These are the schematic outlines of Malraux's theory of the imaginary museum, which for anyone acquainted with modern art criticism is constructed of fairly familiar materials. Malraux's redefinition of "style" is precisely what Alois Riegl meant by his much-discussed and very influential concept of *Kunstwollen,* i.e., a will-to-art all of whose forms were equally valid and valuable independent expressions. Riegl's work inspired the scholarly effervescence in Germany which led to a re-evaluation of what, from the Greek and Renaissance point of view, had long been considered "backward" or "regressive" styles. Nor does Malraux's analysis of modern art, scintillating as it is, offer anything startlingly original. Roger Fry and Clive Bell had codified the lessons of Cézanne, Gauguin, and Van Gogh in their theory of "significant form"; [3] and so had the French painter and critic Maurice Denis, whom Malraux quotes (though somewhat inaccurately).[4] Even Malraux's key idea of the "metamorphosis" of art through loss of function and the rise of the museum is probably developed from hints in the essays of Paul Valéry [5] and the important but little-known Walter Benjamin.[6]

Nonetheless, by bringing together all these currents of thought Malraux creates a powerful and original synthesis that strikingly illuminates the historical situation of modern culture. Malraux takes the universal relativism of styles out of the art seminar; refracts it through the experience of the autonomy of modern art; and then links both together through the key concept of "metamorphosis," whose effects are intensified and magnified by the imaginary museum of photographic reproduction. Only the combined influence of these phenomena can adequately explain the *unique* historical situation of modern man. Scholarship can—and should—help us to understand the metaphysical sources of style; but if we really could *feel* like the first spectators of an African fetish or a Byzantine Christ, it would be impossible, Malraux argues, to endure their coexistence in the museum. All our knowledge of the past, however, is "filtered" by our experience as moderns—that is, by the experience of the complete autonomy of modern art from extra-aesthetic values. Hence ours is the first culture in history to have completely broken down the barriers between conflicting stylistic traditions and to have achieved the possibility of making contact with the entire range of mankind's artistic creations as a totality.

This description of the modern historical consciousness seems to me a definitive insight of permanent value, one of the few really original contributions to contemporary self-awareness. But whether, as Malraux also believes, it enables us to perceive the essential unity of a universal "quality of man" remains to be seen from the remainder of his great work. It is not difficult, however, to indicate at this point the major intellectual obstacle in his path. This obstacle is nothing less than the diversity of historical cultures and, more particularly, his own basic opposition between humanistic and nonhumanistic styles.

Modern art, to be sure, presumably dissolves this opposition by its "metamorphosis" of extra-aesthetic values; but Malraux does not use this latter concept unequivocally. For the most part, it means the approach to past styles as "art," free from extra-aesthetic values; not always, however.

But though a Gothic crucifix [he writes] becomes a statue, as being a work of art, those special relations between its lines and masses which make it a work of art are the creative expression of an emotion far exceeding a mere will-to-art. It is not of the same family as a crucifixion painted today by a talented atheist. . . . A Gothic head that we admire does not affect us merely through the ordering of its planes; we discern in it, across the centuries, a gleam of the face of the Gothic Christ. Because that gleam is *there.*

Malraux, as we can see, does not wish to surrender extra-aesthetic values *entirely* (we shall understand why later). Meanwhile, let us simply note his oscillation on this crucial issue as the thread of Ariadne that will help to guide us through the labyrinth of his bewilderingly rich developments.

II. The Metamorphoses of Apollo

Malraux's book is not composed in any strict order of expository sequence; and it may appear at first sight as though his second volume, *The Metamorphoses of Apollo,* has little to do with the first. Nothing further is said about the museum or about modern art. Instead, we are suddenly embarked on a vast survey of mutations in style which ranges in time from Alexander the Great to Giotto and in space from India and China in the East to Ireland in the West. But, while there is no strictly logical connection between the first and second books, there is most emphatically a thematic one. Malraux has postulated that "style" is primarily an expression of metaphysical and religious values; and the whole of his second volume is a perceptive demonstration of this thesis. Also, the analyses here further illustrate the general action of "metamorphosis," i.e., the fashion in which one culture selects, filters, and transforms what it receives from another in terms of its own values.

Limiting ourselves to the major articulations of Malraux's argument, we can say that the first metamorphosis of Apollo began when the forms of Hellenistic art were brought by Alexander the Great to the frontiers of India. Here they met the religion of Buddhism; and this produced one of the most remarkable events in art history. For the first representations of the Buddha were created by the Greco-Buddhist sculptors of Gandhara. As Malraux remarks, it required the Greek spirit to breathe life into the figure of the Sage and replace "by his bodily presence the vacant throne which until then had symbolized the Illumination."

But as time went on these Greek forms were subtly changed to conform to the Buddhist sense of values. Buddhism is dominated by the "tranquil picture of a meditation. Thus, throughout the centuries of the 'high' periods of Buddhist art, we find a gradual lowering of the eyelids, a tightening of the face that seems, as it were, to seal it fast upon the Buddha's musings." This Greco-Buddhist art eventually traveled through India and China; everywhere it produced ever-new incarnations of the tender smile of pity at the vanity of human life which is the antithesis of its starting point—the Greek joy in the beauty of the human.

Greco-Roman art was metamorphosed in the Far East by Buddhism; in the Near East by Christianity—but a Christianity which Malraux rather dubiously sees as more allied with Islam than with Latin Christendom in the West. Christian art, to be sure, began in the Roman catacombs; but there is no style of catacomb art. Here Malraux finds the concept of "regression" to be applicable, despite his constant search for positive value in styles diverging from the classical norm. "It is primarily the inexpertness, the poverty of their art, that gives the Catacombs their specifically Christian accent"; the simple craftsmen who decorated them merely used the forms of late Roman art as best they could. And, while Roman forms began to be petrified in Palmyra and Fayum (the latter exclusively a funerary art like the Egyptian), it was only in Byzantium that Christianity succeeded in creating its first great style —a style in which man was again negated by the Eternal, as in Buddhism, but with a difference. "The spirit of Byzantium is all a fixed resolve to escape from the mirage of appearances and an aspiration toward a Nirvana in which, however, man attains God instead of submerging his personality in the Absolute."

Malraux's remarks on Byzantine art, however, lack the precision and surety of his best pages. One misses any allusion to the Neo-Platonic and patristic background, which is probably omitted to heighten the contrast between East and West; and the usual exact suggestiveness of Malraux's prose is unfortunately replaced by rather melodramatic rhetoric ("the oldest dynasties of the Orient reigned jointly at Byzantium: gold and the eternal"). Here Malraux's marked taste for picturesque antithesis somewhat gets out of hand and does him a disservice.

The chapters devoted to the evolution of Christian art in the West are much more satisfactory. For Malraux, the progress of Western Christian art is essentially conditioned by its apprehension of destiny as the unique burden of each individual soul. Greek sculpture had never been concerned with individuals, and Roman portraits are character studies but not biographies; they lack any trace of inner life. "Confronted with any prophet whomsoever, Roman patricians have the shut-in faces of prematurely aged children." Christian art in the West, for the first time in history, infused these forms with the unique stamp of sin, suffering, and moral struggle. "It was the individualization of destiny, this involuntary or unwitting imprint of his private drama on every man's face, that prevented Western art from becoming like Byzantine mosaics always transcendent, or like Buddhist sculpture obsessed with unity."

Romanesque art, compared with the Byzantine, already shows the first steps in this reappearance of the human under Christian auspices—though the God who dominates the Romanesque tympanum is still awesome and the ecstatic elongations of Romanesque sculpture aspire to the transcendent. But in Gothic we find the exclusive majesty of the Romanesque Christ now blending with the rest of the composition and endowed with the emblems of earthly royalty as the Christ-King. God and man come together again as once before in Greece; and "once again sharp ridges were to disappear, draperies and gestures to grow supple." The Gothic artists did not imitate the classical style but they could understand it at last, and they put it to use "in the struggle with Byzantium and even Romanesque magniloquence much as, at a much earlier day, it had served to combat Egypt and Babylon." The Gothic sculpture at Rheims has the calm serenity and dignity of the classical style, but its sacred figures radiate an individual soulfulness unknown to antiquity. "The wheel has turned full circle and the smile was coming back into its own, winning admittance to the City of God."

The culmination of this development is the art of Giotto and the early Renaissance. Malraux sees Giotto primarily in the light of his relation to Gothic sculpture; he even prints a detail from "The Resurrection of Lazarus" upside down to bring out Giotto's quest for three-dimensional volume rather than for perspective. Giotto took the decisive step in humanization by substituting psychological for symbolic expression and by grouping the hitherto unrelated Gothic statues into carefully composed dramatic scenes. Inspired by the spirit of St. Francis, he imparts to his best works an accent of "vast compassion" which for Malraux is "Christianity incarnate." "A metamorphosis of Byzantine painting in terms of Gothic sculpture, this art is no less a metamorphosis of Gothic sculpture in terms of the new Christianity, which was to end up by destroying it." With Giotto the art of the Renaissance begins; his innovations revolutionized Western painting and started it on the search for verisimilitude whose consequences were traced in the first book. Hence at the conclusion of *The Metamorphoses of Apollo* we return to the starting point of the tradition whose secularization and ultimate loss of function was to lead to the rise of the museum.

What is style? Malraux asks in summarizing the results of his inquiry. And the answer is that "painting centers much less on seeing the 'real world' than on making of it another world; all things visible serve style, which serves man and his gods." By this time Malraux has amply earned the right to his definition; but we must note that he has made no progress in overcoming the dualism of his basic categories of immanence and transcendence. On the contrary, he has now depicted the whole history of art as a constant struggle between these two fundamental forms of the sacred.

Moreover, even from the very first book these categories had been associated with the values of liberty and humanism on the one hand (immanence) and submission to the absolute or antihumanism on the other (transcendence). "By contrast with the cowering immobility of Asiatic statuary," writes Malraux, in a typical passage, "the movement of the Greek statue—the first movement known to art— was the very symbol of man's emancipation." Malraux's aim, however, is to prove that liberty is just this "quality of man" which emerges from the juxtaposition of *all* styles in the imaginary museum. And his problem, accordingly, is to turn the values of liberty and humanism, which historically have been expressed only in styles of immanence, into a universal category that can embrace styles of transcendence. This is the task he begins to undertake in his third volume, which turns away from style as a collective expression and focuses on the individual artist.

III. Artistic Creation

Malraux's second volume has admirably succeeded in dissociating art from imitation—not only, it should be noted, the imitation of the world of appearances but also the imitation of itself. New styles are never the result of a passive assimilation of an old style (or a foreign one) which has been haphazardly "rediscovered" or encountered. No style is ever reborn as it was or taken over unchanged; it is always re-created in terms of new values that metamorphose it into new forms. The forms of classical antiquity had existed in plain sight all through the Middle Ages, but were not "rediscovered" until Christianity evolved to the point where it could enter into a dialogue with Greece.

Indeed, one of Malraux's most original insights is to have seen this connection between the aesthetic theory of imitation and the historical theory of "influences"; and he carries on a simultaneous polemic against the two all through his book. Both are efforts, whether conscious or not, to submit a creative response of the human spirit to the causality and determinism of nature—in the one case of nature as geography or "environment," in the other of nature as history. And this same effort, which has been all-pervasive in relation to the problem of style as a whole, has also taken tenacious root in a stereotyped image of the psychology of the creative artist. In his third volume, then, Malraux returns to attack these same errors so far as they have crystallized into a false notion of the creative process.

Simplest of all to dispose of is the obvious fallacy that any artist ever directly imitates anything that can be called "nature." For the vision of every artist is always oriented by an already existing tradition interposed between himself and a hypothetically "pure" visual experience. "We know nothing of what a great artist would be like who did not know any works of art, and found himself only face-to-face with living forms." One might reply that child art is an example of such a situation. But Malraux counters that precisely for this reason child art is incapable of development: the child who becomes an artist must first master the forms of his tradition. Nor does Malraux have much more respect for the popular idea that "folk art" or naïve Sunday painting awkwardly (though charmingly) reflects what the artist "sees." A comparison of Russian Orthodox and Polish Catholic folk art, geographically separated by less than a hundred miles, instantly reveals the grip of traditional styles on the folk vision. And the style of *le douanier* Rousseau, the greatest of the "naïve" painters, is incontestably a carefully developed creation which, as he remarked himself, was "the result of persevering toil."

A more sophisticated variant of this theory links art with religion, as Malraux does himself, but makes art merely the *instinctive* expression of religious emotion. This Romantic cult of "inspiration," which first arose in connection with Gothic art, has since been appropriated by the Surrealists and transferred from the cathedral to the fetish. It is not difficult, however, to unmask its implicit absurdities once we take it seriously. If "technique" means nothing and purity of spirit everything, then St. Francis, as Malraux notes acidly, would clearly have been a greater painter than Giotto. And how can we explain the continuity of style in primitive arts if savage artists merely "expressed" what they felt? Why should they always "feel" in forms whose relationships have created the various clearly marked primitive styles?

Malraux acutely traces the persistence of this inspirational fallacy to two causes. One is the hegemony of the aesthetic theory of "beauty" or the imitation of nature. A style whose merits we recognize, but which belies our aesthetic categories, is attributed to "inspiration" because it eludes our conception of "technique." Also, we tend to confuse the level of culture in which an artist works with his consciousness as an artist. Obviously a primitive Negro sculptor or a barbarian designer of Celtic coins did not exist on the same cultural level as Phidias; but his works exhibit no less a degree of *artistic* awareness and intelligence.

An artist, then, does not begin by imitating "nature" or by giving free rein to his instinct. But what *does* he do? Malraux replies in a key passage, which outlines his conception of the truly *creative* artist—the inventor of new forms, whom he carefully distinguishes from the craftsman or epigone who merely carries on an existing tradition.

> A man who is destined to become a great painter [he writes] begins by discovering that he is more responsive to a special world, the world of art, than to the world he shares with other men. He feels a compelling impulse to paint, though he is well aware that his first work doubtless will be bad and there is no knowing what the future has in store. After an early phase of pastiche, during which he usually copies near-contemporary masters, he becomes aware of a discrepancy between the nature of the art he is imitating and

the art which one day will be his. He has glimpses of a new approach, a program that will free him from his immediate masters, often with the aid of the masters of an earlier age. . . . Once he has mastered one by one his color, drawing, and means of execution—once what was a schema has become a style—a new plastic interpretation of the world has come into being.

This passage takes on its full significance only if we use it as a focus to catch the scattered rays of Malraux's metaphysics of art, which now assumes a markedly different aspect. For, while hitherto the metaphysical value of art had derived from its link with one or another historical form of the sacred, we find Malraux here attributing such value to the function of artistic creation *in itself*.

The artist, he tells us, begins by discovering that he prefers the world of pictures to that of reality; and this, whether the artist is aware of it or not, constitutes, in Malraux's opinion, a metaphysical choice. For all art, as Hegel had remarked long ago, is a reduction of the world of reality to one or another significance imposed on it by the artist either as individual or as representative of his culture. "Thus styles are *significations*," Malraux explains, "they impose a *meaning* on visual experience . . . always we see them replacing the uncharted scheme of things by the coherence they enforce on all they 'represent.'"

Life as a whole is stronger than man because implicit in it are chaos and fatality from the human point of view; "but, taken individually, each form of life is weaker than man, since no living form in itself *signifies* life." When he feels the attraction of art, the destined artist is thus inserting himself into the realm that endows the chaos of appearances with significance. Only from this point of view can we truly understand the passionate insistence with which Malraux hunts down every variety of theory that would confuse art with nature (whether as external nature or as natural instinct). All such theories enslave the artist to nature, while art is born, Malraux contends, "from a desire to wrest forms from the real world to which man is subject and to make them enter into a world of which he is the ruler."

The apprentice artist chooses the realm of freedom—not, to be sure, as the result of a rational, self-conscious decision but as the effect of an irresistible passion. But, while he may exist in a realm of freedom relatively to the non-artist, he "is born prisoner of a style." Now begins the struggle to free himself from his masters—a struggle imposed by a new signification of the world which the artist feels obscurely germinating in himself and which he knows only as a dissatisfaction with the already existing forms of his tradition. And if he succeeds in incarnating this new signification into a coherent system of forms, then he takes his place among the masters.

The great artist, then, asserts his freedom not only generically but specifically, in terms of his personal conquest of a signification of the world; and he becomes a symbol for Malraux of the metaphysical power of man himself to create a meaningful human world. *"So far as he is a creator,* the artist does not belong to a collectivity that merely sustains a culture but to one which develops it, whether he cares about doing so or not. His creative faculty does not submit him to a fatality become intelligible; it links him to the millennial creative power of man, to cities rebuilt from the ruins, to the discovery of fire."

It is in defense of this metaphysical value of freedom that Malraux rejects all efforts to "explain" a great artist's conquest of his style purely in terms of historical conditioning. His arguments on this point have aroused a storm of righteous indignation among art historians, who have taken his remarks as an attack on their discipline and have not hesitated to accuse him of intellectual obscurantism.[7] This merely proves that people who carefully study works of art do not always devote the same attention to words and ideas. As a matter of fact, Malraux never denies the importance or the value of the historical study of art; indeed in some ways he makes it more important than do the historians themselves. For Malraux, the "historicity" of a work enters as an integral component into our aesthetic judgment; it is only against the background of a style taken as a whole, or against the entire corpus of an artist's production, that we can truly gauge the new signification embodied in the greatest works.[8]

What Malraux does argue, somewhat analogously to Bergson, is that the conceptual patterns imposed by the historian ex post facto, helpful though they are, do not adequately grasp the existential reality of the creative process. By confusing one with the other, we fall into the illusion of believing that the creations of genius are the natural and inevitable result of a particular historical sequence, as if "values always produce their own art as an apple tree its apples." If a great work were suddenly to disappear, however, it would be impossible to *predict* its creation despite all our knowledge of the historical conditions in which it could come to birth.

History, to use Malraux's formulation, calls forth a response from the artist but does not determine it; each artist responds to a different aspect of his time in terms of his personality (El Greco and Tintoretto were contemporaries, and both studied with Titian). But this does not mean either that the personal biography of an artist "determines" his response; for nothing about an artist's life can ever account for the *quality* of his creations. The works

of a great artist thus always preserve a margin of inde-
termination and mystery—the mystery of human liberty
that Malraux celebrates on a different level in *The Walnut
Trees of Altenburg*. And his third volume culminates in a
veritable hymn of praise to the great creator, whose art
presents man with the incarnation of his own supreme
attribute.

If now we compare Malraux's point of view in his third
volume with that in the first and second volumes we become aware to what extent (and without any overt warn-
ing to the reader) his metaphysics of art has shifted its
ground. "Within every artichoke is an acanthus leaf," he
wrote in the first volume, "and the acanthus is what man
would have made of the artichoke, had God asked his advice. Thus, step by step, Greece scaled down the forms of
life to man's measure, and similarly adjusted to him the
forms of foreign arts." The "humanization of the world"
here is exclusively the work of Greek art and its tradition
of immanence. But in the third volume this "humanization" becomes the appanage of art as a whole.

"Every true style," Malraux now writes, "is the scaling
down to our human perspective of that eternal flux on
whose mysterious rhythms we are borne ineluctably, in a
never-ceasing drift of stars. Apollo, Prometheus—or Saturn;
Aphrodite, or Ishtar; a resurrection of the flesh, or the
Dance of Death." Malraux thus wipes out the distinction
between styles of immanence and transcendence, humanism and antihumanism, by considering all art a reduction
of the chaos of nature to a human perspective independently of the cultural values it may express. Far from solving his problem, however, this inconsequence only makes
it more acute. For now the abyss of an unmediated contradiction yawns between his historical categories, on the
one hand, and his view of art as identical with the meta-

physical value of liberty, on the other. The problems posed by this contradiction are accordingly taken up in the fourth and final volume; and Malraux attempts to resolve them in the light of modern art and its "metamorphosis" of the past.

IV. The Small Change of the Absolute

With his fourth volume, Malraux finally returns to the complex of problems broached in his introductory volume on the imaginary museum. Earlier Malraux had discussed the evolution of modern art largely in terms of the aesthetic revolt against imitation—its rejection of the quest for illusion, and the triumph of formal schema over subject matter. This had been linked with art's loss of function and its total secularization; but since Malraux had not yet established his theory of style as a function of changing crystallizations of the sacred, he had kept this explanation in the background. After his depiction of the "Metamorphoses of Apollo," however, Malraux could assume that he had firmly established his position; and so now he goes back to pick up the thread of historical evolution at the point where secularization first became clearly perceptible. This point is the definitive break of Dutch painting in the seventeenth century with the idealization of Italian Baroque.

Dutch painting of the great period was the first style to abandon Christian iconography on a large scale and to turn to subject matter that was totally secular and mundane. "The Dutch were not the first to paint fish on a plate, but they were the first to cease treating it as food for the apostles." This was the historical moment when the artist began to become alienated from his public (Rem-

brandt was the first *peintre maudit*) and when, as in
Vermeer, we have those first intimations of a "pure" painting which has made the latter one of the godfathers of
modern art. No one was yet aware, though, of what had
really occurred—the beginning of the end of culture's age-
old involvement with the absolute. Always in the past the
waning of one religion had meant the rise of another; but
this was no longer true. "The cult of Science and Reason
that now ensued was not just another metamorphosis of
the religious sentiment but its negation. . . . What is
here in question is not the form assumed by a religion, but
that impulse of the soul which wrests man from his life on
earth and unites him with the Eternal."

Western culture was thus losing its relation with any
supreme metaphysical or religious value; and without such
a value, which forms the basis for spiritual communion
among men, no true culture is possible. "Though there
had been Greek skeptics, there has never been a culture
pledged to skepticism (and ours is not conditioned by our
agnosticism but by our conquest of the world)." But this
loss was masked for two hundred years, first by the deification of Reason in the eighteenth century (which gave men
a new gospel around which to rally and led to Robes-
pierre's cult of a Supreme Being), and then by the exalted
political hopes of the nineteenth. "Modeled no less than
the gods of Greece on human values (though on very different lines), the political deity of the nineteenth century
stepped into the place of the God of the Jesuits." The tri-
umphant bourgeoisie, however, did not bring any values
with it except secular ones. And while the bourgeoisie had
triumphed in the past—in Holland, in Flanders, and in the
Florence of the Medicis—this was the first time it had done
so in a world that had lost all metaphysical coherence.

No one felt this loss more acutely than the artist, whose

function had always been to express the highest values of his culture. And when the bourgeoisie demanded an art of delectation, amusement, or servile flattery, subject to no order of supreme values, the true artist refused to truckle to this debasing demand. Instead, we get the break between the artist and society that is one of the most striking and unprecedented aspects of modern culture. With Manet, Cézanne, and Impressionism, this break was at first only a rejection of the confusion of art with illustration; but with Gauguin, Van Gogh, and the whole development of modern art leading up to Picasso it became an attack on modern culture. This culture was one in which, as in the Hellenistic period of the ancient world, a metaphysical humanism had lost its religious impetus and was running out into the sands of sensualism and self-indulgence. And the modern artist reacted by rejecting humanism in all its forms, bringing back to life instead all the styles of transcendence in which man had either been denied or negated.

Malraux had argued, in his first volume, that the imaginary museum potentially places us in contact with world art as a whole; but he now recognizes that, under the influence of modern art, it has been oriented in the direction of "a barbaric Renaissance." No art that bears the stamp of humanism or civilized refinement really appeals to our sensibility; it is all the others that we hang in a place of honor. And along with these antihumanistic styles, we are once more becoming susceptible to the values that brought them to birth. "Many of our resuscitations," writes Malraux, "call into question not only painting as we know it, but man as he is today."

What has been called into question is the optimism and rationalism, the belief in science and progress, the refusal to face the ineluctable truth of man's fate which marked the nineteenth century. To challenge these dogmas modern art has revitalized all styles which contain either a streak of the diabolic or a spark of the divine; and more the former than the latter. "The devil, who always paints in two dimensions, has become the most eminent artist of our time." Indeed, the specter of modern art hangs over a Europe which has lost faith in itself and its time-honored concept of Man. "Whether dying or not, menaced assuredly, and haunted by the demonic presences she has recalled from oblivion, Europe seems now to contemplate her future less in terms of freedom than in those of destiny."

The conflict between Malraux's metaphysics of art and his historical categories thus reappears dramatically *within* the context of the problem of modern art and modern culture. Moreover, it reappears in a form that seems to land Malraux in a hopeless impasse. For how can he continue to identify artistic creation with the metaphysical value of liberty, when modern art—the most liberated that the world has ever known—has used this liberty only to revive the antihumanism of styles of transcendence? Is not Malraux's own analysis of the meaning of modern culture a refutation of his attempt to make artistic creation a wellspring of metaphysical humanism? At this point in his book Malraux the thinker irresistibly reminds us of one of the heroes of his own novels, facing the dark threat of fate and destruction and striving to assert the dignity of man in the teeth of everything that grinds him to dust. And just as his heroes rise to the full splendor of their humanity only at this moment of crisis, so Malraux gathers together all the conceptual strands of his book to resolve the dilemma that he has stated so forcefully and so candidly.

V. The Two Metamorphoses

Malraux's solution is carried through by means of the concept of metamorphosis, but only by a constant overlapping of the two uses that we have distinguished. Sometimes Malraux stresses the divorce of modern art from all extra-aesthetic values, which allows us to metamorphose past cultural antagonisms into one universal "language." Whether originally savage, humanistic, or transcendental, all past styles have now become transmuted into so many systems of aesthetic forms. "Provided we have art, not culture, in mind, the African mask and Poussin, the ancestor and Michelangelo, are seen to be not adversaries, but polarities." It is easy to understand, however, why Malraux could not rest content with this solution.

For one thing, it fails to explain the orientation of modern art toward styles of transcendence. If all styles are only purely formal systems, why should the modern sensibility prefer one system over another? And even more important, this metamorphosis of styles into "forms" would undermine the very metaphysical value that Malraux wishes to attribute to art—a value that derives historically from the connection of art with the sacred. By stripping art of all extra-aesthetic value Malraux overcomes the dualism of his historical categories; but he turns his metaphysics of art into a gratuitous assertion without any real support.

To support his metaphysics Malraux falls back on the alternate significance of "metamorphosis," which then leads him to a much more subtle and profound view of modern art. Far from being merely the assertion of the hegemony of technique over theme, form over content, modern art is now seen as controlled by a fundamental extra-aesthetic value. "For there *is* a fundamental value of modern art," Malraux asserts, "and one that goes far deeper than a mere quest of the pleasure of the eye. Its annexation of the visible world was but a preliminary symptom of the ancient desire for an autonomous world *for the first time reduced to itself.*" Modern art thus reaffirms art's age-old relation to the sacred without, however, itself having any positive version of the sacred to express; it insists on continuing to exercise a metaphysical function, although deprived by modern culture of any religious substance.

Styles of transcendence have always expressed most forcefully art's relation to the sacred; and this explains the paradox of modern art, which unites the utmost freedom of the artist with his preference for styles in which freedom had been negated. "Akin to all styles that express the transcendental and unlike all others, our style seems to belong to some religion of which it is unaware. Yet it owes its affinity with the former not to the expression of faith in an unseen world, but, rather, to the absence of such faith, and is as it were a photographic negative of the styles of the transcendent." Hence freedom, in modern art, becomes an attribute of styles of transcendence; it is modern art that reconciles Malraux's metaphysics and his historical categories.

By projecting this reconciliation of modern art back onto the past, Malraux arrives at the most brilliant single stroke of conceptual intuition in his entire book. Modern art has revived our sense of art's relation to the sacred per se, without committing us to any of its historical forms; nor does its latent antihumanism negate the individual freedom of artistic creation. Hence it enables us to appreciate sympathetically the values of all the spiritual communions of the past. Even more, we now see their art, on the analogy of our own, as differing but essentially related responses of human freedom and creativity to the eternal question of man's fate.

> For since the great languages of the past reach us only by way of a metamorphosis, they are no longer the original languages; each masterwork, in transmitting one of these languages, gives us the impression that this was the language of a single artist, unique creator of all the spiritual values he expresses. Though we know that behind a Khmer head lie centuries of Buddhism, we look at it as if its spirituality and complexity must have been the invention of its maker. It conveys to us a "relativized absolute." In short, we look at great works of the remote past—whether their purport be cosmic, magical, religious, or transcendental—*as so many Zarathustras invented by so many Nietzsches.*

In other words, we do not feel past styles primarily as products of conflicting cultural traditions—any more than we feel Gauguin and Matisse to be mutually exclusive despite the clashing spiritual worlds in which they live. On the contrary, we unite them as differing expressions of creative freedom; and, in Malraux's opinion, we do the same with the art of the past. The absolutes of history have become "relativized" into symbols that retain their expressive significance as confrontations with the sacred; but the conflict between such modes recedes before our apprehension of the liberty of the creative process. "In ceasing to subordinate creative power to *any* supreme value, modern art has brought home to us the presence of that creative power throughout the whole history of art."

It is in the light of this latter metamorphosis that we must understand Malraux's cryptic but extremely suggestive concluding remarks on the philosophy of history. Malraux, it should be stressed, does *not* believe anything so puerile as that art "frees" man from time or history. He ridicules this very popular pseudo profundity in *The Wal-*

nut Trees of Altenburg,[9] and he explicitly says the opposite in *The Voices of Silence*. "Art does not deliver man from being only an accident in the universe," he emphasizes, "but it is the soul of the past in the sense in which each ancient religion was the soul of the world." Religion, by defending man against destiny, had formerly given a soul to the world; but modern culture has no religion and destiny, too, has now assumed a new guise. "Whenever becoming or fatality usurps the place of being, history usurps that of theology"; it is history that has become the destiny of modern man, who no longer sees himself in the perspective of any religious eternity but exclusively in that of time. Destiny has become the Hegelian intuition of history as an all-engulfing and all-destroying process which, once divorced from Hegel's belief in the Absolute as Spirit and hence as freedom, has culminated in Spenglerian pessimism and in the various other types of historical determinism that rule the modern consciousness.

Against this background, the metamorphosis of the imaginary museum takes on an extraordinary importance. For in Malraux's opinion this metamorphosis enables us to feel all the great cultures of the past as symbols of a creative power which continues to exist in our own day, and which testifies to the ability of man to create a world of human values that assert his spiritual autonomy. Malraux has been consistently misinterpreted to mean that the mere *survival* of works of art somehow accomplishes this feat; but, since a good many things besides works of art have survived from the past, this reduces Malraux's thought to banality.

Art occupies a privileged place because, unlike an ordinary artifact, it bears the impress of man's encounter with the sacred; because we can experience this encounter *directly* without the necessity of the translation or erudition required by literature; and because the metamorphosis of the past by modern art enables us to transform this experience into that of human liberty defending itself against destiny. Hence art allows us to confront historical relativism on its own terms and, while accepting its conclusions, to turn them into a source of inspiration rather than of despair. In this sense modern culture is heir to all the ages—"not so much of this or that value in particular (or of each and all) as of something that runs deeper: that undercurrent of the stream of human consciousness which brought them into being." All art is thus, as Malraux writes, "an antidestiny." It has become the "soul" of a modern world which accepts no absolute other than history and time, but which, if it is to continue to survive, must struggle to preserve its faith in the creative power of human liberty.

VI. The Quality of Man

Malraux's *The Voices of Silence* is such a grandiose and impressive achievement, it is conceived on so majestic a scale and carried through with such mastery and *brio,* that one's first reaction can only be an admiration that far outweighs all criticism or reservations. Nor is this reaction belied after the first impact has begun to wear off. Not since Nietzsche's *The Birth of Tragedy* has there been any work on art which can even remotely begin to compare with Malraux's; only its great predecessor combines such depth with such range or unites so passionate a sympathy for the modern with so penetrating an understanding of the past. And this comparison of Malraux with Nietzsche can be extended much further.

Nietzsche wished to sweep away all merely "aesthetic"

interpretations of Greek tragedy so as to re-establish its relation to the religious and the sacred; and Malraux does the same for the entire realm of the plastic arts. Wagner's music drama provided the contemporary point of departure for Nietzsche's reflections, while Malraux takes his from modern art and the aesthetic of Postimpressionism; and where Nietzsche exploited the fruits of a half century of German classical scholarship, Malraux utilizes the efforts which two generations of art historians have devoted to the study and re-evaluation of transcendental styles. Finally, both writers are concerned with the problem of the nature of art primarily as a clue to the more important question of the condition of modern culture. But while Nietzsche, at the time he wrote *The Birth of Tragedy*, saw hope for the future only in the reawakening of the German spirit by the metaphysical profundity of Wagnerian music, Malraux sees modern art as the herald of a universal humanism founded on the metaphysical dignity of man as creator.

Nietzsche's uncovering of the Dionysian roots of Greek tragedy has become one of the permanent acquisitions of modern culture; and the same, we may predict, will prove true for Malraux's interpretation of the significance of modern art. By placing the adventure of modern art in the context of the millennia of history Malraux illuminates its problems in a remarkably original fashion. For, while modern art has hitherto been considered the most radical break ever made with tradition, Malraux reveals it to be, on the contrary, an unprecedented effort to restore art's immemorial link with the sacred in a desacralized world.

The usual views of modern art are that it tries either to incarnate the visually paradoxical theories of modern science or to explore the irrational depths of the psyche. Both explanations are related, as we can see, by the effort to penetrate beyond the human world to some underlying principle that supports and sustains the visible. Etienne Gilson has acutely spoken of abstract art, with its acknowledged theosophical roots, as an invasion of art by the ancient spirit of Pythagorean mathematical mysticism; and the same mysticism is evident in the exploration of the self, which becomes the vehicle through art for man's contact with the absolute. Malraux's theory provides a common category for both interpretations and places them in a definitive historical perspective. "In this context," he writes, "the religious vocabulary may jar us; but unhappily we have no other. Though this art is not a god, but an absolute, it has, like a god, its fanatics and its martyrs, and is far from being an abstraction."

Does Malraux, however, really succeed in overcoming the opposition between his metaphysics of art and his historical categories? How convincing are his final arguments, which have been presented so far without any criticism?

To answer this question we must make a distinction that Malraux overlooks between the view that all art is a human response, and the related but not identical claim that we experience all these responses throughout the whole range of world art as *equal* expressions of man's freedom. It is certainly true, as Malraux points out, that the combined influence of modern art and art history has taught us to see all styles as human responses. None are any longer relegated to the realm of merely instinctual barbarism or savagery; all are felt as expressions of values. But it does not follow that we have ceased to feel the differences between the values expressed in styles of transcendence from those expressed in styles of immanence. This is the point at which Malraux tries to prove too much, and where, in my opinion, his thesis ultimately breaks down.

It may well be that this breakdown is concealed from Malraux himself because of the ambiguity in his idea of metamorphosis. For, if all the art of the past were metamorphosed into "aesthetic forms," then, as we have already noted, it would be true that we could feel them all as an undifferentiated unity. But this unity would have no metaphysical value because the forms would not endow nature with any "significance." On the other hand, once Malraux concedes that we feel the metaphysical *quality* of past cultures in their styles (and this position not only is necessary for his argument but certainly corresponds far more closely to the facts), then he reintroduces the felt disparity between humanistic and nonhumanistic styles that he wished to eliminate. To get around this difficulty, which he never clearly formulates but which he undoubtedly felt, Malraux occasionally suggests that a great masterpiece somehow conveys the experience of man's creative power in a pure state. But this contention can hardly be taken seriously, especially in the light of Malraux's own historical analyses.*

Even a work of genius comes to us as a particular historical incarnation, which expresses a certain level of cultural development and a certain type of response to destiny. "If an art associated with the most hideous sacrifices holds our interest," Malraux asks, "is this because of the glimpses it gives us of a world of elemental chaos? Or

---

* At least once in the book Malraux offers still another argument that reveals him wrestling with this dilemma. Here he claims that art transcends the historical horizon of its own culture and is not bound to its values. "However closely bound up with the culture whence it springs, art often ranges farther than that culture, or even transcends it, seeming to draw its inspiration from sources untapped by the spirit of the age and from a loftier conception of man." But Malraux fails to pursue this idea or offer any evidence in its support, and we may disregard it as a rhetorical flourish.

is it, rather, for its expression of man's ability to escape from chaos, even though the way of escape lies through blood and darkness?" We can follow Malraux in choosing the second alternative to this question without agreeing to his unconvincing corollary that such an art ranks with the classical Greek as an expression of man's freedom. One has the feeling that Malraux drives his argument to this extreme only because his two meanings of metamorphosis keep blending into each other, and he never really succeeds in disentangling all their divergent implications.

Malraux ultimately fails, then, to dissolve the disparate qualities of historical cultures and their styles into the universal apprehension of the liberty of the creative act. But this by no means invalidates his major argument as a whole; it merely shows that he has been trying to perform an impossible task. What he *has* done is to prove that all art, to use Ernst Cassirer's term, is a universal "symbolic form"; and perhaps the best way to evaluate Malraux's achievement is to compare his main thesis with the startlingly similar one of the greatest modern philosopher of culture.

"Every authentic function of the human spirit," Cassirer has written, "has this decisive characteristic . . . [that] it does not merely copy but rather embodies an original formative power. It does not express passively the mere fact that something is present, but contains an independent energy of the human spirit through which the simple presence of the phenomenon assumes a definite 'meaning,' a particular ideational content. This is as true of art as it is of cognition; it is as true of myth as of religion." [10] No better definition could be given of Malraux's central concept of "style"; and it may not be too fanciful to suggest that, probably without any knowledge of Cassirer's *The Philosophy of Symbolic Forms,* Malraux has nonetheless added a fourth volume on art to Cassirer's three on language, myth, and cognition. However that may be, Malraux certainly shows us man everywhere behaving not only as a symbolic but also as a metaphysical animal, eternally confronting the problem of destiny with a world of values of his own creation.

Malraux's mistake was in wishing to press this *functional* unity of the spirit too far and to turn it into the substantial, or *ontological,* unity of a universal "quality of man" (though Malraux's position is even more complicated because he appears to recognize that such an ontological unity is a historical "myth," arising only as a result of the metamorphosis of the past by modern art). But no such ontological unity can be asserted if, like Cassirer and Malraux, one honestly faces the enormous range of man's historical diversity rather than indulging in the currently fashionable Existentialist sport of postulating pseudo-universal categories. Schooled in the intricacies of Kantian speculation, and far more aware of this pitfall, Cassirer limits himself carefully to asserting only a functional unity, and he grapples superbly with the formidable task of tracing the various stages of development within each of the great cultural forms.

Malraux, it seems to me, could well have done the same without contradicting the true logic of his fundamental position. For to recognize that the human spirit has been more or less free in the course of its history, and that art expresses its temporary defeats and abdications as well as its victories, does not cancel out the qualitative separation of the spirit from nature or the impossibility of explaining its creations as the product of purely natural or nonhuman causes. But Malraux refuses to admit any overt principle of cultural evolution in his book, perhaps because he felt too acutely the danger of implying that a humanistic culture would necessarily produce an aesthetically more valuable style. Or perhaps, just as he finds it impossible in his novels to represent any character who is basely and inhumanly evil (a point perceptively noted by Claude-Edmonde Magny), so in his thought he instinctively refuses to acknowledge that the "quality of man" has not always been equal to the highest potentialities of his freedom.

There are certain failures which, by their very magnitude, dwarf any number of smaller and more timid successes; and after all the objections have been made to *The Voices of Silence,* the first impression of a towering achievement still remains the only adequate response. Malraux has incontestably written one of the great reaffirmations of humanism in our time—a reaffirmation all the more valuable because it breaks through the bounds of the Greco-Roman tradition from which humanism sprang and attempts to endow its ideals with universal meaning. Like Freud, Thomas Mann, and Cassirer, Malraux has refused to surrender the ideal of man inherited from both the classical tradition and the eighteenth-century Enlightenment; but he has tried to widen and deepen this ideal by overcoming its opposition to the primitive, the irrational, and the nominally antihuman. Freud gave us a new understanding of the dream, the unconscious, and the sexual; Mann projected a "dream poem of humanity" that would synthesize the Dionysian and the Apollonian; Cassirer extended Kantian categories, derived from the epistemology of the natural sciences, to the irrational realms of language and myth; and Malraux struggles to show us man affirming his humanity in the fetish, the painted trophy of the head-hunter, and the grinning death mask of the Aztec crystal skull. No more important task could possibly be undertaken in our time, when Heidegger has denied the value of even attempting to restore the ancient luster of the word "humanism" and Sartre has appropriated it for a philosophy in which ethics is declared an impossibility.[11] If we are to look anywhere in modern culture for a truly great expression of an Existentialist humanism outside the ranks of those committed to a dogmatic religion, it is to Malraux's novels and his books on art that we shall finally have to turn.

NOTES

2. MALRAUX'S METAPHYSICS OF ART

1. This is only a minor example of the liberties, sometimes wholly unjustified, that Stuart Gilbert takes with Malraux in his very free translation. On the whole, Mr. Gilbert does a good job, but he has a disconcerting way of leaving out qualifying and amplifying phrases and clauses that are sometimes of great importance.

   I have used Mr. Gilbert's translation of *The Voices of Silence* (New York: Doubleday and Co., 1953), but have made minor alterations in his text to bring him closer to the original in a good many of my quotations.

2. In *The Metamorphosis of the Gods,* Malraux extends this concept to include the Hellenistic period. The Hellenistic spectator, he says, does not admire in Lysippus what he admired in Phidias. With the former, "sculpture had discovered a new power—and the first universe of the aesthetic. The *Athena* was a divine image, the *Aurige* an ex-voto; henceforth one wished a *Praying Ephebe* to be a work of art." *La Métamorphose des Dieux* (Paris: Gallimard, 1957), Vol. I, p. 95.

3. Roger Fry, "Retrospect," *Vision and Design* (New York: Brentano's, n.d.), pp. 295–302.

4. Maurice Denis, *Théories* (Paris: L. Rouart et J. Watelin, 1920), p. 1.

5. "I can well understand," wrote Valéry, "why neither the Egyptians, the Chinese, nor the Greeks, all wise and civilized peoples, were familiar with this system of juxtaposing productions that

mutually devour each other." This remark both places the museum historically and approaches the idea of the metamorphosis of the work in the museum. Paul Valéry, *Oeuvres* (Paris: Bibliothèque de la Pleiade, 1960), Vol. II, p. 1292.

6. Walter Benjamin's influential essay, "The Work of Art in the Era of Technical Reproduction," first appeared in French in 1936 and was cited by Malraux in the same year at a speech before the International Association of Writers for the Defense of Culture in London.

   Benjamin points out that reproduction deprives a work of art of its "aura" of unicity, which is linked with its value in cult and ritual; and he argues that this constitutes an epochal transformation in man's whole relation to art. But Benjamin does not develop the implications of this idea, and he goes on to discuss the movies and their relation to the masses. Walter Benjamin, *Schriften* (Frankfurt am Main: Suhrkamp Verlag, 1955), Vol. I, pp. 366–397.

7. As an example, we may cite Professor James S. Ackerman, editor of *The Art Bulletin.* "A few years ago," he wrote in 1960, "the presentness of all past art was pointed out by André Malraux, whose observations led him to the abandonment (?) of historical consciousness and to a philosophy of pure sensation. Malraux saw the weakness in history without criticism, and found an answer in criticism without history." James S. Ackerman, "Art History and the Problems of Criticism," *Daedalus,* 89 (Winter, 1960), 260.

   Malraux, it might be remarked, is a good deal more sophisticated about problems of historical method than are most of the scholars who feel impelled to read him a lesson. Certainly the best work on historicism in recent years is Raymond Aron's *Introduction to a Philosophy of History* (Boston: Beacon, 1962); and one of the two persons to whom he dedicates the French edition of the book is—André Malraux. Such a dedication would testify, if not to literal intellectual indebtedness, then at least to a lively interchange and communion of ideas.

8. This is the basis for Malraux's interesting discussion of the problem of fakes. Why should a work hailed as a masterpiece one day be relegated to the junk heap the next if it is found to be a forgery? Malraux replies that, once known as a forgery, the work can no longer be felt as part of a historical tradition of forms expressing a particular significance; and the great work no longer appears as the personal conquest of a new variety of such significance.

   Etienne Gilson has objected to Malraux's view as too "literary" and "historical," and has written instead: "It is not true that the intrinsic value of a work of art, taken *qua* work of art, should be in any way affected by the answer given to the problem of its authenticity." *Painting and Reality,* p. 94.

   Malraux's argument at least has the merit of trying to grapple with an observable and omnipresent phenomenon. Gilson's attempt to rule out *all* "knowledge" in determining "intrinsic value" strikes me as self-contradictory. Without some knowledge, how would we even know we were looking at a "work of art"?

   Perhaps the real answer to the problem lies in economics rather than aesthetics: it is scarcity that increases value. But in any case, it is amusing to observe Malraux the novelist and intellectual amateur arguing on the side of knowledge and history, while the learned historian of medieval thought champions the purity of ignorance.

9. In the famous colloquy at Altenburg, Count Rabaud says: ". . . the great artist, gentlemen, establishes the eternal identity of man with himself. By the manner in which he depicts such and such an action of Orestes or Oedipus, of Prince Hamlet and the Karamazov brothers, he brings close to us those destinies otherwise so distant in space and time; he renders them fraternal and revelatory. Thus certain men possess this great privilege, this divine spark, of finding within the depths of themselves— and presenting it to us as a gift—that which delivers us from space, time, and death."

   The narrator, who speaks for Malraux, comments ironically on this position: "The idea he had just developed, subtly banal, was then popular among a good many intellectuals." This idea is then rejected in the course of the debate as inadequate to the tragic reality of the human condition. *The Walnut Trees of Altenburg,* Part II, Chap. iii.

10. Ernst Cassirer, *The Philosophy of Symbolic Forms* (New Haven: Yale University Press, 1953), Vol. I, p. 78.

11. Martin Heidegger, "Brief über den Humanismus" in *Platon's Lehre von der Wahrheit* (Bern: A. Francke, 1947), pp. 53–119; Jean-Paul Sartre, *Saint Genet* (Paris: Gallimard, 1952), p. 177.

3 André Malraux: The Image of Man

"We know that we have not chosen to be born, that we will not choose to die. That we have not chosen our parents. That we can do nothing against time. That between each of us and universal life there is . . . a sort of gulf. When I say that each man experiences deep within himself the presence of destiny, I mean that he experiences—and almost always tragically, at least for certain moments—the world's indifference *vis-à-vis* himself."

These lines are from André Malraux's last novel, *The Walnut Trees of Altenburg* (1943), and they go a long way to explain why, of all the French writers famous before the Second World War, Malraux is one of the few to whom the younger generation still pays homage. Better than any other figure of his epoch, Malraux anticipated and crystallized the postwar Existentialist atmosphere that has become associated with the names of Sartre and Camus. Man's irremediable solitude; his absurd but unquenchable longing to triumph over time; his obligation to assume the burden of freedom by staking his life for his values; his defiance of death as an ultimate affirmation of "authentic" existence—all these Existentialist themes were given unforgettable artistic expression by Malraux long before they became fashionable intellectual catchwords or tedious artistic platitudes. Indeed, the genesis of French Existentialism as a full-fledged cultural movement probably owes more to Malraux than to Heidegger or Jaspers, Berdyaev or Chestov. For it was Malraux, through his novels, who shaped the sensibilities that then seized on doctrinal Existentialism as an ideological prop.

André Malraux has thus taken on the status of a prophetic precursor in contemporary French literature, and at the same time the essential contours of his own work have begun to stand out in much clearer relief. Up to the beginning of the Second World War, Malraux was the radiant symbol of the free liberal intellectual who had dedicated his life to the Communist Revolution and the struggle against fascism; and the focus of critical interest in his novels was their political content. But the Communists were never too happy about Malraux as an ally— and with good reason. For Malraux's heroes were never simply engaged in a battle against a particular social or economic injustice; they were always somehow struggling against the limitations of life itself and the humiliation of destiny. Communist critics were never loath to advise Malraux to shed his "romanticism," i.e., his Pascalian awareness of *la condition humaine;* but while this was unquestionably good advice for a political commissar, it would have been death to Malraux the artist. For what makes *Man's Fate* the greatest of all novels inspired by revolution, what gives it a poetic resonance invulnerable to changing political fashions, is precisely that Malraux was able to experience the revolution in terms of man's immemorial longing for communion in the face of death.

But if Existentialism has now allowed us to see Malraux's work in a more accurate perspective, it also carries with it a new danger of misunderstanding. This danger consists in reading into Malraux's work the fixities of later doctrine and overlooking the extent to which, from his very first serious book in 1926 (*La Tentation de l'Occident*), Malraux has been driven by the need to transcend the dilemmas of claustrophobic egoism and the anguish of rootless liberty which Sartre has absolutized into ontological categories of human existence. It was this need that originally impelled Malraux toward communism and, when the latter displayed its determination to mutilate the total "quality of man," has now led him to search for a human communion in other realms of experience.

An ambitious French book on Malraux, Jeanne Delhomme's dizzyingly dialectical and impressively intelligent philosophical study, *Temps et destin*,[1] attempts to force Malraux's work into a system of categories derived from Kierkegaard, Heidegger, and Sartre (with a dash of Bergson to boot); but while such categories are applicable to isolated characters and moments in Malraux's novels, they are entirely misleading when used to interpret Malraux's dominating artistic impulse as a whole. This is particularly true for the latest phase of Malraux's evolution, which comprises *The Walnut Trees of Altenburg* and the great series of works on art and aesthetics that have continued to appear since the end of the Second World War. For here if anywhere in contemporary literature is a major effort to restore some of its former luster to the tarnished image of the species Man or, as Malraux himself puts it, "to make men conscious of the grandeur they ignore in themselves."

I

André Malraux's *The Walnut Trees of Altenburg* was written in the early years of the Second World War, during a period of enforced leisure after the fall of France. The manuscript, presumably after being smuggled out of the country, was published in Switzerland in 1943. The work as it stands is not the entire book that Malraux wrote at that time—it is only the first section of a three-part novel called *La Lutte avec l'Ange;* and this first section was somehow preserved (there are always these annoying little mysteries about the actual facts of Malraux's life) when the Gestapo destroyed the rest. If we are to believe the list of titles printed in Malraux's latest book, *La Métamorphose des Dieux* (Vol. I, 1957), he is still engaged in writing a large novel under his original title. But as he remarks in his preface to *The Walnut Trees,* "a novel can hardly ever be rewritten" and "when this one appears in its final form, the form of the first part . . . will no doubt be radically changed." Malraux pretends, perhaps with a trifle too self-conscious a modesty, that his fragmentary work will accordingly "appeal only to the curiosity of bibliophiles" and to "connoisseurs of what might have been." Even in its present form, however, the first part of Malraux's unrecoverable novel is among the greatest works of mid-twentieth century literature, and it should be far better known than it is.[2]

The theme of *The Walnut Trees of Altenburg* is most

closely related to its immediate predecessor in Malraux's array of novels: *Man's Hope* (1937). This magnificent but greatly underestimated book, which bodies forth the very form and pressure of its time as does no other comparable creation, has suffered severely from having been written about a historical event—the Spanish Civil War—that is still capable of fanning the smoldering fires of old political feuds. Even so presumably impartial a critic as W. H. Frohock has taken for granted that the book was originally intended as a piece of Loyalist propaganda. And he has then gone on to argue, with unimpeachable consistency, that all the obviously nonpropagandistic aspects of the book are simply inadvertent "contradictions." [3]

Nothing, however, could be further from the truth. The whole purpose of *Man's Hope* is to portray the tragic dialectic between means and ends inherent in all organized political violence—and even when such violence is a necessary and legitimate self-defense of liberty, justice, and human dignity. Nowhere before in Malraux's pages have we met such impassioned defenders of a "quality of man" that transcends the realm of politics and even the realm of action altogether—both the action of Malraux's early anarchist-adventurers like Perken and Garine and the self-sacrificing action of dedicated Communists like Kyo Gisors and Katow in *Man's Fate*. "Man engages only a small part of himself in an action," says old Alvear the art historian; "and the more the action claims to be total, the smaller is the part of man engaged." These lines never cease to haunt the book amidst all the exaltations of combat and to make an appeal for a larger and more viable human community than one based on the brutal necessities of war.

It is this larger theme of the "quality of man," a quality that transcends the ideological and flows into "the human," which now forms the pulsating heart of Malraux's artistic universe. To be sure, Malraux does not abandon the world of violence, combat, and sudden death which has become his hallmark as a creative artist, and which is the only world, apparently, in which his imagination can flame into life. *The Walnut Trees of Altenburg* includes not one war but two, and throws in a Turkish revolution along with some guerrilla fighting in the desert for good measure. But while war still serves as a catalyst for the values that Malraux wishes to express, these values are no longer linked with the triumph or defeat of any cause— whether that of an individual assertion of the will-to-power or a collective attempt to escape from the humiliation of oppression—as their necessary condition. On the contrary, the frenzy and furor of combat are only the somber foil against which the sudden illuminations of the human flash forth like the piercing radiance of a Caravaggio.

II

The Walnut Trees of Altenburg is composed in the form of a triptych, with two small side panels framing and enclosing the main central episode of the novel. This central episode consists of a series of staccato scenes set in the period from the beginning of the present century to the First World War. The framing scenes, on the other hand, both take place in the late spring of 1940, just at the moment of the defeat of France in the second great world conflict. The narrator is an Alsatian serving with the French Army, and he has the same name (Berger) that Malraux himself was later to use in the Resistance. Like Malraux, he was also serving in the tank corps before being captured, and we learn as well that in civilian life he had been a writer. These biographical analogies are obvious, but far too much time has been spent speculating on their possible implications.

It is much more important to grasp the feelings of the narrator (whose full name is never given) as he becomes aware of the disorganized and bewildered mass of French prisoners clustered together in a temporary prison camp in and around the cathedral of Chartres. For, as his companions gradually dissolve back into a state of primitive confrontation with elemental necessity, as they lose all the appanage of their acquired culture, he is overcome by the feeling that he is at last being confronted with the essence of mankind. "As a writer, by what have I been obsessed these last ten years, if not by mankind? Here I am face to face with the primeval stuff."

The intuition about mankind conveyed in these opening pages is of crucial importance for understanding the remainder of the text; and we must attend to it more closely than has usually been done. What does the narrator see and what does he feel?

Many pages of the first section are taken up with an account of the dogged determination of the prisoners to write to their wives and families—even when it becomes clear that the Germans are simply allowing the letters to blow away in the wind. Awkwardly and laboriously, in stiff, unemotional phrases, the soldiers continue to bridge the distance between themselves and those they love; they instinctively struggle to keep open a road to the future in their hearts. And by a skillful and unobtrusive use of imagery (the enclosure is called a "Roman-camp stockade," the hastily erected lean-to is a "Babylonian hovel," the men begin to look like "Peruvian mummies" and to acquire "Gothic faces") Malraux projects a fresco of human endurance—which is also the endurance of the human—

stretching backward into the dark abyss of time. The narrator feels himself catching a glimpse of prehistory, learning of man's "age-old familiarity with misfortune" as well as his "equally age-old ingenuity, his secret faith in endurance, however crammed with catastrophes, the same faith perhaps as the cave men used to have in the face of famine."

This new vision of man that the narrator acquires is also accompanied by a *re*vision of his previous view. "I thought I knew more than my education had taught me," notes the narrator, "because I had encountered the militant mobs of a political or religious faith." Is this not Malraux himself alluding to his own earlier infatuation with the ideological? But now he knows "that an intellectual is not only a man to whom books are necessary, he is any man whose reasoning, however elementary it may be, affects and directs his life." From this point of view the "militant mobs" of the past, stirred into action by one ideology or another, were all composed of "intellectuals"—and this is not the level on which the essence of mankind can be discovered. The men around him, observes the narrator, "have been living from day to day for thousands of years." The human is deeper than a mass ideology, certainly deeper than the isolated individual; and the narrator recalls the words of his father, Vincent Berger: "It is not by any amount of scratching at the individual that one finally comes down to mankind."

The entire middle section of *The Walnut Trees* is taken up with the life of Vincent Berger himself, whose fragmentary notes on his "encounters with mankind" are now conveyed by his son. "He was not much older than myself," writes the narrator, "when he began to feel the impact of that human mystery which now obsesses me, and which makes me begin, perhaps, to understand him." For the figure of Vincent Berger Malraux has obviously drawn on his studies of T. E. Lawrence (though Berger fights on the side of the Turks instead of against them), and like both Lawrence and Malraux himself Berger is a fervent admirer of Nietzsche. A professor at the University of Constantinople, where his first course of lectures was on Nietzsche and the "philosophy of action," Vincent Berger becomes head of the propaganda department of the German Embassy in Turkey. As an Alsatian before the First World War he was of course of German nationality; but he quickly involves himself in the Young Turk revolutionary movement to such an extent that his own country begins to doubt his patriotism. And, after becoming the right-hand man of Enver Pasha, he is sent by the latter to pave the way for a new Turkish Empire embracing "the union of all Turks throughout Central Asia from Adrianople to the Chinese oases on the silk trade route."

Vincent Berger's mission is a failure because the Ottoman nationalism on which Enver Pasha counted does not exist. Central Asia is sunk in a somnolence from which nothing can wake it; and amid a dusty desolation in which nothing human any longer seemed to survive, Vincent Berger begins to dream of the Occident. "Oh, for the green of Europe! Trains whistling in the night, the rattle and clatter of late cabs . . ." Finally, after almost being beaten to death by a madman—he could not fight back because madmen are sacred to Islam—he throws up his mission and returns to Europe.

This has been his first encounter with mankind, and, although he has now become a legendary figure in the popular European press, it leaves him profoundly dissatisfied. Despite Berger's report, Enver Pasha refuses to surrender his dream of a Turkish Blood Alliance; and Vincent Berger learns that political ambition is more likely to hide than to reveal the truth about men. But as he discovers shortly, on returning among intellectuals obsessed by *le culte du moi,* his experience of action had also taught him a more positive lesson. "For six years my father had had to do too much commanding and convincing," writes the narrator, "not to understand that man begins with 'the other.' "

And when Vincent Berger returns to Europe, this first result of his encounters with mankind is considerably enriched and deepened by a crucial revelation. For a dawning sense of illumination occurs in consequence of two events which, as so often in Malraux, suddenly confront a character with the existential question of the nature and value of human life. One such event is the landing in Europe itself, when the mingled familiarity and strangeness of the Occident, after the blank immensities of Asia, shocks the returning traveler into a realization of the infinite *possibilities* of human life. Significantly, Malraux compares this shock to that undergone by a man who has just committed murder. "This evening he [Vincent Berger] felt released . . . with a poignant liberty indistinguishable from license." The other event is the suicide of Vincent's father five days after his landing and just two days after a conversation in which Dietrich Berger had said: "Well, you know, *whatever happens,* if I had to live another life again, I should want none other than Dietrich Berger's."

Both these events pierce through the thin film of the quotidian, the horizontal surface on which most of human life is spent, and disclose the vertical depths of the contingency of human existence and the anguish of human liberty. This anguish of liberty is a familiar phenomenon to all readers of Malraux—it possesses Malraux's adventurers, as well as the terrorist Tchen in *Man's Fate*—and always, in the past, it had resulted in a release that was equivalent to a condemnation. The answer to this anguish had always been a paroxysm of the will-to-power: a convulsive attempt of human liberty, freed of all attachments, to prove its own autonomy by an impossible duel with the power of inhuman fatality. But the release that now occurs in Vincent Berger is of an entirely different order:

The human adventure, the world. And all of it, like his father's fulfilled destiny, could have been other than it was. He felt himself gradually possessed by an unknown sensation, as he had once been at night in the highlands of Asia by the presence of the sacred, while around him the velvet wings of the little desert owls fluttered in silence. It was the same agonizing sense of freedom, only far more pronounced, that he had felt that evening at Marseilles watching the shadows glide in the faint odor of cigarettes and absinthe —when Europe had seemed so unfamiliar, when he had watched it as if, liberated from time, he might have watched an hour of the distant past slip slowly by with all its strange retinue. In the same way, he now felt the whole of his life becoming strange; and suddenly he felt delivered—mysteriously a stranger to the earth and astonished by it, as he had been by that street where the people of his rediscovered race slid by in the greenish twilight.

The experience of the contingency of existence thus leads Vincent Berger to an intuition of "the sacred." But the category of the religious—as we have learned from Kierkegaard and could have learned even earlier from Job —transcends the category of the social or ethical; and in this sense Perken, Garine, and Tchen had also been initiated into the mystery of "the sacred." But the sacred is no longer the equivalent of the demonic (also a religious category); nor is it, as in Asia, a sense of the nothingness of man before the awfulness of the infinite (the desert is monotheistic, as Renan remarked in a once famous phrase). Rather, "the sacred" is now for Malraux an intuition of the infinite mystery of human liberty, of a world and a life which "could have been other than it was" and which, in being what it is, testifies to the existence of a human essence that endures and persists underneath the equally infinite vicissitudes of time and history. Vincent Berger's "agonizing sense of freedom" is, as it were, only the coming-to-consciousness of the freedom that exists as an inchoate but irreducible and immortal possibility at the center of human life itself. And this is the intuition of "the sacred" in man that Vincent Berger defends in the famous colloquy at the old abbey at Altenburg.

III

This debate is certainly one of the most brilliant scenes of its kind in contemporary fiction. Nothing is more difficult than successfully to dramatize serious intellectual discussion; and Malraux does so with an aphoristic intensity and an emotional vibrancy that can be matched only in the very best pages of Thomas Mann. Indeed, Malraux's formulations are so striking and so luminous that they have provided an irresistible temptation for critics to overstress their importance.

In a view which is generally accepted, W. H. Frohock has maintained that Vincent Berger is "rationally" defeated by the Spenglerian arguments of the ethnologist Möllberg; and that at the end of this sequence he can only fall back on an "irrational" vision of the walnut trees of Altenburg to establish his faith in an essence of man.[4] But such an interpretation is inadmissible for a number of reasons. For one thing, Malraux is too well acquainted with Spengler, who prided himself precisely on his "intuitive" view of history, to identify Spengler's position with any kind of "rationalism." For another, it is perfectly clear in the novel that Möllberg's views spring from the same existential level as Vincent Berger's, but reflect a temperament and an outlook that lead to despair instead of to a grave and sober exaltation. And on this level, the refutation of Möllberg already has been given both in the opening pages of the book and in Vincent Berger's intuition of "the sacred."

"Is there something given on which we can base the notion of man?" This is the issue at stake in the great debate as formulated by Vincent's uncle, Walter Berger, the famous intellectual impresario who orchestrates the colloquies at Altenburg. The first answer proposed is that man's essence can be founded on the creation of "culture," that is, on great works of art, the gift of individual genius to mankind, which free us "from the bonds of space, time, and death." * This "subtly banal" view, however, is rejected by Edmé Thirard, who sounds much like the great literary critic Albert Thibaudet and whose words receive the silent approval of Vincent Berger. "Culture," Thirard asserts, "doesn't teach us about man, it merely teaches us about the cultured man, in proportion to the degree of his culture." In other words, the religion of culture isolates culture from the roots of life and fails to make contact with "the commonplace human misery . . . in hospitals, in maternity wards, and in the rooms of the dying."

The next answer suggested is that we can get at the essence of man by psychology, that is, by "scratching at the individual" in search of his "secrets." Vincent Berger's experience of "the other" has already implicitly rejected this answer according to the artistic logic of the novel; and

---

* The entire passage is quoted in Note 9, p. 102.

now, intervening directly in the argument, he attacks the emphasis on psychology as Occidental cultural chauvinism, a consequence of the influence of Christianity on the Western psyche. "It's our old struggle against the Devil . . . which makes us confuse our knowledge of man with our knowledge of his secrets." The mystery of man is precisely that no secrets can ever explain his inviolable freedom. And when Thirard remarks that our knowledge of man is always dubious because "we can hardly ever foresee the really important actions of those nearest to us," the figure of Dietrich Berger rises before Vincent's eyes as a vital confirmation of this assertion. This is the manner in which, underneath the glittering swordplay of ratiocination, Malraux constantly appeals to the deeper level of experience portrayed elsewhere in the book; and unless we situate the ideas in this framework we can hardly understand either the underlying movement of the discussion or the nature of its resolution.

In place of man as the creator of culture, or as the repository of secrets which, once brought to light, would eliminate the mystery of freedom, Vincent Berger proposes another image of man: as eternally engaged in a struggle with destiny, as eternally striving—and succeeding—in transforming fate into freedom. Here again art is invoked as evidence, just as in the thesis about culture; but it is very important to grasp Malraux's distinction (not, it must be admitted, made very clearly) between the two. Art is no longer a miraculous gift of individual genius to mankind which *creates* a freedom from destiny; now it is only a symbol that *expresses* man's collective and eternal struggle to transcend the conditions of his servitude:

To me [Vincent Berger says] our art seems to be a rectification of the world, a means of escaping from man's estate. The chief confusion, I think, is due to our belief—and in the

theories propounded of Greek tragedy it's strikingly clear—
that representing fatality is the same as submitting to it. But
it's not, it's almost to dominate it. The mere fact of being
able to represent it, conceive it, release it from real fate, from
the merciless divine scale, reduces it to the human scale.
Fundamentally, our art is a humanization of the world.

It is this "humanization of the world"—a humanization
that stems from the assertion of human liberty in the face
of destiny—that Vincent Berger has already felt in his intuition of "the sacred"; and the validity of this intuition
is denied by Möllberg in the speech that follows.

Möllberg's presence in the book is far from being merely
that of a disembodied voice grinding out a string of irref-
utable arguments. And if critics had paid a bit more attention to his human contours, perhaps they would have been
able to place his arguments in a juster perspective. In any
case, it is certainly not accidental that when Vincent Berger enters Möllberg's room (in a scene preceding the debate) he finds it filled with grotesque little figurines—
imaginary gargoyles with animal traits incongruously
scrambled together, all looking curiously like their creator
and all with an "air of gripping sadness, like Goya's monsters which seem to remember they were once human."
Möllberg, who has been molding these figurines for many
years, is clearly a sensibility haunted by the infinite mal-
leability of nature and by the extent to which man is
merely another element in the eternal flux.

Moreover, when he is asked, at the end of the debate,
what "concept" drove him to the conclusions he presents,
he snaps back angrily: "Not a concept. Africa!" Upon
which follows a hallucinatory parade of images: "The
succession without end of days under the dusty firmament
of Libya or the heavy, gray sky of the Congo, the tracks
of invisible animals converging toward the water holes,

the migration of famished dogs under the empty sky, the hour when all thought becomes weariness, the gloomy thrust of giant trees in prehistoric boredom." This should be enough to show that Möllberg's views are no more "rational" than Vincent Berger's intuition of "the sacred." What resounds in the background of Möllberg's impressive speech is the thwarted bitterness of his defeat by "Africa," that is, by a nature so savage and so terrible that it has confirmed his latent fear of nature's ultimate triumph over man.[5]

Projected on the plane of ideas and buttressed with an impressive amount of ethnological evidence, this fear amounts to the Spenglerian thesis that every culture cycle is an airtight and self-enclosed whole imprisoned in its own assumptions. There is no possibility of communication between cultures, hence no escape from the determinism of fate (in the form of the isolated mental structure of each culture) and no essence of man based on the continuity of his struggle against destiny. Directly addressing himself to Vincent Berger, Möllberg affirms: "Men are, perhaps, more thoroughly defined and classified by their form of fatalism than by anything else." The mental structure of our own civilization is dominated by the idea of history, and even more fundamentally by the discovery of "time." Time is the fatality of modern man, and, while earlier cultures had believed in some sort of eternal value impervious to time, we make no exception to the inexorable iron grip of fatality on all of human life.

Now, it is simply not true, as has been asserted over and over again, that Möllberg crushes all his interlocutors into a helpless mutism by the power of his arguments; the fact is that he is forced to concede a very important point to Thirard. For Möllberg's whole position hinges on the identification of man with what he "thinks," i.e., with being what has been called an "intellectual" in the opening pages. Malraux thus expects the attentive reader to know that Möllberg's argument is humanly fallacious from the very start; and he brings out this point in Thirard's question. Even if an Egyptian high priest and a Catholic cardinal exist in different psychic realms, Thirard asks, would not an Egyptian laborer and an Alsatian one have something in common? Möllberg cannot deny the pertinence of this thrust; and here is where the issue is joined. Möllberg is speaking:

> "The less men partake of their civilization, the more they resemble each other. I agree! But the less they partake of it, the more they fade away. The permanence of man can be conceived, but it's a permanence in nothingness."
>
> "Or in the fundamental?"
>
> It was my father [Vincent Berger] who put the question. *The point at issue was no longer the history of man, but the nature of each one present; everyone felt himself at stake.* [Italics added. J. F.]

The debate has now become a reflection, in the last analysis, of the nature of the individual participants; what is at stake is *their* quality as men. And Möllberg's position is a perfect illustration of the arrogance of the intellectual who has not learned, like Vincent Berger, that man begins with "the other" and who, equating "humanity" only with his own subspecies, contemptuously relegates everyone else to the realm of "nothingness," i.e., animality. The reverse side of this arrogance is the susceptibility to despair, the self-hatred and *Schadenfreude* (the German word is appropriate) that impels Möllberg to say "with sardonic self-satisfaction" that "there's no better way of concentrating on man than looking at an anthill." Erich Heller has pertinently written that "Spengler's history is untrue because the mind which has conceived it is, despite its learning and seeming subtlety, a crude and wicked mind. The image of man which lurks behind Spengler's vast historical canvas is perverted. . . . For Spengler has no idea of the true stature of the problem of human freedom. Therefore his historical vision is lacking in depth as well as in love, pity and pathos." [6] Malraux is saying nothing else in his portrait of Möllberg, though with a nuance of sympathy for his character that Heller finds it impossible to muster for Spengler.[7]

During the discussion Möllberg exemplifies the nothingness of nonintellectual man by pointing to some statues on the wall carved from the walnut trees surrounding the abbey of Altenburg. These, he asserts, are either statues—the product of a specific cultural tradition—or they are nothing, mere logs; there is no "fundamental walnut" intermediate between the two, just as there is no "fundamental man" intermediate between intellectual or ideological man and the brute. Trees also take on symbolic value in another context, for Möllberg has explained earlier to Vincent Berger that the pages of his proposed (and now abandoned) book demonstrating civilization as a conquest by man "are hanging from the lower branches of various types of trees from the Sahara to Zanzibar. Right. In accordance with tradition, the victorious carry off the spoils of the defeated." With these words as well as Möllberg's reference to the statues still in his mind, Vincent Berger strolls across the fields of Altenburg and looks at the rows of carefully cultivated walnut trees receding in the distance and framing the cathedral of Strasbourg in their perspective.

"Between the statues and the logs there were the trees," he thinks, "and their design which was as mysterious as life itself." The walnut trees of course figure forth the reality of "fundamental man" (neither intellectually self-conscious nor mere blank nothingness); and the human effort embodied in their cultivation is no doubt intended to contrast with the wilderness that broke Möllberg's spirit. Nonetheless, although the meaning of Malraux's symbolism is clear enough, one cannot help feeling a certain disharmony in the prominence given the tree metaphor by Malraux's title. It is true that the sight of the trees evokes an impression of "will and metamorphosis without end" in Vincent Berger's consciousness; but trees are still only a part of nature, and the use of this symbol clashes with Malraux's central thematic focus on *man's* freedom and creativity.[8]

IV

Vincent Berger's defense of man's eternal capacity to "humanize" the world, to transcend the circumstances in which the fatality of history may imprison him, is the spiritual climax of the middle section of the novel. And the remainder of the action of this section, which ends with Berger's death by poison gas, is a magnificent projection of this capacity in one of the most moving scenes of the contemporary novel.

After the outbreak of the First World War, Vincent Berger is assigned to German Intelligence on the Eastern Front; and he is detailed to look after a scientist who has invented a new poison gas which is ready to be tested in combat. Malraux again punctures the pretensions of the subspecies "intellectual" by sketching the innocently obtuse inhumanity of the scientist with merciless skill. By contrast, the naïve and childish chatter of the ordinary German soldiers, waiting in the trenches before the attack, is dense with the warmth of an all-pervasive humanity. The most absurd legends, myths, and suggestions flash out like Roman candles as the voices sound in the enveloping darkness; but all of them bear the unmistakable stamp of man. One soldier ferociously advocates that all the enemy be castrated, but then adds this reflection: "It's not humanitarian, perhaps, but that way we'd finish them once and for all, and without killing anyone." Stories of adultery and lust end in the laconic comments: "But he let it go on, because of the kid"; or: "So the chap, instead of appearing in court, he went home, and then he hung himself."

Exactly as his son was to do twenty-five years later, Vincent Berger senses that he is at last coming close to "the fundamental" in man. "Listening in this live darkness, my father was conscious for the first time of the people of Germany. Or perhaps just of people: men." And what men really are, or what they can become in certain privileged moments, is gloriously shown in the "human apocalypse" unleashed by the gas attack. For when the Germans reach the Russian trenches, pushing their way through fields turned by the gas into an eerie universal putrefaction, the sight of the Russians in the terrible convulsions of strangulation releases an instinctive combination of anguish and fraternity that cannot be denied. Instead of advancing, the German soldiers return to their own lines and hospital units, bearing the bodies of men who have become their brothers out of an impulse far deeper than pity. For it seemed to arise from a need for *self*-protection against the spirit of evil: each Russian soldier was a talisman. Vincent Berger, abandoning his duty like the rest, meets his end in this fulfillment of his faith.

The power and majesty of this scene are so great that all writers on Malraux (including myself, in an earlier article) have unanimously taken it as the key figuration of the novel's major theme: the fraternity of the human. My opinion now, however, is that such a reading unduly narrows the scope of Malraux's range and that "fraternity" is only one manifestation of his theme rather than its entire substance. This substance is embodied essentially in Vincent Berger's intuition of "the sacred," the "humanization of the world" that arises out of man's liberty to oppose destiny. And this humanization can disclose itself not only in the upsurge of fraternity but also in art—or in the contemplation of the humblest work of human hands and the lowliest of human creatures. This is why Malraux, in the final section of the book, returns to the narrator—Vincent Berger's son—to bring us back to the present and give us a final epiphany of his true theme in its full extent.

This last scene centers on a French tank attack in which the narrator takes part, presumably in the series of battles leading to the French defeat. After being bogged down in a tank trap all night and expecting the pin-pointed artillery to zero in on them at any moment, the narrator's crew finally manage to disengage themselves and stop in an evacuated village at dawn. Still harrowed by his night of terror, the narrator feels the simplest signs of life to be a miracle, an apparition: "The world might have been as simple as the sky or the sea. And at the sight of the shapes in front of me, which are only the shapes of an abandoned, condemned village—I feel in the presence of an unaccountable gift—an apparition. All this might never have been, might never have been as it is! . . . There are other worlds, the world of crystals, of oceanic depths . . ." The wonder of the human world being as it is overwhelms Vincent Berger's son, as it had overwhelmed his father on the night of his landing at Marseilles.

But the greatest miracle of all is man himself, in the guise of an old peasant couple too enfeebled to have gone on with the rest. The narrator looks at the wife:

Harmonized with the cosmos like a stone. . . . Yet she smiles, a slow, pensive smile; beyond the football-field with its solitary goal-posts, beyond the tank turrets gleaming in the dew like the bushes camouflaging them, she seems to be viewing death at a distance and even—oh, mysterious blink, sharp shadow at the corner of the eyelids!—even with irony. . . . Let the mystery of man reappear from that enigmatic smile, and the resurrection of the earth becomes nothing more than a trembling backdrop.

That the earth should not be as simple as the sky and the sea, but everywhere bear the imprint of man; that an old peasant woman should be capable of looking with a smile in the face of death—this is the miracle of the human that Vincent Berger had felt in his intuition of "the sacred," and which now shines forth again, as from a biblical illustration of Rembrandt's, in the debris of a war-torn village. "I can scarcely remember what fear is like," writes the narrator finally; "what I carry within me is the discovery of a simple, sacred secret."

No writer in modern literature can compete with Malraux—at least not with the Malraux of this final scene—in evoking so poignantly what Wordsworth called "the still, sad music of humanity." And this music, despite its stillness and sadness, never ceases to sound in Malraux's novel above the roar of battle and the tumultuous march of the centuries. Malraux manages to wrest an affirmation of an absolute value in man out of the very teeth of the experience which—for example, in Sartre's *La Nausée*—had resulted in Antoine Roquentin's frightening vision of man's absorption into the world of brute materiality. The disclosure of the contingency of existence had led Sartre to portray man himself as a futile excrescence on the blank surface of things; and despite the role that liberty plays in his philosophy, Sartre has not yet succeeded (it is dubious whether he ever will succeed) in transcending the hopelessness of *La Nausée* by any equally powerful artistic expression. Indeed, one wonders whether Malraux's *The Walnut Trees of Altenburg,* consciously or otherwise, might not have been intended to meet the challenge of the vision of man proposed in *La Nausée* (which after all appeared in 1938, and which Malraux very probably would have read).

However that may be, there is no doubt that Malraux has managed by the sheer force of his artistic genius to extend the bounds of Existentialism in an extremely significant fashion. Even when Existentialism is determinedly atheist, as in Heidegger or Jean-Paul Sartre, the movement as a whole has drawn its image of man from the tortured cogitations of Kierkegaard; and that means from a Christianity which emphasizes the fallen nature of man and all the dark and gloomy aspects of human existence. Malraux, on the other hand, might be said to have created —paradoxical as it may sound—an Existentialism of the Enlightenment. For in reading *The Walnut Trees of Altenburg* one thinks of Kant rather than of Kierkegaard —not, to be sure, the Kant of *The Critique of Pure Reason* but the Kant who, in *The Critique of Judgment,* defined the "dynamic-sublime" as man's consciousness of the final inability of the power of nature, however menacing it might be, to force him to surrender his humanity. Malraux's image of man is therefore "sublime" in the strict meaning given that term by the greatest mind of the Enlightenment. And Malraux has performed the remarkable feat, unique in our time, of projecting this image both on the highest level of cultural achievement (through the symbol of the artist as creator in his books on art) and, in *The Walnut Trees of Altenburg,* as equally embodied in the simplest and most unself-conscious human response.

NOTES

3. ANDRÉ MALRAUX: THE IMAGE OF MAN

1. Jeanne Delhomme, *Temps et destin* (Paris: Gallimard, 1955).

2. One of the minor mysteries of American publishing is why Malraux's novel should still not have appeared in this country twenty years after it came out in French. A translation has been published in Great Britain (John Lehmann, 1952), but this is so riddled with errors that crucial passages of the book are entirely meaningless.

   I have, however, used this translation as a basis for some of my quotations, with appropriate corrections.

3. W. H. Frohock, *André Malraux and the Tragic Imagination* (Stanford: Stanford University Press, 1952), pp. 104–125.

4. *Ibid.*, p. 132.

5. See also the following comment of the narrator while Möllberg is speaking: "Discussion and logic, the books in serried ranks on the shelves, were fighting for their rights against the voice of the dark continents."

   Möllberg is the voice of "the dark continents," not of "rationalism"; the very conception of reason is meaningless unless we believe in man as somehow superior to nature.

6. Erich Heller, "Oswald Spengler and the Predicament of the Historical Imagination," *The Disinherited Mind* (New York: Meridian, 1959), p. 193.

7. The French critic and novelist Armand Hoog, now teaching at Princeton, has given us a valuable insight into the genesis of Möllberg which supports the interpretation offered here.

   "One day Malraux wrote me: 'Physically, Möllberg is Leopold Chauveau; ideologically, Frobenius (in so far as the characters of a novel are ever anyone).'

"Leopold Chauveau has not left a particularly great name in literature. However, his memory remains alive for many. A surgeon who no longer practiced, an author of regional novels and children's stories, Chauveau belonged to the Pontigny group (that so highly resembles Altenburg). But why should Malraux have transformed Chauveau into Möllberg? One can venture a guess.

"In one of the Altenburg episodes, we see the little figurines that the ethnologist carries with him everywhere. He has sculpted them himself. Fantastic animals, squirrels with fins, birds of prey with simian bodies, cat-faced penguins, as sad as the phantoms of Goya. Möllberg calls them his monsters and gives them names.

"One should now read the memories of Chauveau in *Galerie Privée*, by the old lady who, for half a century, was at the center of French letters and who hid under the pseudonym of 'M. St. Clair.' Chauveau too sculpted 'half-human monsters.' Were they, queries the memorialist, 'the indirect, exasperated expression of an inner collapse, of an element of malice'?" See Armand Hoog, "Malraux, Möllberg and Frobenius," *Yale French Studies,* 18 (Winter, 1957), 92–93.

The impression that Chauveau gave his friends dovetails perfectly with Malraux's portrait of Möllberg; and we may speculate that Malraux thought of Chauveau precisely because Möllberg's views testify to a state of "inner collapse" and exasperated malice.

8. To make matters worse, Malraux unfortunately stresses the insignificance of man's endeavors at this point compared to the spectacle of the trees:

"And that spire [i.e., of the cathedral] rising like the prayers of the maimed, and all the human patience and the human labor that were the waves of vineyards descending to the river, were only an evening background to the immemorial upsurge of the living wood, for the two thick clumps that wrested the strength from the earth itself to spread in their branches."

One has the uneasy feeling that here Malraux's imagery swept him away and caused him to lose control over his theme.

4 Reaction as Progress: Thomas Mann's *Dr. Faustus*

The literary career of Thomas Mann is certainly one of the most remarkable in modern letters. Beginning at the very close of the nineteenth century, when Symbolism, naturalism, and *fin de siècle* decadence were the reigning international artistic movements, Mann has traversed all the peripeties of the first half of the twentieth century—and he is the only writer of his generation who never ceased to grapple artistically with the chaotic world that replaced the complacent security of pre-1914. Neither Gide nor Shaw, his rivals in longevity, retained sufficient artistic resiliency to renew themselves creatively in the latter period of their lives; and Joyce retreated into a private world of linguistic experimentation whose fascinating ingenuity does not compensate for its total lack of contact with the world of the common reader. But Thomas Mann, after writing one of the great novels to emerge from the holocaust of the First World War (*The Magic Mountain*), performed the astonishing feat of composing what is unquestionably the greatest work inspired by the degrading and horrifying events culminating in the Second. For no other work of our time can compete with Mann's *Dr. Faustus* as a sublime and sophisticated aesthetic expression of the raw reality of contemporary historical experience.

Mann himself, in a letter to a friend, called *Dr. Faustus* his "wildest" book, a work in whose light the immediately preceding *Joseph* novels—and, he might have added, *The Magic Mountain* as well—appear as an "operatic pleasantry." *Dr. Faustus,* indeed, is colored by an emotional chiaroscuro far removed from the bland narrative poise of Mann's other works. Mann always conceived of the artist as the mediator between nature and spirit, the all-reconciling *deus ex machina* playfully harmonizing the contraries out of which human life is formed. The appointed role for the artist is thus that of cosmic master of ceremonies or of supreme ironist (irony being understood not as satirical mockery but as clear-eyed and unbenighted love); and Mann's leisurely narrative manner, with its tongue-in-cheek slyness, is the perfect embodiment of this conception. This typical Mannian tone, however, is conspicuous by its absence in *Dr. Faustus;* nor is it difficult to understand why.

In *The Story of a Novel,* a little book that he wrote about *Dr. Faustus,* Mann remarks on the "curious and licentious spiritual dissolution" that seemed to accompany the writing of this work, the relaxation of inner barriers that turned it into both a "piece of esoterica and a personal confession." [1] To a large extent *Dr. Faustus* is Thomas Mann's own spiritual autobiography in which he makes an unprecedented use of events drawn directly from his own life. And the tragedy he depicts is not only that of his country and his people but also that of the cultural heritage from which he has drawn his spiritual sustenance.

This does not mean, however, as many American reviewers thought in 1948, that *Dr. Faustus* is too "German" to have much interest for other readers. The book was conceived, Mann tells us in his commentary, to express the "situation of art in general, of culture, yes, of mankind itself, of the spirit in our thoroughly critical epoch." Adrian Leverkuhn is a musician because music has a special symbolic relation to the German spirit; but the cultural situation that his music reflects is that of the Occident as a whole in the past half century. This situation has often been expressed in Yeats's famous lines:

> The best lack all conviction, while the worst
> Are full of passionate intensity.

But Mann goes considerably deeper by making us aware of the extent to which the best and the worst have become intermingled, linked in a dialectical unity of opposites which incessantly transforms one into the other and blurs all distinctions. How can we any longer tell the primitive from the avant-garde, barbarism from civilization, reaction from progress? It was German culture, of course, which pressed this dialectic to its terrifying practical and political conclusion. But it would be folly and false pride to believe that Thomas Mann's Devil holds no temptations for those raised elsewhere than among the medieval towers of an old German city.

I

The original plan of *Dr. Faustus* goes back to a note three sentences long that Mann jotted down in 1901, and which, after completing the last volume of *Joseph and His Brothers,* he took up again early in 1943. Mann reports that even while working on the last volume of his *Joseph* series he found himself perusing the *Memoirs* of Stravinsky and leafing through a number of long-familiar works about Nietzsche. "Music and Nietzsche," he writes. "I could give no explanation for such a direction to my interests and thoughts at that particular time." [2] But on March 15, 1943, having cleared away all the material of the *Joseph* novels, he began to look through old papers for his note on *Dr. Faust.*

What was *Dr. Faust?* He hardly knew himself. "A certain long-existing outline of a very cloudy idea that I pursued. At the moment it concerned the diabolic and fatal *release* of an artistic existence through intoxication." [3] At the same moment as this idea was emerging from the mists of the past, Mann's notebooks (cited in *The Story of a Novel*) were also filled with accounts of Nazi atrocities against friends and acquaintances and with comments on the course of the war. Music and Nietzsche, the theme of Faust, the depravities of nazism and the struggle against it—all these motifs were beginning to focus themselves as part of one artistic complex.

The central action of *Dr. Faustus,* the theme of Faust itself, thus goes back to an early period of Mann's work ("the *Tonio Kröger* period," as he calls it himself); and *Dr. Faustus* takes its place in Mann's famous series of *Künstlernovellen,* dealing with the antinomy between art and life. Mann had played many variations on this theme in the past. One of the most famous is the mortal peril in which the artist places himself by his commerce with the sensuous, the demonic and irrational. Gustave von Aschenbach, the great writer in *Death in Venice,* had fallen a victim to this danger by confusing the boundaries between art and life. As an artist himself, whose spiritual education had been conducted under the guidance of Schopenhauer, Nietzsche, and Wagner, Thomas Mann could hardly ally himself with Philistinism against art and the irrational; but *Death in Venice* reveals his acute consciousness of the possible degradation involved in giving the latter any hegemony over conduct. This theme had been only a private and personal one in 1911—an outgrowth of the tension in Mann himself between the amoralism of art and the ethical responsibility of the burgher. But it is an essential part of Mann's genius that, like all great writers, he has been able to exfoliate his quarrel with himself into a mirror of the universe; and the whole course of modern German history conspired to give the theme of *Death in Venice* a vaster and much more terrible scope.

It may well be that Mann did not really know why "music and Nietzsche" began to preoccupy him as the *Joseph* novels drew to a close or why he opened his old packet of notes on *Dr. Faust* (though one suspects him of being a little coquettish on this score). Nevertheless, Mann's political writings of the late thirties and early forties are filled with references to demonism and the Devil in speaking of the capitulation of the German people to Hitlerism. The German people, he wrote in 1939—to select only one example among many—had now become the "Enemy of Mankind," i.e., the Devil incarnate; and alluding to the ideals of freedom, truth, and justice, he says: "We hold them out before the Enemy of Mankind, as the medieval monk held out the crucifix before Satan in person." [4] The Faust theme of a pact with the Devil, as we can see here, had clearly become associated for Mann with the political triumphs of nazism and the surrender of the German spirit to the irrational forces of blood and soil. But this same surrender, on a higher level, had long before become linked in Mann's sensibility with the work and figure of Nietzsche.

After the defeat of Germany in the First World War, German culture was inundated by a flood of doctrines and attitudes exemplified by such names as Spengler, Ludwig Klages, Bachofen, Ernst Jünger, Stefan George, *e tutti quanti*. All these novelists, philosophers, and poets, Mann noted in an important article on Freud (1929), stress "the impotence of spirit and reason . . . while by contrast the powers of the lower regions, the dynamic of passion, the irrational, the unconscious, is exhibited with bellicose piety." [5]

Whether intentionally or not, the writings of these men served as the intellectual and spiritual precursors of nazism; and Thomas Mann, who felt this whole movement as a perversion of his own deepest values, recommended Freud as an antidote in the courageous struggle he waged as both publicist and artist against this current. Freud too had called attention to the dynamism of the irrational and the importance of the instinctive; but he had done so with the ultimate aim of harnessing this dynamism in the service of reason and enlightenment. And while the postwar irrationalists appealed for support to the German Romantics, who had pitted the idealization of the sacred past and the cult of death against the "shallow" reason and clarity of the Enlightenment, Mann points out that the Romantics had never attempted to conceal their reactionary nature by taking the offensive against reason in the name of revolution.

"The word 'revolution,' " Mann writes, "is here given a paradoxical and, according to logical usage, inverted sense. For while we are accustomed to link the idea of revolution with the powers of light and the emancipation of reason, in short, with the future, the message proclaimed here sounds quite the opposite. For it points to the great return into the nocturnal, the primevally holy, the fecundity of the pre-conscious, to the mythical, historical and romantic womb." [6] Mann labels this whole movement with a phrase taken from Nietzsche: "Reaction as Progress"—a phrase that Nietzsche had used to characterize German culture as a whole as typified by representatives like Luther and Schopenhauer.[7] Even more, Nietzsche's own relation to this tendency, as Mann points out, is a highly ambiguous one. For, while Nietzsche saw himself as carrying forward the banner of Enlightenment inscribed with the names of Petrarch, Erasmus, and Voltaire, there is little doubt that his own work had given a mighty impulse to the counter-Enlightenment holding the field in the twenties. "Following in Nietzsche's footsteps," Mann writes, "whose battle against Socrates' enmity to instinct so pleases our prophets of the unconscious . . . following in his footsteps all the anti-rational tendencies of the nineteenth century have continued to our own day; in the more extreme cases, of course, not so much in his footsteps as over his body." [8]

This essay is of first importance for *Dr. Faustus*. It shows us how early Mann had begun to equate the growing influence of nazism with the idea of "reaction as progress"— the typically German transformation of a return to the past into a revolutionary principle; and this dialectic not only was baptized by Nietzsche but also incarnated by one aspect of his own career. But Nietzsche's life and intellectual history also reveal a heroic struggle for the self-conquest and self-transcendence of his own Romantic primitivism. "All its [the present's] conflicts and convulsions," Mann writes, "seem like a satyr-play and a ludicrous repetition of his [Nietzsche's] experience reduced to a trivial everyday scale . . . in him, through him, they were settled long ago in the grand manner." [9] The two levels of *Dr. Faustus*—the tragically sublime sufferings of Adrian Leverkuhn, with their distorted image in the mirror of contemporary German cultural life—are already implicit in these pages. And in the years when Germany rose to her horrible apogee of power, enjoying the fruits of her fatal pact with the chthonian powers of blood and soil, it is little wonder that Mann should have turned to meditate again on the figure of Nietzsche and use his life as scaffolding for his fictional Leverkuhn.

It is thus easy to see how the Faust theme of the demonic fused with the Nietzsche theme of "reaction as progress" under the pressure of Mann's experiences in the late thirties and the early war years. But to these two themes we must add a third—German apoliticism and *Innerlichkeit,* which Thomas Mann has always loved to symbolize under the aspect of music. "If Faust is to represent the German soul," wrote Mann in an essay that serves as an ideological overture to *Dr. Faustus,* "then he must be a musician; for the relation of the German to the world is abstract and mystic, i.e., musical." [10] Nothing has stirred up more antagonism to *Dr. Faustus* than this coupling of music with Faust and the demonic; Mann has been accused both of slandering Germany's most precious spiritual heritage and of distorting the nature of the most seraphic of the arts. To the latter charge one might reply that *Dr. Faustus* is a novel and not a treatise on aesthetics; to the former, that the symbolic value Mann attributes to music is by no means his individual invention.

It was Schopenhauer who first interpreted music as the direct expression of the metaphysical reality of the will; and it was Nietzsche and Wagner, Schopenhauer's disciples, who seized on music as the typically "German" art precisely because of its presumed relation to the tragic, irrational depths of the world soul. To be sure, Mann himself did much to popularize this symbolism of Germany as the "unliterary land," the land of music, whose rhetorical inarticulateness is a consequence of the intensity and purity of its emotions. But after *The Magic Mountain* he was also concerned with the dangers involved in German *Innerlichkeit,* the inadaptation of such a "musical" culture to the nonmetaphysical and "human" realm of social and political reality. It was thus inevitable and suitable that Mann should place music symbolism at the center of *Dr. Faustus*—not only because of its previous use in his own artistic world, but also because this use coincides with the dominant modern image created for itself by German cultural self-consciousness.

II

The structure of *Dr. Faustus,* as Mann has noted, is based on a "montage-technique" that he chose to employ for a number of reasons. In the first place, it allowed him to attain a certain distance from the material that he felt was humanly necessary if he was to write the book at all. The history of Adrian Leverkuhn, accordingly, is not narrated in the third person by the author himself; it is written as a biography (with interjected comments) by Leverkuhn's boyhood friend Serenus Zeitblom. This narrative method "allowed me," Mann explains, "to divert into indirection all the emotion caused by everything direct, personal and confessional that lay at the root of this uncanny idea. I could portray it in travesty as the perplexity, the trembling hand of that fearful soul." Even more, this technique gave Mann the possibility of constructing his narrative "on a double time-plane," so that "the experiences which shake the narrator as he writes interweave polyphonically with those he is recounting. Hence the trembling of his hand from the vibrations of distant bomb-explosions and from inner terrors can be explained both doubly and yet again unitedly as one." [11] The montage-technique allows the career of Adrian Leverkuhn and the catastrophe of the Third Reich mutually to reflect and illuminate each other; but this does not mean that they are to be considered absolutely parallel. Indeed, one of the commonest errors in the interpretation of *Dr. Faustus* is to make this identity more absolute than Mann does himself.

The story, then, is told through the eyes of Serenus Zeitblom, a lifelong friend of Leverkuhn's and a teacher of Latin, Greek, and theology in a German high school and seminary. Zeitblom's very name, with its faintly grotesque and pedantic mixture of Latin and German, immediately evokes the atmosphere of his character and his symbolic function in the book. By birth and conviction a Catholic humanist, Zeitblom represents a tradition of cultural unity that corresponds to the *via media* of "the human" between the competing extremes of Western civilization. "For my part," he says, "I feel very truly at home in that golden sphere where one called the Holy Virgin *Jovis alma parens*." And as a human being, too, Zeitblom incarnates a golden (but naturally rather unexciting) mean. For he is a touching and sympathetic but hardly inspiring figure— a decent man revolted by Hitlerism but, for all his personal probity, timorous and ineffectual. There can be little doubt that Thomas Mann's rather pathetic portrait of Zeitblom represents a good deal of what he feels about himself and his relation to Germany—not, to be sure, as a private individual (for Mann was anything but timorous and ineffectual in the fight against nazism), but as the representative of a German humanism that was impotent to check the course of catastrophe.

If there were any doubt on this score, it would be removed when Zeitblom, in the opening pages of the novel, evokes Hans Castorp's famous vision in the snow from *The Magic Mountain*—the vision of the harmonious fusion of the Apollonian and the Dionysian, the human and the awesomely irrational, in the higher unity of the *Homo Dei:* "When I stood at the place of the initiation itself, in the district of Eubulus at the edge of the Plutonian cleft overhung by rocks, I experienced by divination the rich feeling of life which expresses itself in the initiate veneration of Olympian Greece for the deities of the depths; often, later on, I explained to my pupils that culture is in very truth the pious and regulating, I might say propitiatory, entrance of the dark and uncanny into the service of the gods." Zeitblom's point of view is thus the very ideal of Mann himself as expressed in *The Magic Mountain*—and Zeitblom's helplessness, sadness, and sense of resignation certainly represent one facet of Mann's own feeling as he describes the defeat of this ideal in the history of Adrian Leverkuhn. For, instead of the unity he had once envisaged in Hans Castorp's "dream poem of humanity," instead of enlightened human intercourse in silent recognition of the blood sacrifice, it was the blood sacrifice that had found its voice and was now shouting its supremacy from the housetops—or, to be more accurate, through the loudspeakers.

Dr. Faustus is thus narrated through the perspective of *The Magic Mountain,* but this perspective, appropriately enough, no longer controls the pattern of the symbolism.

In *The Magic Mountain* the elaborate dialectic play of opposites was intended to reveal the necessity for the higher synthesis embodied in the major theme. Each character, both humanly and ideologically, was driven into self-contradiction by the necessary limits of his being and point of view; all were to be reconciled and transfigured by "life's delicate child," Hans Castorp, who represents the precarious balancing point of "the human" and is lord of counterpositions. But the world of *Dr. Faustus* is precisely one from which "the human" has been eliminated except as helpless onlooker; and the symbolic structure is thus controlled by the *fusion of extremes without mediation*—exactly as in the "morally chaotic all" represented by the Catholic-Communist Naphta, the antagonist of the dogmatic Enlightenment humanist Settembrini in *The Magic Mountain*. From Naphta's point of view, "God and the Devil were at one in being opposed to life, to bourgeoisiedom, reason and virtue, since they together represented the religious principle." The confusion and identity of "reaction as progress" is the very principle of Naphta; and it is his dialectic (though not in the specific political form that he embodied) which now shapes the entire symbolic structure.

The first chapters of the novel hold up before us an image of untroubled childhood unity and harmony. But when we come to the description of the Leverkuhn family, and Adrian himself, this is replaced by a treacherous process of metamorphosis in which opposites become confused and identified and extremes merge with each other in such a fashion that one cannot disentangle opposing categories. This symbolism is developed in relation to the experiments in biology and natural science carried on as a hobby by Leverkuhn's father. Mann's description here strikes the note of the uncanny, the mysterious, and the terrible that swells in volume as the novel proceeds, and which reaches its piercing peak of expression in Adrian Leverkuhn's greatest music. For all these experiments hover on the uncertain borderline between the organic and the inorganic, natural law and miracle, science and witchcraft; it is impossible, in any given case, to draw a hard-and-fast line between the two. And Zeitblom speaks of the senior Leverkuhn in medieval terms, as "speculating the elements" (like the hero's father in Goethe's *Faust*) because "a tinge of mysticism was perceptible in them [the experiments] which would once have been suspect as a leaning to the black arts."

Two points should be made about this episode, aside from its illustration of the diabolic transposition of "reaction as progress" that controls the entire symbolic structure of the book. One is the picture given here of Adrian Leverkuhn's supercilious and mockingly distant personality, which is symbolically associated both with Lucifer's Satanic pride and with German national arrogance. Another is the introduction of the motif of a "yearning for life" in connection with one of the experiments in question. The senior Leverkuhn takes a group of chemicals and develops them into what appear to be underwater plants: these give all the appearance of life but are really dead. Still, being exposed to the rays of the sun shining from one direction, they all poignantly turn toward the source of light. "Indeed, they so yearned after warmth and joy that they actually clung to the pane and stuck fast there." Despite Adrian Leverkuhn's silent laughter at this spectacle, which moved the other onlookers to tears, this motif, so to speak, remains in the family. Adrian himself will ultimately yearn for "warmth and joy" and for a life and a soul that his nature cannot attain. And this secret, irresistible yearning for "the human" is what saves him in the end, or at least gives his life an aura of self-sacrifice and martyrdom that keeps it quite distinct emotionally from the historical plane of the book.

The background of Leverkuhn's early life is masterfully depicted by Mann in chapters where the dialectic of the imagery evokes the interpenetration of late nineteenth-century Germany with the atmosphere of the Reformation. The Reformation is of course the period of the original *Faust* chapbook, whose theme of damnation in return for knowledge and power over nature—the theme taken over and used by Marlowe in the Elizabethan *Dr. Faustus*—expresses the Lutheran opposition to the humanism of the Renaissance. And it is this atmosphere of regressive folk fanaticism and folk superstition, of religious ardor reverting to mass hysteria, that Zeitblom feels lingering in the old streets and buildings where one still sensed "a morbid excitement, a metaphysical epidemic latent since the last years of the Middle Ages."

This Reformation atmosphere is an essential element of the symbolism of the book and, as part of the general coloring of the Faust theme, its employment is explicable enough. Yet, since Hitler and nazism have very little (indeed nothing) directly to do with Luther and the Reformation, one may well wonder why Mann uses it so insistently. The answer is that Mann, along with many historians, views Luther's sharp distinction between spiritual and political freedom as having exercised a nefarious influence on German culture. Luther imposed a strict religious obligation to obey political authority; and this accounts for the musical "interiority" of German culture, i.e., the political irresponsibility of its greatest representatives (Nietzsche is the most relevant example), and for German docility to authority of any kind. Luther's extremism in separating the realms of the religious and the social is thus the prototype of the German fusion of opposites, which turns the highest concerns of the spirit into the breeding ground for the most ruthless tyranny.

III

Ortega y Gasset once remarked very acutely in his *The Dehumanization of Art* that most of the radical movements in modern art and literature could be analyzed as quite simple changes in the normal perspective with which the world is seen or described. Depending on whether the artist places himself closer or farther away than the normal distance, or shifts the accepted relation between background and foreground, his work will appear more or less startling and daring.[12] One of the secrets of Thomas Mann's art is a mastery of such shifts in perspective— shifts so slight, however, that the normal perspective is never destroyed, while we gradually become aware of a reality existing below or beyond or behind the one we are nominally regarding. Every reader of Mann will recall such effects, which are usually obtained by a careful choice of incongruous detail, by the repetition and slight variation of leitmotifs, and by stylistic stress and insinuation. Nowhere in Mann's work is this palimpsest technique employed with such mastery and effectiveness as in *Dr. Faustus,* since every step of Adrian Leverkuhn's career must be felt both as humanly free and yet as guided by a hidden diabolism working itself out at the same time.

Leverkuhn's life is indissolubly linked with music from his earliest days; and the major music symbolism is first expounded in the lectures of Wendell Kretschmar, town organist of Kaisersaschern and Leverkuhn's music teacher. Kretschmar sees modern music (his example is the later Beethoven) as longing to transcend its individualism and romantic subjectivity by a return to its old role as the expression of a collectivity like the Church. Not that any simple return is possible—but the way forward would be a reimmersion in the powerful currents of the mythical, the collective, and the supernatural under new conditions. These lectures make a profound impression on young Leverkuhn; but their result is to drive him to study theology instead of music, as if to ward off the imminent danger he feels in his attraction to the latter.

Leverkuhn, in effect, is fleeing from the demon to the protection of God; futilely, as it turns out, because he finds no refuge in the ancient sanctities which are themselves exposed to the same dialectic that Kretschmar had foreseen in music. When theology is not ridiculous and ludicrous (in the guise of the professor who apes Luther's grossness and vulgarity), it is brilliantly sinister in the lectures of Dr. Schleppfuss (Dragfoot, the Devil), *Privat-docent* in the psychology of religion. For Schleppfuss ingeniously demonstrates the dialectical unity of good and evil, equates "freedom" with the power to sin, "humanity" with the concern for the salvation of the soul shown by the pious witch burners of the Middle Ages, and belief in the evil eye with a "humanistic" elevation of spirit over matter. Schleppfuss insinuates—without expressly saying so—that these theological redefinitions of Enlightenment ideals are far more "advanced" than their ordinary, banal meanings. And in the same way, in the conversations of Leverkuhn's student friends, any concern with political matters is immediately "raised" to the level of metaphysics or to speculations about the "folk soul." All the clichés of German high-brow jingoism are rehearsed in these pages; and it is interesting to see how, in this theological atmosphere, they blend with the growing influence of Kierkegaard and his contempt for both "objective" truth and a "herd" existence (Kierkegaard was discovered at the turn of the century by the German avant-garde).

Leverkuhn finally abandons theology for the study of music; but in doing so he is well aware of the disparity between his own nature and the traditional concept of art. For art is always, in a certain sense, a compromise and reconciliation between genius and convention, between the individual and the social. But Leverkuhn writes to Kretschmar: "I am embarrassed at the insipidness which is the supporting structure, the conditioning solid substance of even the work of genius, at the elements thereof which are training and common property, at use and wont in achieving the beautiful." All this seems to Leverkuhn's icy haughtiness the peak of absurdity: "Why must I think that almost all, no, all the methods and conventions of *art are good for parody only?*" The answer, within the symbolic structure of the book, can be found only in Leverkuhn's incapacity to experience or express feeling except negatively, jeeringly, derisively. And his inability to participate in the median sphere of "the human" would seem to doom his art to be merely "parody and critique" instead of truly creative.

This is the point at which the Devil takes a hand. From whence can a genius with such a nature draw the emotional dynamism necessary for positive creation? Only by a dialectical fusion of the negativity of pure spirit with pure (or rather, impure) flesh; not by love—for love is precisely the "human" mediation of both spirit and flesh—but by sex. And Leverkuhn's pact with flesh and the demonic (the two, as Dr. Schleppfuss has luminously explained, have been traditionally the same), is sealed by a sexual embrace with a prostitute that culminates in a syphilitic infection of the brain. This is the poisoned source from which Leverkuhn will draw his inspiration—

not from the healthy heat of sun-warmed feeling but from the smoldering fire hiddenly crackling in the witch's kitchen. In associating art with disease and genius with illness, Mann is of course returning to one of the omnipresent motifs of his artistic career. But, while in the past this linkage had been treated as a piquant though somewhat melancholy paradox, it is now the Devil who announces, "The artist is the brother of the criminal and the madman," and who laughs at the Goethean idea, still clung to by Leverkuhn, of "sane and sound greatness." What was once merely a Nietzschean paradox has become diabolism and the spirit's self-betrayal.

It is only after this event that the musical originality of Leverkuhn begins to flower; and he fictively reinvents Schönberg's atonality to solve his musical problem. This system of composition imposes on music an objective structure that rigidly controls both melody and harmony in a manner paralleling—though without duplicating—the "strict style" of early Church polyphony. The harmonic subjectivity, the freedom, of the atonal composer is totally negated; but in relation to harmonic convention his music sounds wildly iconoclastic. "More interesting phenomena," Leverkuhn observes to the narrator, "probably always have this double face of past and future, probably are always progressive and regressive in one." And at the mid-point of the book, when Leverkuhn's surrender to the demonic has been effectuated both physically (by his contraction of syphilis) and musically (by the invention of atonality, with its inverted relation to early Church music), the Devil in person appears in what Leverkuhn tries to convince himself is only a feverish hallucination.

The burning dialogue between the two is obviously modeled on *The Brothers Karamazov;* and, impossible though it may seem, Mann's pages triumphantly survive the burden of such a comparison. Twenty-four years are given Leverkuhn in which to create those remarkable works that press so far forward (or backward) along the path he must follow; but he shall create them in icy solitude, denied "the human" and the normal love of other "humans." "Not only will you break through the paralyzing difficulties of the time—you will break through time itself," the Devil promises Leverkuhn, "by which I mean the cultural epoch and its cult, and dare to be barbaric, twice barbaric indeed, because of coming after the humane. . . . Believe me, barbarism even has more grasp of theology than has a culture fallen away from cult, which even in the religious has seen only culture, only the humane, never excess, paradox, the mystic passion, the utterly unbourgeois ordeal."

Particular attention must be paid in this discussion to a knotty point in theology. Taxing the Devil with a certain shallowness in his approach to the subject, Leverkuhn warns him not to be too sure of his bargain; for there is a *"prideful contritio"* that may work in Leverkuhn's favor. "The *contritio* without hope, as a complete disbelief in the possibility of mercy and forgiveness, the rocklike firm conviction of the sinner that he has done too grossly for even the Everlasting Goodness to forgive his sin—only that is the true *contritio*. I call your attention to the fact that it is the nighest to redemption, for Goodness the most irresistible of all." But the Devil replies that precisely such speculations, which testify to Leverkuhn's supremely insolent self-possession, will forever prevent him from achieving "the naïve recklessness of despair" necessary for "the sinfull waye to salvacion."

After this fateful interview, the novel widens into a macabre evocation of German culture from the period immediately preceding the First World War through the final triumph of the values of the demonic-irrational in the Third Reich. This section of the book, in a literal sense, is Thomas Mann's autobiography. He pitilessly weaves in tragic incidents from his own family life (the suicide of his sister Carla is narrated, even to the exact reprinting of her suicide note, in the death of Clarissa Rodde); and in Zeitblom's identification with German hopes of a "breakthrough" to world power in 1914 Mann depicts his own spiritual state at the time he wrote his *Betrachtungen eines Unpolitischen* (1918). Mann also settles accounts here with the Munich intelligentsia among whom he lived for so many years, satirizing real figures under assumed names or, in many cases, not even deigning to invent a pseudonym at all.

But this does not mean, as some critics have suggested, that at this point Mann neglects the demands of his major theme for the sake of paying off old scores or unburdening himself of searing memories. On the contrary, each of the major episodes in this section rehearses, on a smaller and less significant scale, some aspect of Leverkuhn's grandiose history. Clarissa Rodde is an artist herself, an actress who, like Leverkuhn, lacks warmth of feeling, and consequently cannot project herself successfully on the stage. She is finally seduced and driven to suicide by a shabby "pseudo Mephistopheles" of the backstage coulisses. Her equally ill-fated sister Inez, who ends up by murdering her unfaithful lover, is married to a simpering art historian infatuated by Nietzschean "ruthlessness"; and the tragedy of her life is described in terms of the opposition between ethics and aesthetics. All this part of the book is literally a "satyr-play and ludicrous repetition" of what Leverkuhn-Nietzsche is undergoing "in the grand manner." And the artists and intellectuals of the Kridwiss circle, who vaunt the creative superiority of irrational "myth" over "abstract" ideas like justice and truth, are clearly the very ones against whom Mann launched his article on Freud in 1929.

IV

All through *Dr. Faustus* we are given superbly expressive accounts of Leverkuhn's music. Far from burdening the novel with a dead weight of unassimilated material, as some critics have contended, these serve as the chief means for characterizing the main figure. Leverkuhn's life is as outwardly uneventful as Nietzsche's; and his spiritual history is entirely portrayed by the description of his musical compositions. Every detail of these descriptions is carefully designed to bring out some facet of his inner conflicts or to express the cultural situation of his time; but the parallel between Leverkuhn and German culture, as we have already remarked, is by no means a total identity.

Leverkuhn's pact with the demonic is a source of continual spiritual torment, not an occasion for emotional titillation or moral license; it leads both to agonizing physical suffering (whose symptoms are taken largely, though not exclusively, from Nietzsche's letters) and to the inner wrestlings of his God-forsaken conscience as revealed through his music. The "yearning for life" never ceases to haunt even his most bitter and uncompromising scores. This is why he speaks so tenderly of the little seamaid in Andersen's fairy tale, who, for love of a human prince, enters into the kingdom of the sea-witch to gain human legs instead of a fish's tail; and who wears her human legs despite the knife-sharp pains at every step "perhaps to win, like human beings, an immortal soul." When the accusation of "barbarism" is leveled against Leverkuhn's composition the *Apocalypse,* with its use of glissando to imitate animal howls, Zeitblom rejects the charge because of certain song passages that are "like a fervid prayer for a soul . . . to call soullessness the yearning for a soul—the yearning of the little sea-maid—that is what I would characterize as barbarism, as inhumanity."

This "yearning for a soul," which contravenes the interdiction of the Devil against human love, is reflected in various episodes of the book; but in none more poignantly than in Leverkuhn's final devotion to his little nephew Nepomuk, whose nickname is Echo. No pages of Mann's work are more charming and touching than his description of the elfin Echo, whose figure is interwoven with allusions both to the Christ child and to Shakespeare's Ariel. Leverkuhn's love for Echo, however, precipitates the last personal tragedy in a book weighted with disaster. The child dies a horrible death in the throes of spinal meningitis, an illness whose symptoms and prognosis duplicate those of Leverkuhn's syphilitic infection of the meninges. Echo's death is the revenge that the Devil wreaks on his unfaithful accomplice; and this crushing blow wrings from Leverkuhn a gigantic cry of despair—his last and greatest composition, a massive symphonic cantata *The Lamentation of Dr. Faustus,* which "takes back" Beethoven's "human" paean to the brotherhood of man in his Ninth Symphony.

In this work, which is described by Zeitblom at the exact moment when the Satanic horrors of Hitler's concentration camps are exposed to the world for the first time, "echo, the favorite device of the baroque, is employed with unspeakably mournful effect." For echo represents the human voice transformed into nature, given back as nature-sound, "Nature's melancholy 'Alas' in view of man, her effort to utter his solitary state." The concealed thematic identity between the voices of Heaven and Hell in one part of the *Apocalypse* is now carried through in the whole of *The Lamentation,* whose structure is rigidly controlled by the twelve syllables of Faust's confession in the old chapbook: "For I die as a good and as a bad Christian." Yet despite its rigid atonality, *The Lamentation of Dr. Faustus* represents Leverkuhn's breakthrough to pure expressiveness. The very rigidity of the structure, the complete absence of any free note, allows the composer, by a dialectical paradox, to take technique for granted. The uttermost constraint resolves itself into "the free language of feeling, the birth of freedom from bondage"; and there is no trace of parody left in the total negation expressed by both the words and the construction of the music.

But in the most often quoted passage in the book—Zeitblom's concluding paragraph on *The Lamentation*—a further and almost inconceivable paradox is also hinted at:

> No, this dark tone-poem permits up to the very end no consolation, appeasement, transfiguration. But take our artist paradox: grant that expressiveness—expression as lament—is the issue of the whole construction: then may we not parallel with it another, a religious one, and say too (though only in the lowest whisper) that out of the sheerly irremediable hope might germinate? It would be but a hope beyond hopelessness, the transcendence of despair—not betrayal of her, but the miracle that passes belief. For listen to the end, listen with me: one group of instruments after another retires, and what remains, as the work fades on the air, is the high G of a cello, the last word, the last fainting sound, slowly dying in a *pianissimo-fermata*. Then nothing more: silence, and night. But that tone which vibrates in the silence, which is no longer there, to which only the spirit hearkens, and which was the voice of mourning, is no more. It changes its meaning; it abides as a light in the night.

The religious paradox alluded to here is of course that of the *"prideful contritio"*; and it should be clear that Leverkuhn's "yearning for a soul" has brought him to the "naïve recklessness of despair" that the Devil had thought impossible.

This despair is revealed in Leverkuhn's terrible demented address to his assembled "friends," in which he utters all the horror and agony of his demon-haunted spirit and acknowledges his guilt for not having striven so that "among men such order shall be 'stablished that again for the beautiful work living soil and true harmony be prepared." And then, with a gesture of crucifixion, he sinks into total mental darkness. But this confession is the light abiding in the night of Leverkuhn's madness, faintly illuminating his wasted features, from which all intelligence has fled, with the aura of martyrdom. Nothing similar, however, occurs in the world symbolized and foreshadowed by Leverkuhn's tragic end; the satyr-play continues its tumultuous course, and its protagonists feel personally untouched by Leverkuhn's prophetic collapse. The question remains open whether the German people too can achieve his naïve recklessness of despair; and perhaps part of the answer may be found in what one hopes (but does not really believe) is only a failure of critical acumen. For ironically enough the most popular accusation made against *Dr. Faustus* in German criticism is that Mann condemns his people to "hopelessness" and leaves them no way of attaining salvation.*

* This point is worth illustrating at some length since it reveals so much about the present German state of mind. I shall quote a passage from Wilhelm Grenzmann, *Dichtung und Glaube* (Bonn: Athenaeum, 1957), p. 57. Grenzmann's book, now in its third edition, is a critical survey of postwar German literature written from a "Christian" point of view and with no pretensions to originality. The book thus obviously represents the views of a substantial body of German literate opinion. Here is what Grenzmann writes:

"One feels the inner emotions of the otherwise so detached writer over

V

Lengthy as this analysis has been, it is far from having begun to exhaust the complexities of *Dr. Faustus.* Hermann J. Weigand once called *The Magic Mountain* the "most highly integrated" of all novels conceived on so vast a scale; [13] but it is quite likely that the palm must now be awarded to *Dr. Faustus* (the only other possible contestants are *Ulysses* and *Finnegans Wake,* and it may be argued that neither of these is a novel in the sense in which Thomas Mann continued to write such works). *Dr. Faustus* is clearly composed in the "strict style" that defines Leverkuhn's music: every incident, episode, and detail is paralleled, varied, and transposed in an incredibly elaborate variety of correspondences. But no matter from what angle

---

the fate of his hero [Adrian Leverkuhn], over himself, over all of mankind. But here no perspective and no power becomes visible that leads out of this self-enclosed circle. In whatever direction one turns, there is no breaking out of this enclosure—all exits are barred, all windows darkened.

"Or does the brief passage referring to a 'light in the night,' conceal a hope against all hope? Can an unknown, rejected and unimplored God come to pity and save a world entangled in its own misery?

"We understand the lament—we do not understand the accusation. We know that Thomas Mann has not spared the latter; and even the last words of his great novel, in which he turns with no transition from the tragedy of Leverkuhn to the fate of the German people struggling with death, contain a mixture of lament and accusation. Has he the right to accuse after this book? What means of renovation does he provide his people, after he has become the messenger of such despair? In what order of universal meaning would he domicile a people wishing to renew themselves? A presupposition for any conversion is that one believes that the world has order and meaning. A transgressor, who defies and violates a structure of values, a blasphemer, who challenges and insults the majesty of God, can be reclaimed; but not he who does not believe in being. Under such circumstances are not words useless—and more than useless?"

This sort of mealy-mouthed hypocrisy, I regret to say, is quite typical of the "pious" school of contemporary German criticism.

one approaches *Dr. Faustus*—whether from that of content or of form—the entire work reveals itself as a dialectical transposition of opposites whose paradigm may be found in Mann's original analysis of "reaction as progress." All the thematic material is controlled by this dialectic—and the same is true of the structure. For, while the density of its symbolic texture makes *Dr. Faustus* the quintessence of the Symbolist novel, this is combined with the most primitive narrative form of fictitious biography. Or from another perspective, the raw materials of historical events, family disasters, and real personages are assimilated into the recital of Leverkuhn's rarefied aesthetic adventures and blended with the Faust myth.

Not the least originality of this remarkable work springs from its endeavor—unique in the history of the novel—to narrate the life of an artist primarily through an account of his creations. With the exception of one or two novellas of Balzac (notably his *Chef-d'oeuvre inconnu*) nothing similar has ever been attempted. Proust's beautiful analyses of Elstir's paintings and Vinteuil's sonata are the only comparable pages one can think of in modern writing; but Proust strove to communicate the impressions imparted by an art work to a particular sensibility, not to re-create the art work itself as an objective structure. *Dr. Faustus* is the first great work in which an artist comes to life, not primarily as a special kind of picturesque or exotic personality but truly and solely as a creator of his art; and for this reason it seems to be the first successful novel about an artist that has ever been written.

All previous works of this kind deal exclusively with what, for any artist, is merely peripheral—namely, the circumstances of his life. The author desperately tries to convince us that the life of his artist-protagonist has overwhelming importance, but this importance is never "realized" as part of the book—it derives from an activity whose quality we are required to take on faith. For nothing about any aspect of an artist's life can really persuade us that he is capable of producing first-rate art. It was no doubt some such thought that impelled Henry James to remark, in the preface to *The Tragic Muse,* that the artist as subject is interesting only to the extent that he is an artist *manqué.* "Any presentation of the artist *in triumph,*" James writes, "must be flat in proportion as it really sticks to its subject—it can only smuggle in relief and variety. For, to put the matter in an image, all we then—in his triumph—see of the charm-compeller is the back that he turns to us as he bends over his work." [14] Thomas Mann magisterially solves this problem by expressing the inner "reality" of the artist's life exclusively through a depiction of his work; and the works themselves thus become an integral part of the dramatic realization of the theme.

As we know from *The Story of a Novel,* Mann felt the technical problem outlined above with particular acuity; but the solution he adopted has far more than a purely technical function. It is by maintaining his focus constantly on Leverkuhn's music that Mann succeeds, despite the intense "Germanity" of *Dr. Faustus,* in raising the book to the level he wished to attain—the level on which he portrays the situation "of mankind itself, of the spirit in our thoroughly critical epoch." Indeed, without wishing to add another paradox to those of the book itself, we may yet argue that *Dr. Faustus* is an "international" novel in a far deeper sense than *The Magic Mountain.*

For in spite of the latter's Swiss setting and cosmopolitan cast of characters, the theme depends on a special thesis about German culture that few but Germans would accept. This thesis considered Germany to be "the land of the center," the country destined by fate (or the *Weltgeist*) to reconcile the conflicting cultural antagonisms of Western civilization. The European surface of the book, then, was sustained by a thematic foundation with a strong nationalistic bias. In *Dr. Faustus,* however, the strongly accentuated national coloring of the surface does not conceal the "international" character of Adrian Leverkuhn's music; his work bears the characteristic stamp of twentieth-century European culture as a whole. And who can fail to recognize in Leverkuhn's compositions a dialectic to which all of modern culture has fallen prey in a greater or lesser degree?

It is hardly possible any longer to overlook the union in modern art of the most daring intellectual and aesthetic modernity with a rejection of humanism and liberalism, and a preference—both formally and ideologically—for the primitive, the mythical, and the irrational. To be sure, this has not necessarily resulted in an alliance with the forces of political retrogression; nor did it do so, we should remember, in the case of Leverkuhn himself, whose music was considered *Kulturbolschewismus* by the masters of the Third Reich. Still, the careers of Knut Hamsun, Ezra Pound, and Drieu la Rochelle; the political pronouncements of Yeats, Eliot (in the mid-thirties), Wyndham Lewis, and Gottfried Benn; the proto-Fascist tendencies in the work of D. H. Lawrence and Stefan George—all this reveals to what extent Thomas Mann has managed to raise to the level of sovereign art the problematic nature of modern culture itself. As modern life has become more and more rationalized, mechanized, and industrialized, art has been driven into a more and more frenzied and violent assault on a world in which the total dimension of the spirit has been reduced to a stiflingly materialistic utilitarianism. The legitimacy and necessity of such a revolt is beyond question; yet its danger is no less evident. For it is an uncomfortable but inescapable truth that, if some of our noblest artistic expressions were to be translated tomorrow into practical, political terms, the result would only be to play into the hands of some form of tyranny and oppression.

The parallel between Adrian Leverkuhn and nazism has aroused much criticism, and, even among writers generally friendly to Mann, has been rejected as unconvincing. The gap between the two phenomena, it has been said, is too wide to eliminate an ultimate sense of incongruity. But, on the contrary, it seems to me that the stature of Mann's book as a symbolic projection of the crisis of modern culture derives precisely from the tension of this incongruity and the dialectic it suggests. The images of our greatness are far more intimately connected with those of our misery than we are willing to admit; and it is the genius of Thomas Mann, sharpened by the tragedy of his culture, that has discerned and portrayed their hidden interconnection. All the significant movements of modern times, whether in art, politics, philosophy, or theology, have driven straight for one type or another of extremism; nothing has seemed so paltry and contemptible as counsels of caution or recommendations of prudence. It is only the final paradox that out of Thomas Mann's "wildest" book, which captures the spirit of our apocalyptic era as no other comparable work, the peaceful, bourgeois *via media* of "the human" should finally emerge as the true Promised Land.

NOTES

4. REACTION AS PROGRESS: THOMAS MANN'S *Dr. Faustus*

1. Thomas Mann, *The Story of a Novel,* tr. by Richard and Clara Winston (New York: Alfred A. Knopf, 1961), p. 32.

   The various drafts of this essay were written before Mann's book on *Dr. Faustus* was translated into English, and I made my own translation. My quotations, as a result, do not exactly correspond in wording with those of the page references given, but there is no major difference in the meaning.

2. *Ibid.,* p. 11.

3. *Ibid.,* p. 17.

4. Thomas Mann, *Altes und Neues* (Frankfurt: S. Fischer, 1953), p. 655.

5. Thomas Mann, "Freud's Position in the History of Modern Thought," *Past Masters* (New York: Alfred A. Knopf, 1933), p. 174.

6. *Ibid.,* p. 173.

7. This phrase is the title of Paragraph 26, Book I of Nietzsche's *Human, All-Too Human.*

8. *Past Masters,* p. 177.

9. *Ibid.,* p. 169.

10. Thomas Mann, "Deutschland und die Deutschen," *Die Neue Rundschau,* 1 (1945–1946), 8.

11. *The Story of a Novel,* p. 31.

12. José Ortega y Gasset, *The Dehumanization of Art* (Garden City, N. Y.: Doubleday Anchor), p. 31.

13. Hermann J. Weigand, *Thomas Mann's Novel, Der Zauberberg* (New York: Appleton-Century Co., 1933), p. 159.

14. Henry James, *The Art of the Novel,* ed. by R. P. Blackmur (New York: Charles Scribner's Sons, 1934), p. 96.

5 The Dehumanization of Art

Few works in modern aesthetics have enjoyed such widespread acceptance and influence as José Ortega y Gasset's *The Dehumanization of Art.* If its brilliant and provocative author had not achieved world-wide notoriety for his famous book on politics, *The Revolt of the Masses,* it is safe to say that his little brochure on the tendency of modern art would have assured him a similar status. First published in Madrid in 1925, Ortega's book immediately made its mark and had a considerable influence on the gifted young rising generation of writers and artists in the Spanish-speaking world. But Ortega's ideas have also had a wide circulation elsewhere, and it is impossible to consult any book on modern art without coming across a reference to his terms and ideas. Within the context of the present volume, Thomas Mann's *Dr. Faustus* can easily be seen as a gigantic dramatization of the moral perils lurking in the "dehumanization" that Ortega defines; and the attempt to conjure these perils is central to Malraux's aesthetics of modern art.

Despite its wide acceptance, however, Ortega's book has been the subject of a good deal of misunderstanding. For one thing, it is universally accepted as a *defense* of the movement it sets out to investigate, although Ortega emphatically declared that he was not attempting to assume the role of judge or advocate but solely that of philosophical observer. And when Ortega abandons this role for a moment, as he does from time to time, he makes it quite clear that his tastes by no means incline him toward modern art. "It may be said that the new art has so far produced nothing worth while," he observes at one point, "and I am inclined to think the same." Even more, Ortega's interest in modern art derives far more from his own philosophy than from any attraction to this art itself. And his reflections lead him into a *depreciation* of the function of art in modern culture which has gone largely unnoticed, and which, if understood, would hardly please the partisans of the moderns. Now that the passage of time has somewhat dimmed the immediate sense of illumination provided by Ortega's scintillating pages, it may thus prove useful to go back and reassess his book from a more balanced perspective.

Certainly the most valuable and perennial section of the work is Ortega's *description* of the main tendency of modern art. This remains as fresh today as when it was first written. Whether or not Ortega coined the word "dehumanization," it was first given currency by his book; and it has been used ever since to fix one of modern art's most dominating traits. What Ortega means is most obvious in the plastic arts, where the importance of recognizable human forms is no longer dependent on their specifically *human* expressiveness. We are not interested in Cézanne's portrait of his wife, or for that matter his self-portrait, because of any sense the canvases may give us of the inner lives of the people portrayed; these canvases are paintings, not portraits, unlike the works of Rembrandt devoted to the same type of subject. The forms of the visible world, whether human, organic, or simply material, are treated solely as aesthetic objects and distorted at will to meet the artistic necessities of the painter's vision. Ortega, it might be noted, does not apply this idea to so-called "pure" abstract art, which in any case he thinks impossible; and he remarks that the few attempts made by Picasso in this direction have been "failures."

A similar evolution has taken place in modern literature, and particularly modern poetry. In the past, simile and metaphor had been used to decorate and embellish the "real" subject or content of the poem, just as form and color had been used to express and convey the "real" subject of the plastic work of art. But now, exactly as in the plastic arts, the order of importance between these elements has been reversed, and what was merely instrumental has become essential. "Before, reality was overlaid with metaphors by way of ornament; now the tendency is to eliminate the extra-poetical, or real, prop and to 'realize' the metaphor, to make it the *res poetica*." The "substance" of the poem is no longer the reality which the metaphor expresses, but the metaphor itself crystallized into a curious linguistic world "distinct from human flora and fauna." This objectification of metaphor, which Ortega finds beginning with Mallarmé, is the most radical method of dehumanization in literature. But he also discerns another method in such writers as Proust, Ramón Gomez de la Serna, and Joyce, who change the normal perspective on reality by shifting attention to, and placing in the foreground, aspects of life which are usually kept in the background or which escape attention altogether.

All these experiments of modern art move in the same direction—a direction that Ortega defines in terms of the epistemological relation between idea and thing. Ordinarily, ideas are used to orient action, to help us grasp reality; and so unconscious are we of this process that we constantly define reality in terms of our ideas, as if the two were naturally identical. "By means of ideas we see the world," Ortega notes, "but in a natural attitude of the mind we do not see the ideas—the same as the eye in seeing does not see itself." But modern art, by shifting attention away from the "reality" expressed in art, has inverted this natural relation between idea and thing. The artist no longer focuses on reality, surreptitiously using his ideas as a controlling framework, but rather turns back and displaces the artistic center of gravity to a *direct* expression of his ideas. The portrait painter is far more interested in *his* perception of the pattern created by a sitter than in the sitter himself; and Cubist paintings are what Ortega calls a "symbolic cipher" for certain ideas about the structure of reality. In his immensely suggestive essay "On Point of View in the Arts," which serves as a valuable supplement to *The Dehumanization of Art,* Ortega sees modern art as the culmination of the entire history of Western painting. For the law which he persuasively deduces from its historical evolution is that "first, things are painted; then sensations; finally, ideas." [1]

This displacement by modern art of the normal focus of interest—i.e., reality, the world, people and passions as they present themselves in ordinary human life and human affairs—has thus resulted in a purer distillation of the essence of art than ever before. And, while Ortega may have his doubts about the permanent value of the products of modern art, there can be no question that he is wholeheartedly in sympathy with this endeavor of the moderns to define boundaries rigorously and stringently. Ortega's thought, violently in reaction against the eclecticism of the second half of the nineteenth century, welcomes modern art's rejection of the confusion between art and life fostered by realism and naturalism—movements which he calls "a maximum aberration in the history of taste." Also, he favors modern art, unexpectedly enough, for what he labels "sociological" reasons.

Modern art, he points out, separates its audience into those who are capable of a "pure" aesthetic experience and those who are not. It thereby distinguishes the select from the vulgar, and becomes an invaluable catalyst for the formation of that new aristocracy of the spirit which Ortega believed indispensable to the salvation of modern culture. Since this aspect of Ortega's aesthetics has usually been ignored, it is worth quoting a key passage. "Through its mere presence," he argues, "the art of the young compels the average citizen to realize that he is just this—the average citizen, a creature incapable of receiving the sacrament of art, blind and deaf to pure beauty. . . . On the other hand, the new art also helps the élite to recognize themselves and one another in the drab mass of society and to learn their mission which consists in being few and holding their own against the many."

For all these reasons, Ortega spoke warmly and enthusiastically of the new trend as an inevitable and salutary historical phenomenon (which no doubt accounts for the mistaken belief that he was concerned to defend its particular manifestations and experiments). And in any case his irreverent and witty thrusts against the immediate past were certainly calculated to hearten the young artists then undertaking the hazardous mission of totally breaking with their predecessors. "To insist on neat distinctions is a symptom of mental honesty," Ortega assured them. "Life is one thing, art is another—thus the young set think or at least feel—let us keep the two apart. The poet begins where the man ends." Ortega's pages are filled with the same dash, defiance, and willful injustice toward the past that inspired modernism in its heyday; no other work communicates so vivid a sense of the youthful élan and bravado of this effervescent era. Nor has any writer since been able to compete with Ortega's trenchant book in synoptic grasp and power of conceptual penetration.

II

As we pursue the train of Ortega's ideas, however, we soon begin to find ourselves in strange and rather quagmirish territory. Dehumanized modern art, cutting itself off from the natural relation of mind to reality, has ceased, we are told, to have any "connection with dramatic social or political movements, or with profound religious or philosophical currents." Art during the nineteenth century, particularly in the Romantic period, had been ready to take on itself nothing less than "the salvation of mankind"; but modern art and the modern artist, Ortega asserts, will no longer have anything to do with such ponderous pretensions. Art has renounced its role, apparently voluntarily, of being the spokesman and interpreter of the highest values of its culture and has retired to a realm where the pleasures and refinements of the aesthetic sensibility are cultivated exclusively for their own sake.

Most writers on modern art have seen this increasingly predominant aestheticism as stimulated by a sense of art's superiority to vulgar and "impure" reality. But here Ortega paradoxically takes the opposite view, that modern art is being modest rather than proud; and he points to the irony and self-mockery so characteristic of modern art (or at least of the modern art of the twenties) as proof of his contention. Indeed, one source of Ortega's lack of interest in the possibility of "pure" abstract art lies in his desire to conceive of modern art as actively engaged in the *process* of dehumanization rather than simply neglecting the human entirely. What he wishes to find in modern art is an explicit and self-conscious inversion of tradition, which has to be embodied in the work itself by some recognizable deformation. "For the modern artist, aesthetic pleasure derives from such a triumph over human matter. That is why he has to drive home the victory by presenting in each case the strangled victim."

Modern art, then, is essentially negative, derisive, ironic. *It does not take itself seriously,* nor, in Ortega's opinion, does it expect anyone else to do so. "Art is appreciated," he writes, "precisely because it is recognized as a farce. . . . A 'farce' in the bad sense of the word it would be if the modern artist pretended to equal status with the 'serious' artists of the past, and a Cubist painting expected to be extolled as solemnly and all but religiously as a statue by Michelangelo. But all he [the Cubist artist] does is to invite us to look at a piece of art that is a joke and that essentially makes fun of itself." Rather than being concerned with the serious and profound issues on which the fate of humanity was once supposed to hang, modern art, the new style, "only asks to be linked to the triumph of sport and games."

Ortega does not undertake the task of explaining in

The Dehumanization of Art why art should have traveled this road in modern times; he refers the reader for more details to an earlier work, *The Modern Theme*. And if we turn to this book we discover that Ortega's interpretation of modern art clearly derives from his general philosophical position at this period. *The Modern Theme* is the written version of a group of lectures, given in 1921–22, in which Ortega launches a Nietzschean attack on "culture" as a watered-down religion that places the ends of human existence in a sphere transcendent to life. "Culturalism," he declares here, "is a Christianity without God." ² According to Ortega, culturalism locates the values of life in the infinite future; it sets up a hierarchy of abstractions—science, art, ethics, justice—divorced from the possibility of their fulfillment under concrete biological and historical conditions. Ortega's thought is bitterly hostile to this deification of "culture," and he searches for symptoms in modern life that a new era is impending. Such a symptom he finds in the disagreement over modern art which, in the early twenties, pitted the younger generation against the old.

Here is a key passage on art, that gives us a glimpse into the genesis of his book on dehumanization:

> The art of the young does not differ from traditional art so much in its objects as in its radical change of subjective attitude to art itself. The general symptom of the new style, evident in all its multiform manifestations, is to be found in the circumstance that art has been dislodged from its position in the "serious" zone of life, has, in fact, ceased to be a centre of vital gravitation. The semi-religious character, cultivating pathos of a sublime type, which aesthetic taste has been acquiring for two centuries, has now been completely extirpated. Art, in the consciousness of the new race, becomes philistinism or not-art as soon as it is taken seriously.³

On this basis Ortega argues that the gap between the generations (a point he also stresses in *The Dehumanization of Art*) is one that cannot possibly be bridged. For the older generation, the lack of seriousness in art disqualifies it immediately; for the younger, this very lack of seriousness is the supreme value. And Ortega contends that the attitude of the younger generation reveals "one of the most widespread features in the new reaction to existence; it was what I long ago called the sense of life as a sport and as a festivity." [4]

These last words take us back to Ortega's remark that the dehumanization of modern art is "linked to the triumph of sport and games." For in the early twenties Ortega genuinely believed that the whole character of modern life was about to change. We must keep in mind that he was writing during the heyday of Dadaism in France, Ultraism in Spain, and the *Jugendbewegung* in Germany. Youth, vitality, athleticism, bullfighting, nude sunbathing, and the emancipation of the senses were being glorified almost everywhere. There was a gigantic explosion of frenzied *joie de vivre* (or what easily could be seen as such, despite its undertone of tragic despair) as a reaction against the intolerable psychic tensions of the war years.

At that moment it might well have seemed that biological values would replace those of the cultural "beyond"; that the present would replace the future as the dominating temporal horizon; that youth would take precedence over age, and that the cult of the body would triumph over the moribund and senile cult of the mind. And a consequence of this triumph would be not only the dehumanization of art but its *devaluation,* its relegation to a secondary zone of cultural importance, the refusal any longer to invest it with the dignity and reverence it had formerly claimed—and received. "What is behind this disgust at seeing art mixed up with life?" Ortega asks suggestively. "Could it be disgust for the human sphere as such, for reality, for life? Or is it rather the opposite: respect for life and unwillingness to confuse it with art, so inferior a thing as art? But what do we mean by calling art an inferior function—divine art, glory of civilization, *fine fleur* of culture, and so forth." Thus Ortega ironically poses the problem; and though he pretends to dismiss these questions as "impertinent," there can be little doubt regarding his choice between these alternatives.

Ortega's thought, then, lands him in the awkward position of maintaining that a *victory* for the biological and organic values of life in our time has been responsible for the dehumanization of art. And just how awkward this position is becomes clear when we juxtapose it against the diametrically opposed thesis of Wilhelm Worringer in *Abstraction and Empathy*. Ortega never mentions Worringer by name, but, with his fine flair for the very latest and intellectually exciting in German culture, it is inconceivable that he should have missed the stir caused by Worringer's book. Indeed, of the two alternative explanations that Ortega proposes for dehumanization, one is clearly Worringer's; and the paradoxical nature of Ortega's position stands out in full relief only when we become aware of this background. For if modern culture is really moving—or has already moved—in the direction that Ortega indicates, why should modern art have become dehumanized instead of glorifying the body and the senses? Worringer had traced the dehumanization of art, far more logically, to a rejection of the organic values of life, and to a flight from them into the metaphysical and transcendental caused by disillusionment and spiritual malaise. But Ortega, as we see, refuses to adopt this view because of his conviction that dehumanization is merely a negative symptom of art's relegation to a subordinate cultural status. Hence Ortega's argument obviously stands or falls with the validity of this last contention.

III

Once we become aware of Ortega's underlying point of view, the dazzling sparkle of his perceptions cannot altogether blind us to the weak links in his chain of argument. To begin, we may note a purely internal contradiction. Ortega does not seem to be aware that, if art were really to shift to a secondary zone of interest in modern culture, then the beneficial sociological result he expected from such a shift would not occur. Such a result, we recall, was to be the polarization of society into the vulgar and the élite, the touchstone of selection being the capacity of each group to respond to the purely aesthetic appeal of a dehumanized art. The average citizen would become aware in this way that he was incapable of receiving "the sacrament of art," and would thus, presumably, acknowledge his limitations. But this assumes that the average citizen will continue to think of the appreciation of art as conferring some sort of sacrament; in other words, it assumes that art will continue to retain its importance as one of the highest cultural values. If neither the average citizen *nor* the artist believes that art has any importance, it is difficult to understand why either should feel inferior or superior as a result of his response.

Another objection to Ortega is that the permanent unpopularity of modern art, which he unquestioningly accepted as an axiom, simply has been disproved by the passage of time. Movements such as Cubism and Expressionism, which seemed so scandalous and inacceptable when Ortega was writing, have now become thoroughly assimilated and domesticated. The new art created a new sensibility capable of absorbing its innovations, but not, as Ortega had hoped, a new culture based on a sharp distinction between the élite and the vulgar. Indeed, it is one of the ironies of modern culture that the most presumably radical and daring works of modern art have now become fodder for the reproduction industry on a mass scale, and that the same process has begun to take place in literature with the rise of the paperback. Sociologically, modern art has not been able to play the role that Ortega assigned it because "the average citizen," whether because of genuinely greater aesthetic capacity or simply out of modishness, has not proved as refractory as Ortega expected.

Ortega's most glaring mistake, however, was to insist on viewing modern art only as its own self-negation—as a game which could be whimsical and witty, or strident and raucous, but which never took itself seriously. From our vantage point it is clear that modern culture did not take the road that Ortega predicted. The farcical phase of modern art had ended almost by the time Ortega's essay appeared; and no modern artist would accept Ortega's definition of his role. Indeed, we can easily argue that modern artists take themselves with a good deal more seriousness than did the artists of the past. Ortega is right in linking the dehumanization of art with a radical crisis in modern culture; but he misinterpreted the meaning of the symptoms of that crisis, and in doing so he misjudged the significance of the most revealing symptom of all—the dehumanization of art.

Art, it is true, did give up its connection with the publicly accepted values of modern culture, particularly so far as these values derived from the Greco-Roman humanism of the Renaissance. But this by no means meant, as Ortega argued, that art intended to abnegate its old cultural responsibilities or that it had moved to the periphery of modern life. On the contrary, we are now aware that art undertook the unprecedented task of *creating by itself* the cultural, religious, or metaphysical content from which art had always hitherto drawn its aims and inspirations. Ortega, it is clear, simply could not conceive of such arrant audacity at the time he wrote; but thirty years later we must agree with André Malraux's comment that "modern masters make pictures as those of older civilizations made gods." [5]

This incisive observation is more than a striking image; it accurately expresses the pressure of the new relation of the modern artist to his work. The fanatical and often heroic dedication of the modern artist to his mission reveals that he has by no means abandoned his age-old status as a transmitter of the highest spiritual values. Now, however, these values are not derived from the "gods" of his culture; they stem exclusively from his own activity as an artist, from his religious devotion to the function of art itself as the *source* of a new realm of "the sacred." Indeed, the more one investigates the origins of the modern movement in art, the clearer it becomes that we are faced with groups whose activities bear all the hallmarks characteristic of the formation of religious sects.[6] This is obvious from the writings (or conversations) of the major modern artists starting with Cézanne and Gauguin and continuing through such representative figures as Mondrian, Kandinsky, and Klee. All use the language of religious mysticism—with differing intonations, to be sure—in justifying their efforts to pierce through the surface of nature and express the "essence" of reality.

Worringer had thus been right in linking the dehumanization of art with a quest for some new and hidden source of spiritual certainty. But this does not, of course, invalidate the fruitfulness of Ortega's analytical pages on the methods of dehumanization; nor does it obscure the insight of a comment like the following: "Who knows what may come out of this budding style?" Ortega writes. "The task it sets itself is enormous; it wants to create from nought. Later, I suspect, it will be content with less and achieve more." The great temptation of modern art has indeed been precisely that of trying to "create from nought"—completely to negate its contact with the tangible and visible world of human meaning in a movement similar to the mystic's flight to the Unknown. Ortega sensed the dangers of this development, and his instinct was perfectly sound.

Ernst Cassirer has noted, in the second volume of his *Philosophy of Symbolic Forms,* that every great religion always undergoes a crisis in which it attempts to break with the mythical elements out of which it has emerged. The religious spirit reaches a point at which it strives to transcend and abandon all the objective correlatives with which it had once been identified. At this point, Cassirer remarks, "mysticism . . . attempts to arrive at the pure meaning of religion as such, free from all encumbrance with the 'otherness' of empirical-sensuous existence and of sensuous images and representations." [7] One feels that modern art, with its exorbitant emphasis on its "purity," exhibits the signs of a similar crisis—not in the name of any particular dogma, but rather as part of the amorphous "religiosity" that has become identified with the function of art itself. Modern art has become a kind of mystical "negative theology," in which the absolute of art can only be affirmed by a denial or suppression of its predicates.

Ortega was highly suspicious of this tendency despite his theoretical defense of its aims; and he would certainly agree with Cassirer's further observation that "even the highest religious truth remains attached to sensuous existence, to the world of images as well as things. It must continuously immerse and submerge itself in this existence which its intelligible purpose strives to cast off and reject—because only in this existence does religious truth possess its expressive form and hence its reality and efficacy." [8] The greatest mystics have known that, to express their visions at all, it was necessary to compromise with the world of images; this is what Cassirer calls the dialectic of bondage and liberation that seems to control the life of all cultural forms. No doubt the limit-movements of modern art are in the process of discovering this dialectic for themselves. And it is not from such limit-movements, as Ortega wisely predicted, that the greatest triumphs of modern art would come. Those who have been content with less—Picasso, Braque, Klee, Rouault, and Chagall, rather than Kandinsky and Mondrian—have succeeded in achieving more.

NOTES

5. THE DEHUMANIZATION OF ART

1. José Ortega y Gasset, *The Dehumanization of Art and Other Writings on Art and Culture* (Garden City, N.Y.: Doubleday Anchor, 1956), p. 117.

2. José Ortega y Gasset, *The Modern Theme* (London: C. W. Daniel, 1931), p. 68.

3. *Ibid.,* p. 81.

4. *Ibid.,* p. 82.

5. André Malraux, *The Voices of Silence* (Garden City, N.Y.: Doubleday, 1953), p. 616.

6. This point has been made with reference to the Surrealists by the French sociologist Jules Monnerot, in his *La Poésie moderne et le sacré* (Paris: Gallimard, 1949). The traits noted by Monnerot in the Surrealist group apply equally well to other groups based on affinities of doctrine and inspiration.

7. Ernst Cassirer, *The Philosophy of Symbolic Forms* (New Haven: Yale University Press, 1953), Vol. II, p. 249.

8. *Ibid.,* p. 260.

6 Romanticism and Reality in Robert Penn Warren

"The philosophical novelist, or poet, is one for whom the documentation of the world is constantly striving to rise to the level of generalizations about value, for whom the image strives to rise to the symbol, for whom images always fall into a dialectical configuration, for whom the urgency of experience, no matter how vividly and strongly experience may enchant, is the urgency to know the meaning of experience." Robert Penn Warren wrote these words in a first-rate critical study of Conrad's *Nostromo*; [1] but, like all creators who also write criticism, Mr. Warren can hardly approach the work of others except in terms of his own preoccupations. Mr. Warren himself is a novelist for whom the image is always striving to rise to the level of symbol, and for whom—to vary his phrase a bit—the meaning of experience always takes on a dialectical configuration. And the excitement of reading his work derives precisely from its combination of spontaneous creative vitality with an artistic ambition continually striving to rise above the level of a banal naturalism.

I

Mr. Warren's first novel, *Night Rider,* appeared in 1939 and his second, *At Heaven's Gate,* in 1943—just at the moment, that is, when the American intelligentsia were emerging from their flirtation with Marxism. As a member of the Southern Agrarian group Mr. Warren had fought the Marxists all through the thirties, in a battle which involved not only social ideas but aesthetic and philosophical ones as well. The politico-economic program of the Agrarians was, to be sure, an amorphous hodgepodge of states' rights, English Distributism, and belated American Populism; it is hard to believe that the leading Agrarians themselves, who were primarily men of letters, ever took it very seriously. In any case, this aspect of Agrarianism quickly faded from the scene after the mid-thirties and never influenced the work of the Agrarian writers in any significant fashion. Far more important were the Agrarian objections to the sociological naturalism and economic determinism which then formed the dominating atmosphere of American liberal thought; and equally noteworthy was their protest against the reflection of this atmosphere in the literature of the period.

One of the best of Mr. Warren's early essays, for example, was devoted to a demolition of the muckraking novels of T. S. Stribling, who might be described as an inferior Southern Sinclair Lewis. Mr. Warren objected to the facile panaceas for Southern issues implied by Stribling's books, and he compared them unfavorably with the sense of the tragic complexity of life in Faulkner's *Light in August* (this was in 1934, considerably in advance of the Faulkner boom of the fifties). Not all human problems, Mr. Warren argued, were susceptible of sociopolitical solutions; to pretend that they were was simply to falsify experience.[2] And this general position, which forms the valid core of the Agrarian attack on liberalism as a metaphysic, also finds expression in Mr. Warren's first two novels.

Irene Hendry, in the best article on these early books, acutely remarked that Mr. Warren wrote proletarian novels which included what the orthodox examples of the genre left out.[3] At the center of each book is a plot machinery motivated by a political or economic conflict—the uprising of small tobacco farmers against price-controlling cartels in the first, the collapse of a big business tycoon who also controls state politics in the second. In both books, however, Mr. Warren represents his characters' involvement in economic-political action as an escape from moral self- scrutiny.

Percy Munn, the protagonist of *Night Rider,* tries to define himself by his participation in the illegal movement of the night riders growing out of the organization of small farmers. And though Mr. Warren, as an Agrarian, would presumably sympathize with such a movement as an expression of regional independence, he impartially depicts Munn's human disintegration as a result of his increasing absorption in a world of illegality, violence, and murder. Exactly the same theme appears in a poem first published in 1941 ("Terror"), set in the context of the violent political events of the late thirties:

So some, whose passionate emptiness and tidal
Lust swayed toward the debris of Madrid,
And left New York to loll in their fierce idyll
Among the olives, where the snipers hid;
And now the North, to seek that visioned face
And polarize their iron of despair,
Who praise no beauty like the boreal grace
Which greens the dead eye under the rocket's flare.
They fight old friends, for their obsession knows
Only the immaculate itch, not human friends or foes.[4]

On a wider canvas, and with a much richer range of social types, Mr. Warren continues to explore the implications of this theme in *At Heaven's Gate*. The chief characters in this novel all seek to escape their own inner vacuity, their lack of any true sense of human values, by some external surrogate—economic power or politics whether of the right or the left (the business tycoon and the labor organizer are both equally inhuman), sex, drink, mythomania, the cynicism of despair. All these are efforts to escape from the inner reality of moral decision and moral choice—a reality represented in the book by the itinerant hillbilly preacher Ashby Wyndham. Mr. Warren has never been given enough credit for Wyndham's remarkable monologue in backwoods dialect, which winds through the book in a series of chapters alternating with the main action, and which manages to achieve a moving effect of genuine pathos and almost biblical gravity while constantly skirting the border of the bathetic. It is the example of Wyndham, who refuses to compromise with the iniquities of the world, that brings about the resolution of the action—the collapse of the crooked financial empire of the business tycoon, Bogan Murdock, and the at least partial conversion of a number of the other figures to a sense of moral responsibility.[5]

II

Both of these early novels of Mr. Warren's may thus be labeled antinaturalist in theme; each represents a conscious inversion of the naturalist emphasis on the manner in which human lives are shaped by amoral instinctual drives and social pressures. To live at the mercy of such drives and pressures, from Mr. Warren's point of view, is a fundamental betrayal of the human self; and the intention of both books is to portray the futility of a world in which the only aims of life are a reflection of such forces. In *All the King's Men* (1946), however, Mr. Warren's third and most famous novel, we find a distinct shift in thematic emphasis. It is not so much that the fundamental theme changes as that it is approached from a new angle. The two earlier books had merely portrayed the dichotomy of the moral self and the world, with the latter always presented as the realm of self-alienation. But *All the King's Men* starts from the premise that the self and the world are necessarily interrelated; and it tackles the far more complex theme of the tragic ambiguities arising from their inescapable involvement.

Although *All the King's Men* was originally conceived as a play entitled *Proud Flesh,* there can be little doubt that, as a narrative work, it owes its origin to the sudden metamorphosis of Duckfoot Blake at the end of *At Heaven's Gate.*[6] This character, like the later Jack Burden, is a lucidly cynical participant in Murdock's political and financial skulduggery out of a Manichaean resignation to the world's irremediable evil. But he finally finds the courage to realize that "everything matters," and that it is impossible to evade moral commitment by intellectual detachment. Blake's richly figurative and eruditely obscene dialogue is a first draft for the brilliant rhetoric of *All the King's Men;* and Blake himself foreshadows the intellectual bravado, wise-guy cockiness, and searching self-despair that make up the character of Jack Burden. But while *All the King's Men* is essentially the story of Jack Burden, it also includes at least two other important involvements of the self and the world.

One is that of Dr. Adam Stanton, who is explicitly called a "Romantic." For "he has a picture of the world in his head, and when the world doesn't conform in any respect to this picture, he wants to throw the world away." It is the bitter and worldly-wise Jack Burden who makes this comment, but, in his own hard-boiled fashion, Jack Burden is just as much of a Romantic as Adam Stanton. For even though Jack is neck-deep in the off-color politics of Willie Stark, he is a Romantic by virtue of his purely imaginary ironical detachment from the events in which he takes part; neither he nor Adam Stanton can accept the "impure" reality of the world that confronts them. But while Adam Stanton avenges himself on the world by committing murder and being killed in turn, Jack Burden succeeds in forming "a new picture of the world." This new picture not only leads him to negate his own earlier negation and accept the guilt for his actions but also simultaneously inspires him to forgive the guilt of others. Jack Burden thus transcends his Romanticism, with its impossible demand for an inhuman "purity," and in this way he "earns" the faith and ideals that once more permit him to affront "the convulsions of the world . . . and the awful responsibility of Time."

The character of Willie Stark, in the same novel, poses the problem of Romanticism—not, we can see, as a literary or historical but as an ethical and ultimately metaphysical category—in still other terms. Willie Stark is of course the domineering "man of fact," who manipulates the "impure" reality of the world with a fine unconcern for the moral involutions of both Jack Burden and Adam Stanton. But Willie, it should be noted, becomes this man of fact only after he finds that he has been played for a sucker —only after the backroom boys have shown him that high ideals are no match for a corrupt and well-greased political machine. This causes Willie to abandon his wide-eyed innocence about politics—another variety of Romanticism —and motivates his decision to beat the politicians at their own game. Willie also undergoes a "conversion to the real," with all the latter's impurities; there is a parallel between what happens to Willie at the beginning of the novel and what happens to Jack Burden at the end. But Willie's "conversion" is not made out of guilt and humility; it springs from bafflement, frustration, and a raging sense of power. Willie accepts too much of the world, just as Adam Stanton accepts too little—or, to be exact, not any at all.

All the King's Men thus presents us with three types of dialectical interaction springing from the dichotomy of Romanticism and reality. There is the total rejection of the world in Adam Stanton, who clings desperately to his "idea" of purity; there is the total acceptance of Willie Stark, who abandons *his* "idea" of honest and able government (in fact, if not completely in aspiration) for the fleshpots of power; and there is the transcendence of this dualism in the moral evolution of Jack Burden, who passes from self-hatred, caused by his disillusionment with the "idea" of purity, to a recognition of his responsibility for realizing the "idea" in however imperfect a form. The theme of Romanticism and reality had thus become central for Mr. Warren by the time he composed *All the King's Men;* but, except for the character of Adam Stanton, it could be discerned only in the background of the central action. With *World Enough and Time* (1950), Mr. Warren's fourth novel, this theme now comes forward and occupies the very center of the canvas.

III

World Enough and Time is Mr. Warren's first historical novel *(Night Rider,* set in the early part of the present century, can hardly be considered "historical," and is not so considered by Mr. Warren himself).[7] Like all of Mr. Warren's work, it encountered considerable misunderstanding on publication. Critics took it to be a book about life on the Kentucky frontier in the 1820's; and its merits or demerits were assessed according to the somewhat amorphous standards for this type of historical reportage. In reality, *World Enough and Time* is no more a stock historical novel, whose purpose is merely to re-create the past, than *All the King's Men* was a fictionalized biography of Huey Long. To be sure, Mr. Warren subtitled the book "A Romantic Novel"; and this was taken as confirmation that he intended to compete with *Gone With the Wind.* But what the subtitle conveys, of course, is that Mr. Warren has chosen a narrative mode appropriate to his theme. The historical novel is the creation of the Romantic movement in literature; and by locating his story in the early nineteenth century, when the names of Byron and Scott could appear in the text as appropriate period props, Mr. Warren is able to dramatize a world in which the high decorum of the Romantic image of the self forms the natural ambience of his figures.

Something of this stately decorousness, along with its mocking antithesis of worldliness, is contained in Mr. Warren's very choice of title. *World Enough and Time*—the source is obviously Marvell's famous poem, "To His Coy Mistress," which begins: "Had we but world enough, and time." This is the complaint of a lover to his recalcitrant belle, who dallies with him as if both were living in eternity. Were it possible, he tells her, he would indeed devote a more-than-human leisureliness to his courtship:

> An hundred years should go to praise
> Thine eyes, and on thy forehead gaze;
> Two hundred to adore each breast;
> But thirty thousand to the rest.

He argues quite cogently, however, that death would intervene before such a flattering program could be carried out; and he urges his mistress to awaken to the facts of life: "Now let us sport us while we may."

The poem, then, is based on the antinomy between the desire for an impossible ideal of courtly love, which we can recognize as the essence of Romanticism, and an awareness of the impossible barriers in our poor human lot that make such an ideal self-defeating. It reveals the contradiction, the necessary conflict, between the world and the idea; and this, of course, is Mr. Warren's fundamental theme. The love story of *World Enough and Time* duplicates the conflict of opposites in the poem, although not on the literal level; the "idea" pitted against the limiting conditions of life is not that of coy flirtatiousness but of perfect justice. And this accounts for the epigraph to the book, drawn from Spenser's *Faerie Queene*—an epigraph which alludes to the long-distant time

> When good was onely for itselfe desyred
> And all men sought their owne, and none no more;
> When Justice was not for most meed outhyred,
> But simple Truth did rayne, and was of all admyred.

Jeremiah Beaumont, the hero of *World Enough and Time,* embarks on the quest for perfect Justice influenced by this ideal; and he ends by destroying not only everything he loves but also himself. Yet the tragic irony of his fate, Mr. Warren implies, may nonetheless have a positive lesson to teach the modern world.

Like all of Mr. Warren's novels, *World Enough and Time* was suggested by an actual occurrence. This was a famous Kentucky murder trial in 1826—so famous, indeed, that it was immediately taken up and used by such American writers as Poe and William Gilmore Simms, not to mention others now forgotten. The murderer was a young man named Jeroboam O. Beauchamp, who left his own account of the events. Eventually, through the agency of Katherine Anne Porter, this account came into Robert Penn Warren's hands.[8] Scholars have already hastened to compare the original with Mr. Warren's treatment; but from the very first pages it is clear that Mr. Warren is creating his own world and not transcribing that of history. For even in sketching the atmosphere of the period and the place he immediately evokes the antitheses that will be dramatized in his account of Jeremiah Beaumont's career: "The dirk (of Spanish steel or made from a hunting knife or a Revolutionary sword) and the Bible might lie side by side on the table, or Plato and the dueling pistols on the mantel shelf."

The extremes of murderous violence, on the one hand,

and religious or philosophical idealism, on the other, are the poles between which Jeremiah Beaumont will oscillate with the sightless solemnity of a sleepwalker; and each pole is represented by a different narrative voice. The groundwork of the book is the (presumed) journal of Jeremiah Beaumont himself, whose style mingles the pulpit rhetoric of the period with the pompous gravity and Johnsonian orotundity of eighteenth-century moral self-assurance. It evokes a time in which men "took their world greatly and were not embarrassed by the accents of greatness, and knew that in study, field or forum they bore the destiny of man and the judgment of history." Mr. Warren does a superb job of rhetorical pastiche in these sections of the book, and they do more than anything else to make Beaumont come alive; one finds it hard to think of any other American novelist capable of such effects. But set against this voice from the past is that of the modern narrator, who might be described as a Jack Burden reluctantly being impressed despite himself. For this voice is that of our modern disillusioned naturalism, looking behind the grand gestures and the noble motives for the sordid "truths" of passion or self-interest; but acknowledging, in this very impulse, our own need for self-abasement and self-pity, our own search for rationalizations, excuses, and evasions.

IV

We have said that in *World Enough and Time* Mr. Warren places the theme of Romanticism and reality at the center of his canvas. This is true not only of the external action and the narrative mode but also of the spiritual evolution of his chief character. For the history of Beaumont is constructed to reproduce the various dialectics of

Romanticism and reality adumbrated in *All the King's Men.*

The first of these dialectics is that of Adam Stanton, who refused to accept the "impurities" of the world out of self-righteousness. As a young man, Jeremiah Beaumont's education imbues him with the same spirit; he nourishes his dreams of glory on the Latin classics, with their "patterns of human greatness . . . and love of the good beyond flesh or suffering." Later, during a religious phase, he had tried to experience "what truth might be beyond the bustle of the hour and the empty lusts of time." And when he learns that his friend and protector, Colonel Cassius Fort, has seduced a young lady of good family, he sets himself up as her self-appointed champion and attempts to provoke Fort into a duel. Beaumont is impervious both to the stifled anguish of Rachel Jordan, his future wife, and to Fort's sorrowful repentance, which causes the latter to refuse to fight despite extreme provocation. In pursuit of his "idea" Beaumont completely ignores the inner complexities of human reality; but Fort's refusal shows Beaumont that he cannot impose his will on the world and maintain his "purity" (to kill in an honorable duel) at the same time.

The second dialectic is that of Willie Stark—the attempt to play the game of the world for the sake of the idea. Beaumont is tricked into believing that Fort publicly denied his old affair and has accused his ex-inamorata, now Beaumont's wife, of having had relations with a mulatto slave. He thereupon forgets his scruples and decides on murder; now "the world must redeem the idea." Like Stark, however, Beaumont discovers that one cannot accept the terms of the world without becoming its victim. For he is caught and sentenced, not on solid evidence but because the murder has become a political *cause célèbre* and because of the handsome reward attached to solving the crime. "All the lies and false witness against me told truth," he later writes ruefully in his journal. Beaumont had thought to defend "justice" by trickery, deceit, and murder; and what he had desired consciously is achieved unwittingly by those who convict him on corrupt and perjured evidence. There is no essential moral difference between the two deeds, both of which display the same ironic disparity between means and ends.

The final dialectic is that of Jack Burden, who clings to his "innocence" in the midst of degradation, but finally realizes his complicity and his guilt. The setting for this concluding phase, which symbolically reflects Beaumont's spiritual condition, is an outlaw settlement in the backwater swamps of the lower Mississippi barely emerging from the primeval slime. Like Jack Burden trying to forget himself in the Great Sleep, or in sex, or in the archetypal flight west to the innocence of nature and a new start, Jeremiah Beaumont gradually descends into the drunkenness, debauchery, and animal-like existence of the other inhabitants of the place. It is only now that he begins to find his communion with mankind—a negative communion in shame and debasement. Here at last is "innocence," for nature knows no guilt; "but that innocence is what man cannot endure and be man." And Beaumont becomes man again when he finally learns that he had been betrayed into murder and hears the bitter truth about himself from his wife.

"You made me hate Fort and you used me," she says, just before committing suicide. "Oh, I didn't hate him, I loved him, and you used me, you used me to kill him, you used me, you ruined me . . ." At last Beaumont sees himself clearly for the first time; and he sets out on the homeward journey to "shake the hangman's hand . . . and call him my brother at last." There can be no pardon for his crime because he is guilty not of an isolated deed but of "the crime of self, the crime of life. The crime is I." His crime is the deadly arrogance and self-sufficiency of the Romantic ego; and whatever the external provocation for his action, there is no way of expiating the "crime of self" except by the assumption of guilt. But Beaumont never succeeds in clasping his guilt and shaking the hangman's hand; he is murdered on the road back by those who, having used him as a tool, fear the political effect of his disclosures.

Interwoven with Beaumont's story is a lively and vivid account of the political conflicts of the day, which is admirably integrated with the main theme and serves Mr. Warren for far more than external motivation. For the chief issue of that period was a law providing relief to the debt-ridden, which had run into opposition from the Kentucky Supreme Court as unconstitutional. Immediately the cry went up to pack the court or to threaten it with violence—to impugn the source and fount of law itself for the immediate end of social justice. There is a clear parallel between this political subplot and Jeremiah Beaumont's willingness to take justice into his own hands. Indeed, as we have noted, Beaumont is eventually tricked into the murder by Fort's political enemies, who desire to get the latter out of their way. The purity of Romantic idealism does not prevent it from being an easy prey to the unscrupulousness of the political fanatic.

The meaning of Beaumont's career is illuminated not only by this political subplot but also by a number of other characters who act as Jamesian "reflectors" to highlight one or another aspect of Beaumont's adventures. Two in particular serve to modulate our sense of Beaumont's culpability. One is the spidery, skeletal, tubercular Percival

Skrogg, the living image of the bodiless "idea," who illustrates the murderous potential lurking in Beaumont's lofty exaltations but whose icy and inhuman zealotry also serves to bring out Beaumont's relative warmth and human involvement. Another is Wilkie Barron, Beaumont's "friend" as a young man and the Mephistopheles who, with Skrogg's connivance, ultimately sends him to his doom and is responsible for his murder. Barron's pliant opportunism is used as a foil to underline Beaumont's idealistic obsessiveness, which, no matter how misguided, still represents a search for moral values. And while Barron ends up a wealthy and respected senator in Washington, he inexplicably shoots himself one fine morning, leaving Beaumont's journal, which he could never bring himself to destroy, moldering among his papers.

A different pair of characters are used to point up Beaumont's blindness and self-infatuation. The old backwoodsman Munn Short, Beaumont's jailer, had once been guilty of the same crime as Fort (and even worse); his tale of pardon and repentance lights up the path that Beaumont might have followed but could not until it was too late. Finally, there is the figure of Colonel Fort himself, who is a development of the Willie Stark type from *All the King's Men*—but a Willie Stark who has faced the question of the final meaning of human life and who, despite his power, is chastened by a melancholy wisdom. "I loved him," writes Beaumont, "because I thought I saw the goodness of strength which could give strength to others, and was sad for the weakness of others." Fort, who has attained the wisdom of humility and hence of goodness, is the major analogue against which to measure Beaumont; and he is killed by the latter, symbolically, at the very moment he had worked out a plan for reconciling the competing political factions that were tearing the state apart.

All these figures give us various perspectives on Beaumont; but the final perspective is that of the narrator himself, who, on the very last page, inserts a passage of nonstop prose in the breathless style that John Dos Passos took over from Molly Bloom's soliloquy in *Ulysses*. "Things went on their way, and the Commonwealth of Kentucky has, by the latest estimate, 2,819,000 inhabitants and the only Shawnee in the country is on a WPA mural on a post-office wall"—and so forth, in a parody of a complacent Chamber of Commerce brochure. Juxtaposed against, this is Jeremiah Beaumont's anguished query: "I had longed to do justice in the world, and what was worthy of praise. . . . And in my crime and vainglory of self is there no worth lost? . . . . Was all for naught?" The answer to this question is contained all through the book, in the grudging recognition of Beaumont's essential nobility forced on the skeptical modern narrator. Or, as Mr. Warren put it more abstractly in his Conrad essay, a year after publishing *World Enough and Time:* "To surrender to the incorrigible and ironical necessity of the 'idea,' that is man's fate and his only triumph." [9]

v

World Enough and Time does not represent any radical new departure for Mr. Warren from the point of view of theme; but it does show him reaching out for more and more subtle and complex ways of dramatizing his moral vision. Once again he centers on the acquirement of self-knowledge—the discovery of moral responsibility and the attainment of the moral life itself through the recognition of a community of guilt. Up to *World Enough and Time,* however, this theme had always been approached in terms of a central conflict between evasion and amorality, on the one hand, and, on the other, some positive image of moral certainty. But now Mr. Warren is attempting to hold a far more delicate balance; the poles are no longer simply morality and its opposite but much subtler discriminations *within* the realm of morality itself—between innocence and wisdom, let us say, or between callow Romantic idealism and sobered moral realism. The multiple perspectives of *World Enough and Time*—with its moving counterpoint of narrative voices and the constant ironic ambiguities of its plot—are themselves a palpable image of the quicksand complexities of the moral life. And the more one reads the book the more it reveals a brooding richness and a perplexed tenderness that make it perhaps the purest and most eloquent expression (in the novel form) of Mr. Warren's sense of life. But to say this is not the equivalent of asserting that the book is an unqualified success; and it seems to me less so, as a fully realized work, than *All the King's Men*.

One of the first problems that confronts a reader of *World Enough and Time* is the melodramatic nature of the action and the uneasy sense that certain scenes would go very well in Technicolor. Take, for example, the following fateful exchange between Beaumont and Rachel Jordan:

> "Love," she said bitterly. "How should I know what love is?"
>
> "I know what it is," he declared. "It is that for which a man would do anything."
>
> "Too late—too late!" she cried. "For all the world is ruined."
>
> He gripped her hand more strongly, and leaned at her speaking rapidly and in a low voice. "One world is ruined,"

he said, "but we will make another. Do you hear? And to make another we must throw the first away. . . . We must crush it. Destroy it. Do you hear?" etc.

Mr. Warren, of course, consciously courted the risk of such scenes by his whole conception of Jeremiah Beaumont as a Romantic idealist; he was not—as some of his critics were only too happy to assume—tailoring a novel to Hollywood specifications. But the fact remains that Mr. Warren does not always succeed in rescuing certain pages from reading like unconscious parodies of *East Lynne;* and these pages detract from the seriousness with which Beaumont should be taken.

A more important defect arises not so much from the theme itself as from the very nature of Mr. Warren's narrative talent. All his novels show that Mr. Warren has enormous verbal, mimetic, and dramatic gifts; he knows, as the French say, how to "camp" a character before the reader in a few strokes and instantly to bring it to life. But if we survey his work as a whole we become aware that he has always avoided attempting to portray a character from the "inside," that is, to engage directly with a severe inner conflict. Perhaps the reason is that Mr. Warren is a moralist, who believes in the inscrutability of free will; and he has an instinctive mistrust of "psychology." But whatever the explanation, Mr. Warren's characters are always either "flat" and unchanging, or, when they do change, the motivation is invariably given by some external arrangement of the plot that serves as a substitute for a direct grasp of consciousness.

Ordinarily Mr. Warren meets this problem by the use of first-person narrative monologue, in which the character tells his own story. This device seems to place the reader in the heart of the character's consciousness, but

Mr. Warren's characters usually confine themselves to a recital of events. Nonetheless, by the proper use of style to indicate feeling and attitude, and particularly by introducing the perspective of the future into the narrative account, the recital can be colored sufficiently to prepare for the psychological shift. This is one reason why Mr. Warren's most satisfactory novel is *All the King's Men,* where such a use of narrative monologue dominates the total perspective. For from the very first pages the reader feels both the disabused irony and cynicism of Jack Burden —his corroding scorn for the hypocrisies of hand-me-down morality—and at the same time his equally savage scorn for himself. It is the emotional tension between these two extremes, as conveyed by the style, that succeeds in carrying the positive affirmation of values at the end.

To a certain extent, somewhat the same technique is used in *World Enough and Time* in Jeremiah Beaumont's diary. Much of the narrative, however, is not direct quotation but résumé and summary; in these parts the style tends to be neutral, and hence to give only an indistinct and muffled access to Beaumont's state of mind. Moreover, while Jack Burden has to undergo only *one* moral transition, Jeremiah Beaumont has to undergo *three*—each representing another phase of the dialectic of Romanticism and reality. For while different phases of this dialectic were given to different characters in *All the King's Men,* the experience of Beaumont encompasses all the phases at one or another stage of his career. It is therefore of the utmost importance to make the shift from one phase to another as vivid and forceful as possible; but Mr. Warren's inability (or unwillingness) to portray a conscience struggling with itself deprives Beaumont of the necessary inner stature to support his role.

As an example, we may cite the following crucial passage, which describes Beaumont's first disillusionment with Fort:

> He thought how little he had in the world. His labor at the law was suddenly a dreary and childish routine. How had he ever thought that the law answered the deep cry of the heart? And his glowing prospects, what were they? A few dollars, a few acres, the envious servility of men. And if he should realize those prospects, his success would have been poisoned at the root. For he would owe all to Fort. To Fort, the villain. Ah, where was the greatness of life? Was it only a dream? Could a man not come to some moment when, all dross and meanness of life consumed, he could live in the pure idea?

One cannot help feeling something perfunctory about this description, a decisive failure on Mr. Warren's part really to project himself into Beaumont's state of mind. The transition to abstract explanation is too hasty, too quick and easy, to convince us that Beaumont's entire life will be unalterably changed from this moment onward.

One thinks of what Dostoevsky might have done with such a scene; and the comparison is not totally unfair because the theme of *World Enough and Time* is very similar to that of *Crime and Punishment*—innocence murdering out of idealism, and learning the truth about the self as the deed develops its own sinister logic. But nowhere do we feel about Beaumont, as we do about Raskolnikov, that the deed springs forth irresistibly from some deep psychic pressure; nowhere are we touched by any inner torment, any agony of conscience or sensibility compelling first the murder and then the final assumption of guilt. Nowhere, in short, does Jeremiah Beaumont seem anything but an automaton, despite the wealth of symbolic incident lavished on him by Mr. Warren to convey the meaning of his history.

This impression of lifelessness given by Beaumont is reinforced by the manner in which Mr. Warren has plotted the action. Every crucial decision of Beaumont's is a result of treachery and deceit; this is true even of his first disenchantment with Fort, for he hears the rumor about Rachel Jordan from Wilkie Barron, who feigns indignation at the villainous seducer. (No adequate explanation is ever given for this first lie; all the later ones have an obvious political rationale.) The reason for this construction is obvious enough: the idea, thinking itself free and pure, is always implicated in the world and at the service of the world, whether it will or no. Mr. Warren's plotting mirrors his theme; but perhaps he has mirrored it here with a too-rigorous consistency. For in so doing he sacrifices the advantage of making Beaumont fully responsible for his own actions. Indeed, Beaumont ends up by seeming a pitiful puppet at the mercy of all kinds of external influences, not a figure whose character is his fate and who derives dignity from his self-determination. No doubt Beaumont is more sympathetic because he is driven to the murder; but here again one thinks of Raskolnikov, who, though he commits his murder in a hallucinatory trance, induces the trance himself by his brooding over the idea of the crime.

These flaws seem to me to prevent *World Enough and Time* from reaching the very first rank as an independent work; but they by no means cancel out entirely its haunting and poignant impact. Indeed, while *Night Rider* and *At Heaven's Gate* exhibit a similar weakness at the center —a failure to endow the leading characters with any convincing depth of inner life—*World Enough and Time,* despite the elaborateness of Beaumont's imputed evolution, seems to suffer less from this congenital deficiency than either of the earlier books. No doubt because it is so highly stylized and formalized, so much a moral allegory or romance rather than a true novel (it is quite fitting that Spenser should stand godfather at the threshold), one is content here with far less psychological verisimilitude and plausible motivation. The core of the book is only nominally in Beaumont; in reality, it lies in the moral musing of the narrative voices and in the lyrical and poetic pregnancy of the symbolic details. This partial success of *World Enough and Time* in reviving a moribund genre—a genre which also includes *Billy Budd* and *The Scarlet Letter*—is impressive evidence of the brilliance, vivacity, and versatility of Mr. Warren's literary gifts. But one cannot help wishing that he could again manage to get as close to another central figure as interesting as Jack Burden, whose ideological and psychological complexity makes *All the King's Men* the most satisfying of Robert Penn Warren's novels.

NOTES

6. ROMANTICISM AND REALITY IN ROBERT PENN WARREN

1. Robert Penn Warren, *Selected Essays* (New York: Random House, n.d.), p. 58.

2. Robert Penn Warren, "T. S. Stribling: A Paragraph in the History of Critical Realism," *The American Review*, II, 4 (February, 1934), 463–486.

3. Irene Hendry, "The Regional Novel: The Example of Robert Penn Warren," *Sewanee Review*, LIII, 1 (Winter, 1945), 84–102.

4. Robert Penn Warren, *Selected Poems* (London: Fortune Press, n.d.), p. 19.

5. There is an interesting comment on these novels in the very revealing interview that Mr. Warren gave to Ralph Ellison and Eugene Walter in Rome.

   "I think I ought to say," he remarks, "that behind *Night Rider* and my next novel, *At Heaven's Gate*, there was a good deal of the shadow not only of the events of the period [i.e., the thirties], but of the fiction of that period. I am more aware of that fact now than I was then. Of course only an idiot could not have been aware that he was trying to write a novel about, in one sense, 'social justice' in *Night Rider*, or for that matter, *At Heaven's Gate*. But in some kind of a fumbling way I was aware, I guess, of trying to find the dramatic rub of the story at some point a little different from and deeper than the point of dramatic rub in some of the then current novels." *Paris Review*, 4, 16 (Spring-Summer, 1957), 120.

6. Explaining that Jack Burden had had only a line or two in the verse play, Mr. Warren remarks: "When after two years I picked up the verse version, and began to fool with a novel, the unnamed newspaperman became the narrator. It turned out, in a way, that what he thought about the story was more important than the story itself." *Ibid.,* p. 135.

Mr. Warren worked on *Proud Flesh* between 1936 and 1939, and, when he returned to the material, he had already written *At Heaven's Gate* and had discovered Duckfoot Blake. The latter character in a new guise then dominated his old theme.

7. Of *Night Rider,* Mr. Warren says in the interview: "Well, that isn't a historical novel. The events belonged to my early childhood. I remember the troops coming in when martial law was declared in that part of Kentucky. When I wrote the novel I wasn't thinking of it as history. For one thing, the world it treated still, in a way, survived." *Ibid.,* p. 116.

8. "Katherine Anne Porter and I," Mr. Warren recollects, "were both at the Library of Congress as Fellows. We were in the same pew, had offices next to each other. She came in one day with an old pamphlet, the trial of Beauchamp for killing Col. Sharp. She said, 'Well, Red, you better read this.' There it was, I read it in five minutes. But I was six years making the book." *Ibid.,* p. 126.

9. *Selected Essays,* p. 45.

7 The Achievement of John Peale Bishop

John Peale Bishop, who died in 1944, was one of the most gifted and sensitive talents among the American writers who came to maturity after the First World War. A classmate of Edmund Wilson and F. Scott Fitzgerald at Princeton, Bishop was the third member of a triumvirate destined to take a prominent place in modern American letters; but his own work never won him the fame of his collegiate friends. Bishop was an exacting rather than a powerful writer, and his limited production, perfect though much of it was, never imposed itself on the American literary scene with the impact necessary to make a lasting impression. Even the posthumous publication in 1948 of his *Collected Poems* and his *Collected Essays* did little to remedy this unjust situation.[1]

One of the criticisms most frequently made of Bishop during his lifetime was that his work lacked unity—that it was fragmentary and peripheral, destitute of any serious focus. R. P. Blackmur once neatly summarized the prevalent impression by calling Bishop a "superlative amateur," who gave the sense of writing poetry as an "avocation" rather than out of whole-souled dedication and passionate purpose.[2] Such an impression can hardly persist, however, if one reads Bishop's work as a whole—both his creative and critical prose as well as his poetry; for what then strikes one most forcefully is the constancy of Bishop's preoccupation with the spiritual dilemma of his generation.

Bishop defined this dilemma himself in a much-quoted article called "The Missing All" (the phrase is from a poem by Emily Dickinson); it is the dilemma familiar to all readers of Hemingway—the breakdown of values as an aftermath of the First World War. All of Bishop's work is a response to this breakdown, which formed the existential horizon of his generation; but Bishop's own evolution is quite unique, and it is impossible to place him in any convenient and familiar category. His feeling for tradition and for formal values in literature, his sense that man needed some ultimate metaphysical justification, linked him with the followers of T. S. Eliot; and he was allied by sympathy and personal friendship with Allen Tate and the Southern Agrarians. Yet the sense of life in his later work reminds one more of D. H. Lawrence than of any other contemporary writer. And his achievement is precisely to have created an original and very appealing synthesis—small in scale though impressive in quality—of these two major antagonistic traditions of modern Anglo-American literature.

I

John Peale Bishop's début in the turbulent literary world of the twenties was not particularly auspicious. His first book of poems, published in 1917, bears the modest title *Green Fruit;* and the suggestion of immaturity is indicative both of Bishop's modesty and of his critical intelligence. For the poems are indeed filled with youthful echoes of *fin-de-siècle* decadence, obviously garnered from the pages of Swinburne and *The Yellow Book*—the favorite reading of literary undergraduates of Bishop's generation.

By the time Bishop published his second book, however, written in collaboration with Edmund Wilson, he had gone through the archetypal war experience of his generation. And the very title of the work—a curious potpourri of prose and verse in celebration of death called *The Undertaker's Garland* (1922)—reveals its typical orientation. *The Undertaker's Garland* unmistakably bears the stamp of its time—a time when Edna St. Vincent Millay was burning the candle at both ends in Greenwich Village, when the revolt against Puritanism was in full swing, and when the contributors to *Civilization in the United States* were jubilantly declaring that no such thing existed. Both young writers, after their contact with war and Europe, found the Puritan materialism of their homeland intolerable. And in a book defiantly dedicated to death, they set out to *épater les Américains* as best they could.

Much the most important of Bishop's contributions to this high-spirited volume is a short story called "Resurrection." Here we feel the naked impact of Bishop's war experience for the first time, uncluttered by the pseudomacabre bric-à-brac marring his other efforts. Little more than an anecdote, the story pictures the disinterment of a dead American soldier for reburial. A young lieutenant almost faints at the sight of the decaying, putrescent corpse, and he returns to his tent haunted by "the pervasive odor of decay; the blanketed mass he had just seen, with its poor upturned face, had broken down within him some last wall of resisting flesh." It is the contrast between this feeling and the images ordinarily evoked by the word "resurrection" on which the story plays; the result is a grim, unspoken irony similar to the minor poems of Hardy. And here is the first groping statement of what was to become Bishop's perennial theme—the bare and brutal facts of physical reality in conflict with the values by which man tries to dignify his brief existence.

The Undertaker's Garland marks the end of Bishop's juvenilia and the beginning of a period of literary stock-taking that lasted for almost a decade. During this time Bishop printed an occasional review or poem; but it was only in 1931 that he brought out a volume of stories, *Many Thousands Gone,* and this was followed in 1932 by a volume of poetry, *Now With His Love.* These books initiate Bishop's mature work; and to follow his development we may start most conveniently with the volume of poetry. This contains work written over the intervening period, and it will allow us to trace the evolution of Bishop's themes from the immediate reflection of his war trauma to the search for a tradition and a metaphysical order that would exorcise its effects.

II

Bishop's poetry, in *The Undertaker's Garland,* had still been filled with the vestiges of late nineteenth-century mannerisms; but in the interval his poetic style had considerably matured. Now the sensuous clarity of Eliot and Pound are noticeable influences, along with the taut symbolic lyricism of Yeats and the Valéry of *Charmes*. Bishop, indeed, experiments in this volume with a variety of poetic styles, as he was to continue to do all through his life. But as Allen Tate has argued, a good poem in a period style is still a good poem; [3] and *Now With His Love* is filled with good poems that have an unmistakably personal note. Moreover, as the title from Chaucer indicates, the book has a good deal of thematic unity as well. For the experience of "Resurrection" has by no means been forgotten; and it is only love that the poet finds to obliterate the horror.

In reading the love-and-war poems of *Now With His Love* we are irresistibly reminded of the early Hemingway, also obsessed with death, also seeking for a source of positive value in naked sensuous experience. It is no accident that Bishop returned again and again to Hemingway in his critical writings, and that his "Homage to Hemingway" is one of the finest studies of that writer. "His vision of life," Bishop writes, "is one of perpetual annihilation. Since the will can do nothing against circumstance, choice is precluded; those things are good which the senses report good; and beyond their brief record there is only the remorseless devaluation of nature, which, like the vast blue flowing of the Gulf Stream beyond Havana, bears away of our great hopes, emotions and ambitions only a few and soon disintegrating trifles." Bishop here is not only analyzing Hemingway; he is defining one essential aspect of his own work.

But this vision of life does not lead Bishop—as it led Hemingway or, to mention a poet of Bishop's generation, Archibald MacLeish—into a glorification of the primitive. It is a fact of particular significance that Bishop's images of sensuous beauty are invariably expressed in terms of art, the art of the Mediterranean world, of Greece and the Italian Renaissance. Bishop, indeed, is one of the few modern writers in English (the early Ezra Pound and D. H. Lawrence are others) who have been able to write genuinely erotic love poetry without falling into either vulgarity or platitude; and the reason lies in the classical purity of his feeling for the body and the senses. The following stanza from his beautiful "Metamorphoses of M," for example, illustrates the precise elegance of his refined and filtered sensuality. Nor should one fail to note the casual complexity of the controlling paradox, with its imagery as from an early Renaissance tapestry playfully reproducing some monkish bestiary of the Middle Ages:

> Your beauty is not used. Though you have lain
> A thousand nights upon my bed, you rise
> Always so splendidly renewed that I have thought,
> Seeing the sweet continence of your breast,
> Mole-spotted, your small waist, and long slim thigh,
> That even the unicorn that savage beast
> If he should startle on you fresh from light
> Would be so marvelled by virginity
> That he would come, trotting and mild,
> To lay his head upon your fragrant lap
> And be surprised.

This is the world of love (real and yet ideal) that Bishop posed against the nihilistic experience of death shared by his generation. "All loveliness demands our courtesies," he writes in a later poem ("Recollection"), which sums up this phase of his work. And the word "courtesy" (the troubadour *cortezia*) could not have been better chosen. For Bishop's attitude toward loveliness is precisely that of a stately formal obeisance, controlled by a discipline for which the senses, like the Platonic Eros, are valuable only as an avenue to a higher realm of the spirit.

III

Bishop knew too much history, however, to believe that such an avenue could be simply the personal construction of an isolated individual. It is culture that mediates between the senses and the spirit in Bishop's poetry; and culture implies tradition. A number of poems in *Now With His Love* deal with the breakdown of such traditions—not only that of Christianity, but those of classical antiquity and of the eclectic modern world as well. "The Return" vividly evokes the despairing torpor of vanquished Rome waiting for the arrival of the conqueror. And in "Ballet"—obviously inspired by the painting of Dali and Chirico, as well as by the poetry of Cocteau—the chaos of the contemporary world is depicted in a frightening *mise en scène*. The best embodiment of this theme, however, is "Perspectives are Precipices," one of the most widely known of Bishop's poems. Allen Tate has sensitively analyzed the manner in which this work achieves the effects of painting; [4] but it also contains a number of Bishop's key symbols and has far more than merely a formal significance.

Bishop uses an incident from the conclusion of the Bluebeard story in Perrault's *Fairy Tales* as a framework for the poem. Bluebeard is about to kill his most recent wife for having looked into the room where his other victims are hanging; but he gives her a few minutes' grace to say her prayers. During this time she calls her Sister Anne, and asks the latter to mount to the tower and see if their brothers are riding to the rescue. Bishop discards all the incidents of the Bluebeard story, but he keeps the question-and-answer refrain of the dialogue between the wife and Sister Anne; and he turns the rescue motif into a symbolic comment on the fate of modern culture. For while in the tale the brothers arrive to confound Blue-beard and save their sisters, the erstwhile rescuer in Bishop's poem recedes rather than approaches and finally vanishes altogether.

What Sister Anne spies when she goes to the tower is a road running through a harshly sunlit desert landscape; and this would appear to be the track of abstract time starting in the past and continuing into the future ("I see a distance of black yews/ Long as the history of the Jews"). On the road is "a man who goes/ Dragging a shadow by its toes"; in his hand is an empty pitcher, mouth down:

Sister Anne, Sister Anne,
What do you see?

His dwindling stride. And he seems blind
Or worse to the prone man behind.

Sister Anne! Sister Anne!

I see a road. Beyond nowhere
Defined by cirrus and blue air.

I saw a man but he is gone
His shadow gone into the sun.

Man's shadow would appear to refer to his past, to history and to time as human continuity (perhaps there is an im-plied reference here to the sundial). But he is "blind or worse" to his past and pursues his path "beyond nowhere" till he vanishes completely into nature. Typical for Bishop is the sun-baked landscape, the symbolic importance of "shadow," and, as Mr. Tate has noted, the "spatial" quality of the imagery ("Wide plains surrounding silence"). The use of such imagery clearly is linked with the theme of time's obliteration.

To counterbalance such a future, only the birth of a new cultural tradition will suffice; and this need furnishes the inspiration for "Speaking of Poetry." The problem of the poet, of course, is the age-old one of maintaining the proper equilibrium between inspiration and discipline, passion and reason. But for Bishop this is the problem of culture as well; and, using symbolism drawn from *Othello,* he takes this as his theme. How can the delicate Desdemona, the flower of Venetian culture, be truly united with the dark and passionate Moor? Othello is still an inchoate force of nature, powerful but undisciplined; any irregular union between the two will lead to disaster;

O, it is not enough
that they should meet, naked, at dead of night
in a small inn on a dark canal. Procurers
less expert than Iago can arrange as much.

The ceremony must be found.

Traditional, with all its symbols
ancient as the metaphors in dreams;
strange, with never before heard music; continuous
until the torches deaden at the bedroom door.

The ceremony must be found. And Bishop's book of short stories, *Many Thousands Gone* (1931), indicates where he thought it might be discovered—or at least where an American could requicken his sense of what such a ceremony had meant in his own past. The stories of *Many Thousands Gone,* all of which deal with incidents occurring in Virginia during the Civil War, are in effect a condensed moral history of the South; and they should be read in conjunction with Bishop's article "The South and

Tradition" (1933). Bishop was himself of mixed New England and Virginia stock; but his boyhood had been spent in West Virginia, and he easily identified himself in feeling with the Southern Agrarians. His relation to the Agrarians, however, should not be overstressed; for he always remained his own man, and what he took from his Agrarian friends was immediately transformed into his own personal terms.

Like the Agrarians, Bishop disliked the world of science, mechanization, and the machine that had dehumanized modern life. What attracted him to the myth of the South —and he had no hesitation in calling it a myth—was the sense of moral certainty that he felt had once existed at the heart of Southern life. This moral certainty had enabled his Southern great-uncles to ride off to war heroically, while his own generation of Americans had gone to face their ordeal by fire with no real beliefs to sustain them. What Hemingway was seeking in the Spanish bull ring at about the same time—a moral code that would enable one to face death unflinchingly—Bishop sought in the image of a society that had seemed to provide such a code, and, moreover, could not be held responsible for the bleak materialism and Puritanical hypocrisy of American life that he had already castigated in *The Undertaker's Garland.*

But, while Bishop might persuade himself intellectually that such a tradition had existed in the South, he was too honest a writer to force his feelings. What he had experienced, as a member of the Lost Generation, was the breakdown of tradition; and when he came to write his stories of the South he chose to portray what he could feel. For he takes the Southern tradition at a moment when it had already hardened into a lifeless and moribund convention or was collapsing under the impact of war and invasion.

All the stories reinforce the same theme of a society in bondage to the past, a society whose conventions are no longer adequate to cope with reality. And in one story, "If Only," he produces a little masterpiece.

All that remains of the Southern tradition here is a pitiful and morbid nostalgia; it has become a dream world of wish and desire, a world of fantasy which is well conveyed in the slightly Kafkaesque quality of detail. The action concerns two Southern gentlewomen, pathetically living on their memories, who hire a miraculous Negro cook named Bones. As if by magic, Bones turns dream into reality: "With this one tall, black, jovial Negro in the house it was as though the War had never been fought or, having been fought, had turned into a triumph for the South." Bones' extravagances soon drive them to the brink of penury; and they finally discover that he is literally mad. But they find themselves unable to drive him away. "With him they lived in terror, but in the tradition. . . . They would keep him, as it were a dear obsession, till they were dead." The unforced symbolism of Bishop's story, which focuses in a microcosm the tragic white-Negro relationship in the South, has the inevitable rightness of a completely realized achievement.

IV

Despite Bishop's volume of stories, American themes had shown up in only one or two of the poems in *Now With His Love*. But in his next volume, *Minute Particulars* (1935), we find one sequence of five poems devoted to New England, and another, called "Experience in the West," dealing with the theme of the American pioneer. The New England group is personal—the poet's return to the land of his ancestors, where he finds abandoned, "dishonored houses" and a countryside scarred by the defacements of industrialism. "There is no sustenance in this ground," he concludes.

"Experience in the West" is more ambitious, and on the whole more successful, in conveying a complex historical experience in Bishop's carefully wrought pictorial symbols. These poems, with their sensuously compelling visual surfaces, appear vivid enough on first reading though somewhat obscure. But just as his fellow Symbolist Yeats provided glosses on his poetry in *A Vision* and other prose works, so Bishop was in the habit of explaining his symbols in his criticism; and the best way to read "Experience in the West" is to see what he says about the American pioneer in his articles of the mid-thirties.

In his brilliant and moving study of the Lost Generation, "The Missing All," Bishop remarks that Puritanism —the New England idea—had gone bad in the Midwest. Puritanism originally had been based on a hatred of nature, and the ordeal of the wilderness had only increased that hatred; but the original transcendental meaning of this emotion was lost in being transplanted. "The meaning of Puritanism is a contempt for mortality; in the Midwest it was forgotten." When the pioneer came out of the forest onto the prairies, he had been toughened physically but emptied spiritually; he had sloughed off all his traditional values and was left with only a hatred-of-life that had lost its religious rationale. This theme begins in Bishop's "The Burning Wheel," which describes the pioneer carrying his culture on his back as Aeneas carried Anchises:

> They, too, the stalwart conquerors of space
> Each on his shoulders wore a wise delirium
> Of memory and age: ghostly embrace
> Of Fathers slanted toward a western tomb.

These burdens stayed "Aloft, until they were as light as autumn/ Shells of locusts"; and were finally deposited in some "Wilderness oblivion."

"Green Centuries" then evokes an image of the forest in which the pioneer lost his soul. "In green no soul was found,/ In that green savage clime/ Such ignorance of time." Time—which is always Bishop's word for history, continuity, tradition, for the ebb and flow of human experience—comes to a stop "when every day dawned Now." And time is replaced by space, quality by quantity: "Time dreams eternity/ Their nights were starred with space." But the end of the poem finds the pioneer's "death-set face" assuming "an idle frown"; his task is done, his virtues superfluous. This is a preparation for "Loss in the West," whose gloss may be found in some remarks Bishop made about the Idaho novelist Vardis Fisher. "The heroic age is past," he writes. "Courage and hope, those two most admirable virtues of the frontiersman, have become in this late and unpromising land [Idaho, the last frontier] cruelly meaningless."

"Cast out of the fray/ The man in the coonskin cap." The pioneer no longer has a place in modern life ("What have we to do with a fear that stalked/ In a savage unlit wood?"). But the world that the pioneer created still continues its restless and never-ending expansion:

> Yet gaunt—bone, gut, sinews—
> Something like man pursued
> And still pursues
> What? Wheel of the sun
> In Heaven? The west wind? Or only a will
> To his own destruction?

And this pursuit is presented in the fourth and final poem —ironically entitled "O Pioneers"—under the guise of a pioneer party that has lost its way in search of gold and perishes in the desert. Thematically, at least, these poems seem to me to stand by themselves in American literature as a direct rejection of the myth of the frontier. And to feel their full force they should be read against the background of those works of Whitman, Hart Crane, and Archibald MacLeish that celebrate the pioneer *mystique.*

It was part of Bishop's cosmopolitanism that, despite his preoccupation with America, he never shared the cultural nationalism that led to the belief in American "uniqueness." As he explains in his important article on "The Golden Bough," the blind forward surge of the American pioneer is merely one aspect of the scientific conquest of nature—the conquest of space—begun in the Renaissance. And this whole movement has had the same effect on Western culture as the pioneer ethos had on American life. It has destroyed all traditional standards of man, without replacing them by anything equally viable. This is the theme of "O Let Not Virtue Seek," one of Bishop's most ambitious poems but not among his most successful; it suffers from the attempt to combine Symbolist obliquity and Shakespearean declamation. But it is instructive to see how he juxtaposes the quantitative universe of science against the qualitative uniqueness of human experience. Astronomy has now given us "unavailable millenniums" but "we stifle for a second/ When desire bends our knees above our love." The two orders are incommensurate; and even worse, as he remarks in the same article, "we have reached the skeptical point where we see the scientific universe as a projection of our own immortal desire for order, yet realize that it leaves all our desires, even that desire, unsatisfied."

V

If Bishop's poetry had done nothing more than dramatize this dilemma, it would be difficult, despite individual successes, to accord him any higher rank than that of a gifted epigone. But Bishop's most original poetry attempts to go beyond despair in an entirely independent direction, and to communicate a sense of a cosmic order in which modern man can believe. "For," he writes, "it is only by perceiving order in those external forces on which his continuance depends, that man can hope to bring his own being into accord with them." In his *Selected Poems* (1941), the last book to appear in his lifetime, Bishop took three poems from *Minute Particulars* and grouped them together. These compose his first answer to the dichotomy of modern culture; and it is regrettable that when these poems have been noticed at all their true impact has been either overlooked or misunderstood.

Even Allen Tate, who has done more than anyone else to keep Bishop's reputation alive, went wide of the mark in commenting on this phase of his friend's work. For Mr. Tate speaks of one of these poems, "Divine Nativity," as attempting "to use the Christian myth" and then collapsing "with a final glance at anthropology." But there is a collapse only if we believe the two are incompatible and that Bishop, as Mr. Tate writes, was attempting "to replace our secular philosophy, in which he does not believe, with a vision of the divine, in which he tries to believe." [5] Bishop's "vision of the divine" is one in which the opposition between Christianity and anthropology has ceased to exist; and the great merit of these poems is precisely that of creating a world in which this antagonism is nullified.

Once again it is illuminating to turn to Bishop's "Golden Bough" article for a commentary. "In Sir James Frazer's pages," Bishop writes, "there is revealed what one may in all simplicity call the true religion of mankind." Bishop argues that Frazer's researches in anthropology, far from destroying Christianity (as the nineteenth century believed), have on the contrary given it a new authenticity. For if we take "religion as a revelation of human destiny, we must see that He is not less divine because of the company of Adonis, Osiris and Thammuz. His divinity is to be found in precisely those attributes which He shares with these other and older incarnate gods." The central mystery of Christianity is the Mass, which "turns out to be a symbolic presentation of the eternal relation of man to a living and sustaining earth." The Mass derives from the immemorial worship of the Vegetable God; but it transforms "what was originally a form of expressing physical concerns to spiritual ends." Religion, we now see, arose out of the fear that life might cease; it succeeds in giving death and disintegration a positive meaning, and endows the elemental lusts and passions with human significance.

From this point of view, the role of death in authentic religion—or at least in Bishop's "true religion of mankind" —must be carefully distinguished from the death-longing of asceticism, "the belief in dying as an escape from time and change into the unchanging and timeless." Bishop argues that the ascetic element in Christianity, its "peculiar taint of death," is closer "to the collapse of the State than to the rise of the Church." In other words, it is not an essential component of that part of Christianity explored by Frazer. For the worship of the Vegetable God, the true religion of mankind, is based on "knowledge of the revolving year and the memory of the season's return"; it is "coeval with the conception of time." Asceticism is an escape from time and change, a residual vestige of the earliest ages when man lived "in a savage jungle of fear . . . and there [were] no gods and no time."

These reflections throw a good deal of light on what Bishop was trying to do in the poems in question. "The Saints," for example, shows us a group of starvelings staggering through a landscape of "bright waste of sands" and "desert rock." These are certainly the ascetics trying to escape from time:

Subduing time
In naked trance,
Construe as crime
Continuance,
All that changes
Confound with scorn.
So each man avenges
A child born.

The saints renounce life in the hope of triumphing over death:

O concreate
And never abandoned
Longing! Dilate
Our loves beyond
All loves that age
Or lust consumes,
O thirst and rage
For the lost kingdoms!

But this attempt to capture divinity outside of time is futile: "Whoever says/ Divine has said/ Dying."

Life and death cannot be separated: this is the theme of "The Tree," whose details are taken from the Adam and Eve myth. Once the first man and woman have eaten what they receive "from a serpent clasp of cold coils," they lose their status as demigods in timeless Eden; they become aware of each other's sex, and "a sudden light" borders the tree with "a bright burnish of desire." Now, like the incarnate god, they have become human; the woman has been "embraced by the lips with death's taste." Debased to the human status, they are drawn into the process of nature:

> From the living stem
> Such sustenance
> Draws into their dance
> Stars follow them.
> Clasping they control
> The coursing light from pole to pole.

And, as with all life, the act of love and the act of death are inseparable. "All delight of leaf and sun/ Dreams of dissolution."

Bishop's own idea of true divinity is the subject of "Divine Nativity." This poem plays with the idea of incarnation, the birth of the gods:

> O fabled truth:
> Did the god's bride
> Know an armored youth
> His bronze cast aside?

The Incarnation is both truth and fable, divine and human, flesh and spirit. The arrival of the gods is always linked with an outburst of sexual passion ("Adoring Leda leaned upon/ A bright encumbrance of wild swan"). But, in whatever form they appear, the gods bring joy, hope, and rejuvenescence; and in this moment the animal, the human, and the divine are inextricably intermingled:

> Eagle, swan or dove
> White bull or cloud

Incarnate love
Alone is proud.
The arrogant know
In the bestial part
Overflow
Of the elated heart.

These poems compose Bishop's answer to the problem first posed to modern culture in *The Waste Land,* a work which also, it will be recalled, took its departure from Frazer and his pupil Jessie Weston. Eliot too uses the pattern of the vegetation myths as the controlling principle of order in his poem, but he already accentuates the Christian element—the idea of the self-sacrifice of the Dying God—as the source of the restoration of fertility. Bishop, on the other hand, takes a direction similar to D. H. Lawrence's in his emphasis on sexuality and his rejection of asceticism. But just as he had spiritualized the mindless sensationalism of the Lost Generation, so now he does not simply surrender to the deification of the primitive and chthonic powers. He refuses to abandon either the physical ("the bestial part") or the spiritual ("the elated heart"), either to abstract man from nature or to submerge him in its tug. And the fine balance of Bishop's humanism, expressed in the firm control of these masterly poems, seems to me to entitle them to a distinguished place in contemporary poetry.

The same balance is maintained in Bishop's only published novel, *Act of Darkness* (1935), which takes on its full significance only in the context of the poems we have just discussed. As a novel, *Act of Darkness* suffers from an annoying technical flaw—an unexplained alternation between a first-person and a third-person narrator. But aside from this minor defect it is a vivid and memorable little work, written with a fine, fresh lyricism lacking in Bishop's earlier prose. At first sight it may seem merely another example of the American discovery-of-life genre, the awakening of an adolescent to the reality of evil (which, as in Sherwood Anderson's "I Want to Know Why," is usually given a sexual guise). Bishop's originality, however, lies in his dissociation of sexuality and evil; it is rather the attempt to escape from sexuality, to evade the inevitable *rites de passage* into manhood and life, which here, as in the poetry, becomes the true evil.

The "act of darkness" referred to in the title (taken from *Othello*) is a rape, committed by the narrator's uncle. The action is seen largely through the eyes of the adolescent narrator, John; and this fateful outbreak of sexual dynamism—a dynamism that John also had felt stirring in himself—brings on a grave psychic crisis in the boy. John stifles his vitality and falls ill, unwilling to face the fact that life and manhood carry the possibility of both suffering and inflicting evil. But one day he finds himself wishing to die physically, rather than continue to linger in a twilight zone of death-in-life; and the spell of fear is broken. "Having accepted death, I returned to life." And he seals his recovery by a visit to a brothel, where he himself experiences the ritual act of darkness—the initiation rites into the true religion of mankind—which prepares for the perils of manhood. But this experience also coincides with the discovery of Shakespeare, who teaches John that art can "impose a sensuous order on the moral disorder of the world." Here again we find Bishop's acute awareness of the primitive roots of life going hand in hand with a sense of its need for aesthetic and human sublimation. Order and vitality belong together, else we get barbarism or desiccation.

VI

Bishop's *Selected Poems* contains a number of new items either written after *Minute Particulars* or, for some reason, not included in that volume. On the whole, however, these poems do not reveal any significant development in Bishop's work; only his accustomed mastery in familiar themes and styles. Bishop wrote little poetry between 1936 and 1940, but beginning in the latter year he had a remarkable spurt which produced some new poems of striking breadth and power and with a significant extension of thematic range. The death of his old friend F. Scott Fitzgerald in 1940 resulted in a moving threnody; and the events of the following years, particularly the fall of France, filled him with foreboding.

"The fall of France was a terrible shock to him; one was astonished at the violence of his reaction to it," writes Edmund Wilson, whose own political isolationism presumably made him impervious to the catastrophe.[6] But Bishop felt himself a son of Western culture to his very fingertips; and for him that culture was inconceivable without France. "I am dismayed," he said in a speech delivered in 1941, "by the dangerous changes that may come to Western civilization and in the end destroy its continuity." He enjoined the American artist, now that France was silent, to take up the French task of preserving this continuity. "We must find a way to reconcile our own past with the vast past of Western civilization." With his own injunction as a guide, Bishop's last poetry meditates on the rise and fall of cultures, on destruction but also on rebirth. And its imagery, derived from the classical Mediterranean world he had always loved, reveals his own effort to fulfill the obligation he had laid on American art.

These meditations compose a group of poems, "The Statues," unpublished in Bishop's lifetime and only made available in Allen Tate's edition of his poetry. Mr. Tate places their composition in 1940, but with no conclusive evidence; in any case, they obviously take up the theme of "The Divine Nativity" group. But instead of replacing the gods in the life-cycle of nature, as he had done earlier, Bishop now explores their relationship with human order and civilization. The sequence is based on a contrast between desert-imagery of space, drought, and barrenness (familiar from "The Saints") and sea-imagery of time and destruction, but also of fecundation and reimmersion in the waters of life.

It is from the sea that the gods are born; but in the first poem they are "The Uneaten Gods," cast up broken and drowned on a shore which is that of modernity. And so the sea, as it were, becomes desacralized ("Only the waves are seen . . ./ Not the force under the waves,/ Nor the forces above the waves"). Once the gods had been "embodiments of time"; and this was the birth of Greek civilization. In a magnificent passage, which recalls the neo-Hellenism of Schiller and Hölderlin, Bishop pictures this event:

> Imaginings of order
> Rose, beyond the lucent headlands,
> Above the marble stairs. And columns rose,
> Voluptuous doves among the capitals,
> Supporting and overcoming azure.
> The gods stood. Men saw their simulacra
> Display immortal visions. So let the wild
> white horses
> Rise from the bay, and run, bestriding spindrift,
> To rock the shores with stormier tramplings!
> The gods stood. And while they stood, the state

And every sea-gaze circled to the same horizon,
All speech proclaimed one tongue of praise.

The following two poems, "Dunes on the March" and "Sojourn in the Desert," show what occurs when the gods remain uneaten. The flowering shore of the sea becomes barren sand dunes "burning the vision/ In excess of space." But the sojourn in this desert could not give rise to any new flowering ("Ascetic drought was there . . ./ But the saint's secret was not there"). Orpheus could not be reborn in this desolation, nor did "the haggard John/ In his wild cloak of camel's hair" hear the Word in this desert. Only in "Return of the Sea" does life come again to the parched landscape—"Rushing as though water were the word/ Death made flesh/ The Word death/ and the Word made flesh!"/

The poem "Statue of Shadow" is the most enigmatic of all: a vision of "that mystery of clearest light," the shadow cast by the body at high noon on a coast of "burning sand." In "Perspectives are Precipices," Bishop had used "shadow" to symbolize human history and continuity. And what "shadow" seems to indicate here, following the re-birth of the return of the sea, is a recovery of the past and hence of the possibility of creating the future. "The shade of all those centuries/ Whose death is longing and fate a crime/ Lay long/ But no longer/ Than the statue of shadow/ The sun at its silent noon laid at my feet." And the last two poems, "The Great Statues" and "The Archi-pelagoes," resolve the sequence in a recovery of serenity arising from this contemplation of past beauty and har-mony and the conviction of its restoration in the future:

The day returns, but not the day
Of these gods. Yet the dawn resumes the amazed
Smile of a brute Apollo,
Dazzling in bronze of sea-encrusted blue-green.

"The Statues" still sees the rise and fall of cultures primarily in the perspective of the primordial rhythms of the "true religion of mankind." But while the earlier poetry, inspired by the revolt against Puritanism, had concentrated on the incarnation of spirit, "The Statues" emphasizes, as it were, the spiritualization of nature and the flesh. Nature may now have only the lineaments of a "brute Apollo," but total brutishness had forever been exorcised for those who preserve the continuity of Western culture. Nor are all cultures any longer dissolved into one; it is the culture and the gods of Greek humanism that have become the pattern for man. "The time-adorning monuments/ Restore the secrets of eternity." Considering the historical background of these poems—the rise and triumph of nazism, with its obscene worship of the fearsome gods of blood, race, and soil—it is hardly surprising that Bishop should have shifted his accents in this fashion.

And this new anthropocentrism is expressed even more clearly in his last important poem, "A Subject of Sea Change." Here again we find the predominant sea-imagery of this last period. But the sea is now no longer simply the source of life; it has also become the paradoxical, ambiguous, Janus-faced image of history itself. The spectacle of the sea, writes the poet, allowed him "To hold in instant contemplation/ The shifting flow of human history/ That seaward sets even as it shoreward moves."

In this poem Bishop directly expresses his trepidations about the fate of Western culture as he hears "the great bombs drop"; and he reminds his readers "That every ordered change of form/ Brings mind's disorder and destroying storm." But in face of the all-destroying flux, characteristically felt as a breakdown of manners ("Death greets us all without civility/ And every color of the sea is cold"), a man must never fall below the noble image of himself immortalized by the Greeks. As with Oedipus, there is no escape from the responsibility of the tragic role in which he has been cast; but he must uphold human dignity to the end:

> I must learn again the great part of Man—
> Though the lines are scant that any man can speak—
> Proclaiming with such passion as I can
> The part first played, and nobly, by a Greek.
> Time is man's tragic responsibility
> And on his back he bears
> Both the prolific and destroying years.
> And so, I swear, he must surround each act
> With scruples that will hold intact
> Not merely his own, but human dignity.

These were John Peale Bishop's last words.

NOTES

7. THE ACHIEVEMENT OF JOHN PEALE BISHOP

1. *The Collected Poems of John Peale Bishop,* ed. by Allen Tate (New York: Charles Scribner's Sons, 1948); *The Collected Essays of John Peale Bishop,* ed. by Edmund Wilson (New York: Charles Scribner's Sons, 1948). All the poems and articles by Bishop cited in this essay are included in these two volumes.

2. R. P. Blackmur, "Twelve Poets," *The Southern Review* VIII, 1 (Summer, 1941), 198.

3. Allen Tate, "John Peale Bishop," *The Man of Letters in the Modern World* (New York: Meridian, 1955), p. 271.

4. *Ibid.,* p. 275.

5. *Ibid.,* p. 276.

6. Edmund Wilson, Introduction, *The Collected Essays of John Peale Bishop,* p. xiii.

8 R. P. Blackmur: The Later Phase

Despite its long dominance on the American literary scene, there seems to be no abatement of the controversy and discussion elicited by the New Criticism. One has merely to open the pages of any literary journal to find it, if no longer defended so ardently, then at least being attacked with unflagging zeal; and we may take the passion of its opponents as an unwitting tribute to its continuing vitality. A great deal of this combative energy, however, now seems to be quite beside the point and even obviously anachronistic. For like all important and vital cultural movements the New Criticism has not remained static. It has evolved and developed over the course of years, and most of the accusations that continue to be leveled against it have long since ceased to have much relevance.

Many years have passed since Granville Hicks, the erstwhile paladin of Marxist criticism in the thirties, dismissed the New Criticism, with specific reference to R. P. Blackmur, as resembling "the impassioned quibbling of devotees of some game." [1] Some years later Alfred Kazin was hardly more complimentary about Mr. Blackmur in *On Native Grounds,* and protested against "a criticism so *driven* to technical insights that it virtually conceived the literary mind as a sensibility machine—taste, conscience and mind working as gears, levers and wheels." [2] Even an admirer like Stanley Edgar Hyman, in *The Armed Vision,* stressed the brilliance of the New Criticism's close reading of poetic texts in his essay on R. P. Blackmur. And so the impression was created that the New Critics were a group of myopic Formalists, who wished to remove literature to some ethereal realm unsullied by contact with the grosser realities of life and history.

To a certain extent, such an impression was an inevitable result of the cultural conjuncture in which the New Criticism came to birth. It should never be forgotten that many of the positions of the New Criticism were thrashed out in polemics with Marxists or Marxist-influenced opponents during the thirties; and it is curious that the very writers who attack the New Criticism in the name of "history" should never have tried to interpret its positions in their historical context. Faced with the attempt to appropriate literature for purely social and propagandistic purposes, it was only natural for the New Critics, defending the autonomy and integrity of art, to exaggerate and overemphasize its purity and independence from immediate social and political concerns. The concentration of criticism on "form" was a natural result of this reaction, which was based on the belief that the defense of the freedom of art was itself a vital social imperative.

The Marxists, however, were not the only antagonists with whom the New Critics crossed swords. Many of their thrusts were directed against the academic champions of historical positivism, who had managed to side-track any living concern for literary values in the never-ending hunt for "facts." Both the Marxists and the positivists, poles apart as they were in other respects, were united by the tribute they rendered to the idol of "history." And the vigorous onslaught against these two opponents by the New Critics led to the misunderstanding that the latter were rejecting the study of history *in toto* as irrelevant to the understanding of literature.

In reality, as a glance at a few texts will show, this was not true at all. Certainly one of the major sources for the aesthetics of the New Criticism was T. S. Eliot's observation on the dissociation of sensibility, the separation of thought and feeling, which occurred in the seventeenth century as a result of the rise of modern science; like Whitehead, Eliot makes this dissociation responsible for the birth of Romanticism.[3] And what is such an observation if not an illumination of literature by the contemplation of history? Or we may take Allen Tate's view, developed in relation to Emily Dickinson and the New England mind, about the most propitious time for poetry. This, in his opinion, is the moment when a culture has emerged from the grip of a strict religion that still continues to retain its affective hold on the sensibility.[4] Here again we find a historical *aperçu* used to define and clarify a literary issue and, even more, a particular poet. The work of the best New Critics is filled with similar first-rate insights into the relations between literature and history; but this relation is conceived differently by the New Critics than it had been by the academic positivists.

For the New Critics, history was no longer a collection of "facts" and "sources" whose uncovering would "explain" the work of art exactly as a physical event is explained by the combination of the various laws of nature that enter its composition. History, rather, became for them a locus of spiritual and cultural forces, whose study can help us to grasp and "understand" the artistic response to a particular cultural environment or situation. In their own way, the New Critics were developing in practice the dichotomy that Wilhelm Dilthey had drawn between *Erklären* and *Verstehen* in his rejection of the positivist approach to the study of *Geistesgeschichte*. It is true, however, that the New Critics had little awareness of their own theoretical presuppositions, particularly with regard to the problem of historicism. It is also true that part of their critical strategy was to postulate their standards as a priori aesthetic norms, and to mask their historical judgments and cultural preferences under the guise of formal analysis. This unquestionably led to a confusion which, in the hands of their epigones, tended to narrow the horizon of literary studies and to turn the latter, all too often, into a bloodless display of scholastic ingenuity.

Partly for this reason, perhaps, and certainly as a response to the changes in the cultural climate caused by their own success, a number of the original New Critics made notable efforts during the fifties to broaden their position. The way was paved by T. S. Eliot's retraction of his earlier arbitrary dismissals of such writers as Milton, Tennyson, and Goethe. And a winning symptom of this effort may be discerned in a little interchange that took place between R. P. Blackmur and John Crowe Ransom.

For if we compare what these writers have said about each other over the past ten years, we become aware of a charming and amusing mock-ballet of mutual eyebrow raising and mildly astonished admonition which has far more significance than merely that of a private joke between two old friends.

In his essay "The Lion and the Honeycomb," which appeared first in 1951, Mr. Blackmur points out a limitation in Mr. Ransom's famous piece on Milton's *Lycidas.* Mr. Ransom dealt excellently with the rhetoric (the formal structure) of Milton's poem, says Mr. Blackmur, but he neglected to touch on those matters that the rhetoric composed—"the theology and politics and personal experience which are the intellectual and poetic subject of the poem." Three years later Mr. Ransom reviewed Mr. Blackmur's collection of essays, *Language as Gesture;* in that review he rightly praises them as the strongest, sharpest, and most perceptive criticism written on the major modern poets. But then he reproaches Mr. Blackmur with a regrettable narrowness in his critical approach; for Mr. Blackmur, it seems, concentrates too exclusively on the formal structures of the poems he writes about and overlooks the "substantive" elements which are also contained in the poetry.[5]

Both these criticisms were justified about the essay (or book of essays) to which they referred, and which represented comparatively early work on the part of both writers; neither was relevant to the essays Mr. Blackmur and Mr. Ransom were writing when each made his good-humored charge against the other. In the case of R. P. Blackmur in particular, a noticeable widening of scope and approach had already become apparent by his second book *The Expense of Greatness* (1940). This development has continued until it has become difficult to recognize the old Blackmur in the new; and recent commentators have emphasized the disparity between the early work collected in such a volume as *Language as Gesture* and the selection of later essays in *The Lion and the Honeycomb*.[6] Rather than belabor the obvious, however, we should like to try to show that there is a clear line of intellectual continuity between the earlier and the later Blackmur, and that his later criticism represents a development of possibilities implicit in his fundamental ideas from the very start. In so doing, we may perhaps be able to cast some light on the thought processes that guide the performance of our most baffling and rewarding literary critic.

II

Nothing is easier than to catch Mr. Blackmur in the act of apparently changing his mind. In the programmatic essay that gives its title to *The Lion and the Honeycomb*, he explains that his critical ideal is now a fusion of Coleridge and Aristotle, whose names he takes as representative of two basic critical tendencies. Coleridge stands for all the criticism devoted to the psychology of imagination as it applies "to the behavior of words and . . . the attributes of imagination in words." Aristotle stands for all that is contained in the idea of mimesis, which applies not to words "but to the behavior of the things indicated by the words." These latter are the "substantive" values that both Mr. Blackmur and Mr. Ransom wish to include again in their critical purview. It is not only rhetoric, Mr. Blackmur writes, but all the modes of the mind—dialectic and poetic as well as rhetoric—that the critic must handle in the art work.

In passing, Mr. Blackmur remarks that his own early work also falls a victim to his strictures against rhetoric;

but the fact is that Mr. Blackmur was always one of the least dogmatic of the New Critics. It is true that, in his memorable essay on "A Critic's Job of Work," Mr. Blackmur spoke of his own approach to literature as being through the study of "technique." But he immediately added that he was not only concerned with technique on the plane of words or of "intellectual and emotional patterns"—he also meant "that there is a technique of securing and arranging and representing a fundamental view of life." In reality, then, Mr. Blackmur's ideas about criticism have changed far less radically than might be thought at first sight; but there is no question that in the past his emphasis lay on the first meaning of the word "technique." What we have now is a shift in Mr. Blackmur's emphasis (and critical practice) to the second sense of technique as a means of representing a fundamental view of life. How this shift was accomplished may best be seen by an examination of his key critical term, "the symbolic imagination."

No reader of Mr. Blackmur can fail to have been struck by the frequency with which he cites T. S. Eliot's answer to Paul Elmer More. The latter had remarked on the contradiction between Eliot's praise of tradition in his criticism and the stylistic radicalism of his poetry. In critical prose, Eliot replied in *After Strange Gods,* one can legitimately be concerned with ideals; while in poetry one has to deal with actuality. This is of course one of Eliot's typical paradoxical inversions of Romantic doctrine (poetry for the Romantics was the language of the ideal and prose that of the real or the actual); but Mr. Blackmur often prefers to take his paradoxes straight, and he accepted this idea of Eliot's at face value. There is an excellent study of Eliot's criticism in *The Lion and the Honeycomb,* and, though this passage is not cited, Mr. Blackmur offers a gloss on it just the same. Eliot, he writes, "excluded thought as such from poetry and said that poetry dealt with the experience or feeling of the thought which might or might not—probably not—have been the poet's thought." Poetry, in other words, deals with the actual because it deals with thought so far as it comes alive as experience or feeling; critical prose can express abstract ideas as ideals, independently of their emotional actuality.

How seriously Mr. Blackmur took this notion is revealed all through the early essays collected in *Language as Gesture*. Time and again he reiterates that he is not interested in the ideas contained in poetry for their own sake; he is concerned only with the amount of experience and feeling that the poet is able to actualize *through* these ideas. To make this point clearer, Mr. Blackmur distinguished between a literal and an imaginative approach to ideas—much in the manner of Santayana, whose benignly skeptical tolerance of dogmatism pervasively colors the mood of Mr. Blackmur's mind. Whether or not a writer like Eliot or Yeats accepted the doctrines in his own work (i.e., Christianity or Yeatsian theosophy) as literally true, Mr. Blackmur never had to bother about these doctrines in abstract terms; his focus was always on their imaginative use in the work of art. "Our labor," he writes, speaking of literary critics, "is to recapture the imaginative burden and avoid the literal like death."

In *Language as Gesture,* this imaginative approach to doctrine is still used largely as a critical working principle. Mr. Blackmur was determined not to fall into the error of various kinds of ideological critics, who analyzed and evaluated literature in terms of their agreement or disagreement with its "ideas." But it is revealing to see Mr. Blackmur generalizing this imaginative approach, and applying it not only to literature but to all attempts to interpret the meaning of experience.

In "A Critic's Job of Work," he praises the skepticism and dramatic irony of the early Plato and of Montaigne because neither wishes to be fixed in any doctrine. And Mr. Blackmur's sympathy with such writers, it is clear, stems from his own facility in imaginatively entering any framework of ideas without feeling obliged to come to terms with it literally as doctrine. Even more, Mr. Blackmur begins to feel the tendency of thought to take *itself* seriously, its insistence on being literal rather than imaginative, as a tragic limitation inherent in all doctrine. "Thought is a beacon not a life-raft," he writes somewhat fancifully, "and to confuse the functions is tragic. The tragic character of thought—as any perspective will show—is that it takes a rigid mold too soon; chooses destiny like a Calvinist, in infancy, instead of waiting slowly for old age." Any perspective thus becomes tragic when, instead of being used to illuminate some particular area of experience, it is clung to desperately as an absolute and literal truth.

III

This observation on the tragic character of thought is only an incidental remark in *Language as Gesture;* but in *The Lion and the Honeycomb* this idea—or rather, a remarkable efflorescence of this idea—moves into the center of Mr. Blackmur's critical preoccupations. And in essays like those on Henry Adams, T. E. Lawrence, and Irving Babbit, we can see how Mr. Blackmur has magnified this critical working principle into a metaphysical dialectic. "To think straight," Mr. Blackmur writes, "you must overshoot your mark"—which means that you must take your doctrine literally for the whole truth, while at best it can never be more than a partial version of the truth. Every perspective is necessarily tragic when pushed to its limits; for at these limits "reason falters and becomes abstract, or faith fails and pretends to be absolute." Each perspective is thus like the hero in Hegel's theory of tragedy (to which Mr. Blackmur's dialectic bears an intriguing resemblance), asserting its partial truth as absolute and being destroyed in the very act of taking itself as omnipotent.

Under various guises, and with constantly shifting terms, this dialectic now provides the deepest driving force of Mr. Blackmur's cogitations. Adams, as Mr. Blackmur depicts him, had the rare value of pursuing his quest for an ultimate perspective on experience and knowing the necessity for its final failure. Irving Babbitt imposed and asserted an abstract intellectual perspective whose blindness and inflexible dogmatism was its own refutation. T. E. Lawrence, the most complex case of all, did not assert any perspective as absolute but rather the absence of all perspective; and he forced himself to the limits of degradation in an effort to achieve some sort of affirmation through denial and self-nullification. In each case the dialectic between unity and chaos, or order and disorder, or orthodoxy and heresy, controls the framework of Mr. Blackmur's reflections. And the sharp edge of his criticism is inserted at the point where he senses an imbalance between his two terms—a failure of orthodoxy to make room for and absorb heresy, a failure of chaos to keep alive some positive ideal of order.

Once we have grasped the nature of Mr. Blackmur's dialectic, the function and the value that he attributes to the symbolic imagination becomes almost self-explanatory. What Mr. Blackmur wants, what the internal logic of his sensibility impels him to postulate, is a dialectical balance that maintains the proper relationship between his two terms; and in the essay on Babbitt he defines "the religious imagination" in a manner that explains what this relationship must be. "It is only the religious imagination," he writes, "which has the advantage of including the traditional standards of life along with a minute knowledge of its immediate experience; hence it commonly keeps, along with its principles, escape from them through intercession, repentance, sacrifice, grace, as forms of behavior."

In other words, the religious imagination creates an order that does not exclude disorder or a unity that does not exclude chaos. But since for Mr. Blackmur, as he has made clear on a number of occasions, the religious imagination is no longer viable, he remarks in the Babbitt essay "that it is both necessary and possible that we make a secular equivalent of the religious imagination." This is precisely the purpose for which Mr. Blackmur has invented his symbolic imagination, operating through art and primarily through literature. The symbolic imagination is the secular equivalent of a religious imagination that has become moribund; it embodies and actualizes the same sense of life as a dialectical opposition whose extremes do not exclude but interact with and complement each other.

It is in terms of the symbolic imagination that Mr. Blackmur writes his intellectual biographies; and this is what gives them their unmistakable metaphysical cast. For what Mr. Blackmur does is to stylize his material so that the conflicts of his subject are ultimately seen as some local and historical incarnation of his dialectic. Nothing quite like this sort of criticism has been written in English since Emerson's *Representative Men.* Perhaps its closest modern analogue is Nietzsche's idea of "monumental" history— the kind of history that Nietzsche himself wrote in *The Birth of Tragedy* when, with a fine disregard for chronology, he turned the figure of Socrates into a symbol of the eye of Reason under whose ironic scrutiny Greek tragedy withered and died. The great merits of this approach are that it focuses on elements of enduring cultural interest and leaves ample scope for poetic and imaginative insight in historical interpretation. These merits are fully evident in Mr. Blackmur's remarkable studies, written with incomparable verbal *élan* and with an unerring eye for the symbolic detail and the revelatory citation. Its chief danger is that of turning historical experience into a kind of mythology, of making history too transparent, as it were, so that the density of fact becomes only a medium to reveal the latent metaphysical meaning. Neither Carlyle, Emerson, nor Nietzsche, all of whom approached history in this way, wholly escaped this danger; nor does Mr. Blackmur on occasion. But, like them, what he gives us in illumination and understanding more than compensates for some excess in manipulating his material.

IV

Mr. Blackmur's dialectic, however, is not used only as a scaffolding for his studies of individual figures. It also receives a more concrete aesthetic application in a notable essay on "The Loose and Baggy Monsters of Henry James," and here results in an important revision of an earlier position. For Mr. Blackmur, the struggle between the two basic forces of his dialectic—forces whose names are legion —has now become the underlying classic form of life; and he argues that individual novels each depict "a particular struggle between manners and behavior, between the ideal insight and the actual momentum in which the form of life is found." And just as Mr. Blackmur has rejected the pretension of any one perspective on reality to be absolute, so now he rejects the same claim for any one method of objectifying this underlying classic form and giving it artistic shape.

No one technique or executive form is an absolute standard for the novel; and the interest of this assertion is heightened by other essays in which we can trace the course of Mr. Blackmur's thought on this key question. For Mr. Blackmur's masterly study of James's *Prefaces,* written in 1934, did more than any other single work except Percy Lubbock's *The Craft of Fiction* to canonize the Jamesian conception of dramatic form in the novel—a conception derived, as James himself was never tired of explaining, from the drama and the plastic arts. This criterion of dramatic form is the one that the New Criticism advocated when it paid attention to the novel at all; and Mr. Blackmur has been one of its most zealous defenders.

But already in 1938, in a study of the craft of Melville, the canker of doubt had begun to fester. Mr. Blackmur here puzzles over the problem of why *Moby Dick* indubitably manages to hold the interest of its readers, and why some of these readers even think it has a story, when it is "a book of which Henry James would have said that it told no story to speak of." Instead of being led by this to question James's narrowly anecdotal notion of a story (*Moby Dick* is based on the far more fundamental narrative element of epic action), Mr. Blackmur can only conclude that those readers who think Melville had a story were deceived. In his latest essay, though, Mr. Blackmur reaches the point of repudiating the Master himself. For in the teeth of James's declaration that *War and Peace* lacks "deep-breathing economy of organic form," Mr. Blackmur replies that Tolstoy's book has every quality of organic form that James admired although "in a different relation to executive form than any he [James] could accept." It is good to get this a priori notion of dramatic form finally out of the way, useful though it has been in the hands of Lubbock and Mr. Blackmur in sharpening our eye for the aesthetics of fiction.

Mr. Blackmur's essay on the later novels of James is an intense and wide-ranging effort to seize the moral terms in which James dramatized "the permanent struggle between the human condition and human aspirations." So far as Mr. Blackmur confines himself to the characters and themes in these books, his insights are unsurpassed for penetration and suggestiveness; one feels that at last these novels have found a critic who measures up to their intricate delicacy and moral refinement. But Mr. Blackmur throws out so wide a net as he goes along that one cannot help being surprised at some of the catch that is hauled in. Maggie Verver in *The Golden Bowl* becomes James's version of Dante's Beatrice; we are also told that she learns in a London drawing room two of the lessons that Dostoevsky found in the enormous abyss of *The Brothers Karamazov.* And before the essay is ended we have heard about the rise of art for art's sake, the great growth of population in modern times, the disestablishment of culture as a result of shifts in the bases of society—as well as about a great number of other interesting matters which, in spite of Mr. Blackmur's assurances, have only the loosest connection with anything we can find in a late James novel.

From a criticism that moved in the direction of making finer and finer discriminations within the work of art, Mr. Blackmur now is moving in the direction of an analogical affability that dissolves all formal, historical, and cultural boundaries in the warmth of its embrace. Nor is it hard to understand the natural evolution by which this change has been gradually accomplished. Mr. Blackmur sees all cultural movement proceeding under the form of his dialectic; and ever since Plato it has been an inherent movement of the mind to let essential similarities take precedence over accidental differences. Still, the danger for criticism here is very close to the one that Mr. Blackmur points out with reference to Kenneth Burke—except that where Burke substitutes his study of rhetorical strategies for literature, Mr. Blackmur, if he is not careful, may find himself substituting his dialectic or his general form of life for the concrete literary form of life he is nominally talking about.

These dangers become all too evident in Mr. Blackmur's outline for a theory of literature, intriguingly entitled "Between the Numen and the Moha." The symbolic imagination, we have been told, is at work in literature and the arts; and Mr. Blackmur, naturally enough, sees the arts as a theoretic form (he takes the term from Croce) creating "the sort of order which is responsive to every movement of behavior and every pulse of inspiration: an order which gives room to fresh disorder whenever it occurs." Mr. Blackmur's theory of literature turns out to be a series of brilliant verbal variations on this idea; and perhaps, since he calls his effort "a kind of critical poem," it is unfair to ask for anything more than he gives. But occasionally he introduces the name of a specific text as example; and this is when one begins to feel an uncomfortable discrepancy between the particular and the general. "This is how," he tells us, "Tolstoy's *War and Peace* and *Anna Karenina* regard emotions: as the shaping blows of raw force: the emotion we crave *and* shun." But why Tolstoy and these two novels in preference to any other? There is something missing here—the leap of critical illumination and *specific* insight—which shows that Mr. Blackmur for the moment is more interested in his dialectic than in its particular and local literary incarnation.

This leaning toward the general over the particular also betrays itself in a disconcerting vagueness and imprecision of vocabulary, especially when Mr. Blackmur reaches the point of making some crucial definition. As an example, here is how Mr. Blackmur defines his most important term in *The Lion and the Honeycomb:* "The symbolic imagination perhaps can be put as the means of bringing to significance, to order, the knowledge we have above and below the level of the mind. It is, in short, the chief mode of participation in the life common to all men at all times." This is more a shot in the dark than a definition; but to attribute its deficiencies either to carelessness or to incapacity would be a serious mistake. Rather, by using such blanket terms Mr. Blackmur is trying to avoid getting caught in his own dialectic—he is struggling to escape the ultimate treachery of language, which commits you to one position and one perspective when you are so agonizingly aware of all the others at the same time. To circumvent such treachery Mr. Blackmur defines his terms as sweepingly as possible, or he uses some emotive or metaphorical image to give the "feel" of what he means rather than any meaning which would hem him in too tightly.

Here, it seems to me, is one explanation for the celebrated increase in the difficulty of Mr. Blackmur's style which has aroused so much unfavorable comment. To be sure, Mr. Blackmur, who very early came under the stylistic influence of the later Henry James, was never an easy writer to read. Like James, his style appeared to translate his thought into what might be called ideated sensations rather than into concepts. But since Mr. Blackmur's early work was devoted to the analysis of poetic texts, this was more an advantage than a defect—and the extraordinary felicity of his criticism of poetry stems at least in part from the proximity of his style to its subject matter. Not that Mr. Blackmur was an Impressionist critic like Pater, who used his style to re-create his personal sensations and impressions of the work of art. On the contrary, Mr. Blackmur's gift is to evoke in a remarkable fashion the sensations latent in the text itself—at a remove where these sensations become articulate without ever seeming abstract.

The trouble, however, is that as Mr. Blackmur's dialectic of the literal and imaginative became that of the ideal and the actual and more and more advanced into the foreground of his criticism—as it expanded from a critical working principle into a controlling metaphysic—he has increasingly been tempted to talk about *It* rather than about its incarnations; and the sybilline quality of his prose has increased in direct proportion. Ultimately, though, it is in terms of his own metaphysics that one can make the most telling criticism of Mr. Blackmur's later style. For is this style not, in the end, simply an attempt to evade the conditions of all rational discourse? Is it not Mr. Blackmur who rightly tells us that "to think straight you must overshoot your mark"? Mr. Blackmur, somewhat inconsistently, tries desperately not to overshoot, and he pays the penalty for this *hubris*—he sometimes lands so lamentably short of his target that he fails to communicate any apprehensible meaning whatsoever.

v

In addition to the literary and critical essays, *The Lion and the Honeycomb* also contains a number of items devoted more directly to sociocultural problems. Curiously enough, these do not at all create the impression of a blurred focus which occasionally emerges from their literary companions. One feels that pure literature has become too narrow to contain the scope of Mr. Blackmur's intellectual ambitions, and that, as in the Henry James essay, he cannot resist the pressure to move out into wider and more fertile pastures even at the risk of some incongruity. But when he deals directly with larger historical problems, such as the artist as hero or the American literary expatriate, the very broadness of the horizon and the mass of example seem to impel him to rigor and specificity. All these pieces are lively, shrewd, and informative, prophetic in their ability to spot the bedrock issues (Mr. Blackmur was worrying about the effects of mass culture in the euphoria of 1945) and entirely original in their treatment of endlessly rehashed topics such as expatriation. Nothing better has ever been written on this last subject, whose American form, Mr. Blackmur argues, only dramatizes overtly the modern tension between the artist and his society; this is why the Americans James and Eliot could become such internationally representative figures.

All these articles are presages for the future; and it is no surprise to see Mr. Blackmur in his most recent work, *Anni Mirabiles,* 1921–1925—four lectures delivered at the Library of Congress in 1956—making a large-scale effort to place all of modern literature against the background of the crisis of culture that has brought it into being. This remarkable brochure,[7] which has attracted hardly any attention, is certainly one of the peaks of Mr. Blackmur's achievement and one of the great attempts to sum up and define the modern scene. Here are the things we all know about modern culture: the industrialization of intellect, the new illiteracy, the alienation of the artist, the society of the lonely crowd and the organization man, the struggle to impose private order on public chaos—or to destroy what last vestiges of public order exist in the nihilism of despair. None of this is new; nor would Mr. Blackmur, who is scrupulous in citing his authorities, claim for a moment that it is. But nowhere else has it been expressed with such synoptic power and lapidary intensity, or with such a rare combination of sympathy, personal commitment, and discriminating critical rigor.

What *is* new in this work, however, is a kind of criticism so unusual and so scarce that it is likely to go unnoticed. It may be defined as criticism by aphoristic assertion rather than by explanation, criticism as the sudden flashing phrase or sentence that pins down the essence of a life's work (and a lifetime of preoccupation with that work) in a concentrated moment of insight. This is criticism that itself has the gnomic quality of the great, late works of art and literature—works in which the artist focuses the compacted essence of his vision in its purest form. We have noted that Mr. Blackmur's early criticism excels in its capacity to transcribe and communicate the experience of poetry through ideated sensations. And now he does the same thing, not with individual texts but with the totality of a writer's production or with a major literary or cultural development—depending on his own linguistic gifts to strike off exactly the right words to transfix his subject.

The only way to approach this criticism is to read it, and then to wait and see if the shock of revelation occurs. Needless to say, it does not always come off; for the critic runs the same risk as a poet inventing a new metaphor and becomes, as it were, a poet of thought. Not all metaphors work in poetry, but when they do they are extraordinarily exciting; and when Mr. Blackmur's succeed they create the excitement of a true "critical poem." Mr. Blackmur failed when he tried to make such a "poem" out of his dialectic alone in "Between the Numen and the Moha"; but he does not fail when he relies on his concrete perceptions. And now for some examples.

D. H. Lawrence: ". . . the hysteria of direct sensual experience destroys every structure of sensibility, and there is only as much human relation as there is possible in the swoon of the blood, which is a very powerful and very destructive relation indeed."

The alienated artist: "To be either a dandy or dirty, and especially where out of keeping, is always a good role; and to be an anchorite or an oracle combines the advantages of both. You are in any case among enemies."

"In Kafka you have religious novels of rebirth where only the agony, not the birth, takes place."

"In Whitman you find the sprawl of repetition, in Pound the heap of ideographs; in either case we ourselves make the thought emerge."

Neo-movements: "The neo-classicists and the neo-humanists were alike driven to tyranny and suffered from the tyrant's characteristic privation—the lack of direct knowledge of the actual state of affairs, whether in life or in letters."

Emily Dickinson: "This is the best that could be done with the puerile marriage of the self with the self; a sensorium for the most part without the senses, it is sometimes the vision of sense itself."

These should be enough for a sampling of Mr. Blackmur's expressiveness and wit, and for his uncanny ability both to quicken response and to crystallize and clarify literary and cultural experience. As one reads and rereads *Anni Mirabiles* (the rereading is obligatory), what stands out most strongly is the quality of such sharp and striking formulations; they have the imperishable and definitive air of inscriptions carved in stone. But other things of course remain to be noted.

One such is Mr. Blackmur's disapproval of what he calls the "expressionism" of most of the literature between the wars—that is, the failure of the artist to struggle for the imposition of some sort of order on his material. "Instead, we have the apparition of the arts asserting authority in a combination of the spontaneous and the arbitrary, in pure poetry and pure expression and pure trouble. Instead of creation in honesty, we have assertion in desperation; we have a fanaticism of the accidental instead of a growth of will. The true anarchy of spirit should always show (or always *has* showed) a tory flavor." Mr. Blackmur's touchstones are accordingly Joyce, Yeats, Eliot, and Thomas Mann—the artists who have felt and assimilated the greatest amount of the reigning disorder and have made the most strenuous efforts to dominate it most rigorously in their works.

These names show that Mr. Blackmur is not on the side of any particular orthodoxy; but he is on the side of the human effort intrinsic to the order of art itself. And to stress this allegiance Mr. Blackmur now makes an intriguing substitution of the term "bourgeois humanism" for his earlier catchall "symbolic imagination." "Bourgeois humanism," he writes, "(the treasure of residual reason in live relation to the madness of the senses) is the only conscious art of the mind designed to deal with our megalopolitan mass society: it alone knows what to *do with* momentum in its new guise, and it alone knows it must be more than itself without losing itself in order to succeed." One hopes that Mr. Blackmur is right, and that there *is* some such "art of the mind" really capable of dealing with the momentum of our world. But whether such an art exists or not, the momentum makes it more than ever important to keep alive our *need* for the kind of "true" humanism defined by Mr. Blackmur in the essay on Babbitt—a humanism that would be "the median, focusing, balancing point, at the fulcrum of higher and lower, the one and the many, the intuitive and the rational, the inner and the outer, the expansive and contractive tendencies of the human imagination."

The ideal of such a "true" humanism brings us back again to Santayana, perhaps the most powerful intellectual influence among the many that Mr. Blackmur has assimilated, and in any case the one which best helps us to grasp his later evolution. It is not so much that Mr. Blackmur took from Santayana this or that idea, as that he accepted —and still accepts—Santayana's alluring image of the Life of Reason. "The Life of Reason," writes Santayana, "is the happy marriage of two elements—impulse and ideation— which if wholly divorced would reduce man to a brute or a maniac. The rational animal is generated by the union of these two monsters." [8] Mr. Blackmur has performed a great service to modern culture by indefatigably hunting down these monsters and bringing them to bay, wherever they are to be found in the jungle of modernity. But perhaps the chief value of his later essays, whatever their ostensible subject, is that they are finally dedicated to honoring the happy marriage out of which the rational animal is born.

NOTES

8. R. P. BLACKMUR: THE LATER PHASE

1. Granville Hicks, *The Great Tradition* (New York: Macmillan, 1935), p. 283.

2. Alfred Kazin, *On Native Grounds* (New York: Reynal & Hitchcock, 1942), p. 440.

3. T. S. Eliot, *Selected Essays* (New York: Harcourt, Brace, 1932), p. 247.

4. Allen Tate, *The Man of Letters in the Modern World* (New York: Meridian, 1955), pp. 211–226.

5. John Crowe Ransom, *Poems and Essays* (New York: Vintage, 1955), pp. 102–108.

6. For example: Richard Foster, "R. P. Blackmur: From Criticism to Mysticism," *The New Romantics* (Bloomington: Indiana University Press, 1962), Chap. V.

7. Published by the Reference Department of the Library of Congress, and sold only by the U.S. Government Printing Office, Washington, D.C.

8. George Santayana, *Reason in Common Sense* (New York: Collier Books, 1962), p. 18.

9 Lionel Trilling and the Conservative Imagination

The career and reputation of Lionel Trilling as a literary critic pose something of an anomaly. Not, we should hasten to add, that Mr. Trilling does not deserve all the encomiums that have been lavished on him or the considerable influence he enjoys as a spiritual guide and mentor. But Mr. Trilling is by no means the kind of critic who has dominated the American literary scene since the end of the Second World War. His concern with literature has always been broadly moral and historical—like that of his master Matthew Arnold—rather than more strictly aesthetic or formal—like the group of New Critics who sprang into prominence exactly at the time Mr. Trilling's own star was on the rise. The anomaly posed by his career is that of explaining his reputation, when the whole drift of American literary opinion seemed to be moving in the direction opposite to the one he chose to take.

Part of the answer may be found in an observation of Mr. Trilling himself about such men as John Crowe Ransom, Allen Tate, and R. P. Blackmur. It is an illusion, he writes in *The Liberal Imagination*, to believe that these critics are as free from ideology as they pretend; in reality their so-called aesthetic judgments are profoundly steeped in concealed cultural preferences and moral assumptions. This remark is perfectly just. In defending the autonomy and integrity of the work of art, the New Critics were repulsing the claims of the liberals and radicals to appropriate it for social or political ends; their influence was part of the wave of disillusionment with politics that marked the generation of the fifties. And, though Lionel Trilling approached art with overt moral and historical assumptions, the substance of what he had to say was by no means dissimilar to what the New Critics were advocating in their own way. For the pervasive disillusionment with politics was given its most sensitive, subtle, and judiciously circumspect expression in the criticism of Lionel Trilling—and this is the real answer to the anomaly of his success.

Mr. Trilling's strategy was far more elaborate than that of the New Critics and was deployed with far more finesse. Instead of pretending to immure himself in a confining aestheticism, he showed himself open to all the currents of the political and social life; but in his famous attack on "the liberal imagination" he criticized liberalism for attempting to measure the complexities of reality exclusively by a sociopolitical yardstick. Only literature, he argued, could truly cope with the intricacies of the moral life; and he recommended that politics appropriate for itself some of the suppleness of literature.

"Unless we insist that politics is imagination and mind," he declared in *The Liberal Imagination,* "we will learn that imagination and mind are politics, and of a kind we will not like." It was never made clear just how politics was supposed to metamorphose into "imagination and mind"; but phrases of this kind, turned with Mr. Trilling's consummate skill, show how perfectly he was able both to crystallize the temper of the moment and to appear to escape its limitations at the same time. For while he rejects the crudities of politics in one breath, in the very next he holds out the hope of a new politics that will incorporate all the discriminations of literature.

It is hardly necessary to say that no such latter politics has ever existed—or ever will exist. As R. P. Blackmur remarked in an acute review of *The Liberal Imagination:* "The politics of existing states is always too simple for literature; it is good only to *aggravate* literature." [1] No political ideology of any kind can compete with literature in the delicacy of its reaction to human experience. Even Mr. Trilling would agree that his favorite Edmund Burke, whom he so often quotes with approval, hardly rivals Wordsworth in the range of his responses to the French Revolution. In other words, Mr. Trilling's criticism of the liberal imagination revealed nothing that was not equally true of any politics that set itself up as a total view of human reality; and he actually criticizes politics from the point of view of art—a point of view happily free from the limiting conditions of all political action. Yet by confining his criticism to the *liberal* imagination, and not extending it to politics in general, Mr. Trilling implied that his views had immediate practical and political relevance. He thus, as it were, filled the intellectual vacuum left by the New Critics. For Mr. Trilling's readers among the erstwhile liberal and radical intelligentsia could continue to feel that they were actively engaged in the political life, while in fact they were tacitly rejecting it from the standpoint of art that the New Critics defended with less tact and more belligerency.

II

The delicate poise of *The Liberal Imagination* was thus based on an unresolved tension in Mr. Trilling's thinking between art and politics. This tension has since been resolved in his succeeding volume, *The Opposing Self*. For this latter volume of essays is a development of those aspects of Mr. Trilling's thought—aspects that were already present even in his books on Matthew Arnold and E. M. Forster—which come closest to constituting a rejection of the political imagination as a whole.

The best way to approach *The Opposing Self* is to turn to one of the key essays in *The Liberal Imagination,* the essay entitled "Art and Fortune." Here Mr. Trilling speaks of the modern will dying of its own excess; and he suggests that literature, particularly the novel, might be of great service in renovating and restoring the will to health. How can this be done? "The novel has had a long dream of virtue," Mr. Trilling answers, "in which the will, while never abating its strength and activity, comes to refuse to exercise itself upon the unworthy objects with which the social world tempts it, and either conceives its own right objects or becomes content with its own sense of its own potential force." The way for the modern will to renovate itself, according to Mr. Trilling, is to abnegate its action on the unworthy objects of the social world and attain a state of pure contemplative being; and the chosen agent for this renovation is literature.

Mr. Trilling's antipathy to the will, as we can see, is thus of long standing; and there are moments when, for all his candor, alertness, and receptivity to the historical moment, we seem to feel the "inner check" of Babbitt and More—not to mention the Nirvana of Schopenhauer—lurking ominously in the background. But in any case Mr. Trilling's essays in *The Opposing Self* are all devoted to exploring this theme of the abnegation of the will which he had broached in *The Liberal Imagination*. Indeed, he now argues that this abnegation of the will, this substitution of contemplation for an active grappling with social reality, is an important key to modern culture.

The modern self, he writes in the preface to *The Opposing Self*, has an intense and adverse imagination of the culture in which it exists. But this opposition of the modern self to culture takes a very special form. "What virtually every writer of the modern period conceives," he states, is "the experience of art projected into the activity and totality of life as the ideal form of the moral life." Dissatisfied with its habitual life in culture, the modern "opposing self" seeks to transcend culture's moral burdens in the free play of imagination and desire; and this, Mr. Trilling adds, "makes, I believe, a new idea in the world."

One may doubt whether all this is as new as Mr. Trilling would like to think. The Hellenistic self of the Alexandrian era and the Christian self of the first centuries after Christ were also, one suspects, "opposing selves" by Mr. Trilling's standard. But he insists, nonetheless, that the modern self has given birth to a new cultural mutation; and to prove the point he invokes the formidable authority of Hegel. Hegel, he writes, "understood in a remarkable way what he believed to be a new phenomenon of culture."

> This is the bringing into play in the moral life of a new category of judgment, the category of quality. Not merely the deed itself, he said, is now submitted to judgment, but also the personal quality of the doer of the deed. . . . For Hegel, art is the activity of man in which spirit expresses itself not only as utility, not only according to law, but as grace, as transcendence, as manner and style. He brought together the moral and aesthetic judgment. He did this not in the old way of making morality the criterion of the aesthetic: on the contrary, he made the aesthetic the criterion of the moral.

It is unfortunate that Mr. Trilling decided to venture into such deep philosophical waters because, strictly speaking, the ideas he so generously attributes to Hegel are entirely of his own devising.[2] Hegel, it may flatly be asserted, never made the aesthetic the criterion of the moral; and if Mr. Trilling thinks he did, then he should read Hegel's criticism of Friedrich Schlegel and Romantic irony in the lectures on aesthetics.[3] From the reference to style and grace as providing a standard from which law and utility may be judged, it is possible to infer that Mr. Trilling is here confusing Hegel with a recollection of Schiller's *Letters on the Aesthetic Education of Mankind;* but these questions of attribution and accuracy are of course picayune. What is important is to see that Mr. Trilling *himself* now wishes to make "the aesthetic the criterion of the moral," just as previously, in *The Liberal Imagination,* he had made the aesthetic the criterion of the political. This is the point, however, at which it is necessary to tread very cautiously—at least as cautiously as Kant, for instance, who (in *The Critique of Judgment*) also viewed art as a projection into nature of the ideal form of the moral life, but who hastened to add that this ideal was realized *only* in the state of aesthetic apprehension, or, more completely, in that of aesthetic creation.

For it is one thing to make the experience of art—the experience of pleasure and beauty, of harmony and reconciliation—the *ideal* form of moral life. It is quite another to attribute the virtues of this aesthetic ideal to concrete social behavior which, quite independently of any relationship with art, merely exhibits an abeyance or absence of the will. In other words, it is of the utmost importance not to confuse the boundaries of the ideal and the real, the aesthetic and the social; not to endow social passivity and quietism *as such* with the halo of aesthetic transcendence. Mr. Trilling regrettably does not always keep this boundary well defined, and he tends occasionally to identify all forms of being in which the will is absent or quiescent with the ideal values of the aesthetic attitude. As we shall see, this leads him, by a devious path, to end up in justifying a good many of the degrading objects of the social world which the will had once been required to shun and to despise.

III

The best essay in *The Opposing Self,* as might be expected, is the one in which Mr. Trilling portrays the true transcendence of the artist at its highest peak of aspiration and achievement. This is done in his admirable study of Keats's letters, which ranks with the essay on *The Princess Cassamassima* among the finest performances of contemporary criticism. The central purpose of Mr. Trilling's article is to show how Keats's self, while accepting the immitigable reality of evil, was yet capable of affirming a faith in life through aesthetic transcendence. The point is very force-fully made in Mr. Trilling's gloss on the famous conclu-sion to *The Ode on a Grecian Urn.*

When Keats wrote that "Beauty is truth, truth beauty" he was not evading issues but confronting them. What he meant, according to Mr. Trilling, "is that a great poet (e.g., Shakespeare) looks at human life, sees the terrible truth of its evil, but sees it so intensely that it becomes an element of the beauty which is created by his act of per-ception. . . . Keats's statement is an accurate description of the response to evil or ugliness which tragedy makes: the matter of tragedy is ugly or painful truth seen as beauty." By transcending the reality of evil in this fash-ion, Keats affirmed "the creativity of the self that opposes circumstance, the self that is imagination and desire, that, like Adam, assigns names and values to things, and can realize what it envisions." (This last, presumably, means to "realize" artistically.)

What Mr. Trilling so rightly admires in Keats is the courage and resilience of the self, the gallantry of the spirit accepting the challenge of circumstance and the world's evil and asserting its heroic resolution nonetheless. This spirit, according to Mr. Trilling, is no longer of our time. "We have lost the *mystique* of the self." This mystique does not consist in the struggle of the will against fate, but rather in the transcendence of the will by a self that feels capable of rising superior to any onslaught. "Shakespeare suggested the only salvation that Keats found it possible to conceive, the tragic salvation, the soul accepting the fate that defines it." Certainly when man is faced with the problem of ultimate evil, the Keatsian heroism of accept-ance may be seen as the finest flower of the cultivation of the self. But not every evil is ultimate, not every accept-ance is heroic; and while there is no need to stress this point for Mr. Trilling, with his acute sense of moral nuance, the fact remains that he does not always keep it in mind in developing his arguments.

As an example we may take the wide-ranging essay on "Wordsworth and the Rabbis." This title is a pretty *jeu d'esprit* that Mr. Trilling works out with graceful ingenuity; and there is no reason to take it more seriously than he does himself. Wordsworth has as much (or as little) to do with the rabbis as with the lamas, the fakirs, the gurus, or the bonzes. What Mr. Trilling wishes to bring out by this comparison is the "sentiment of being" in Wordsworth's poetry, a sentiment very close to the natural piety shared by disciples of all the great spiritual religions.

This sentiment of being is perfectly expressed in the lines from *Tintern Abbey* (though Mr. Trilling does not use this passage himself), where Wordsworth speaks of

> that serene and blessed mood,
> In which the affections gently lead us on,—
> Until, the breath of this corporeal frame
> And even the motion of our human blood
> Almost suspended, we are laid asleep
> In body, and become a living soul:
> While with an eye made quiet by the power
> Of Harmony, and the deep power of joy,
> We see into the life of things.

Mr. Trilling believes that Wordsworth's loss of contemporary reputation, his relegation to the status of a school classic, is caused by the preference of our time for the apocalyptic and the charismatic, our inability to experience the sense of being illustrated by these lines as anything but alien and repugnant. "The predilection for the powerful, the fierce, the assertive, the personally militant is very strong in our culture," he writes. Wordsworth's sentiment of being is thus foreign to our sensibility.

To prove this point Mr. Trilling refers to T. S. Eliot's *The Cocktail Party*—specifically, to the scene in which Eliot depicts the way of life of the "common routine" as contrasted with that of the saint or the martyr. Many critics have objected that Eliot's picture of the common routine is far from appealing—that it is, in fact, perhaps even more terrifying than the way of martyrdom. There is no reason, of course, for a Christian like Eliot to glorify ordinary earthly existence. But in the context of his evident desire to make the resolution of the common routine a plausible one, his failure to brighten up its colors a bit more is unquestionably an aesthetic defect. Mr. Trilling attributes this weakness in the play to our modern insensitivity to the values of the nonassertive, which he now associates both with Wordsworth's "sentiment of being" and with "the common routine" to which Eliot had failed to do justice. He argues that even the way of martyrdom is made factitious by Eliot's inability to portray the simple joys of the common routine. And Mr. Trilling castigates this "system of feeling which sets very little store by—which, indeed, denies the possibility of—the 'beatitude' which Wordsworth thought was the birthright of every human soul."

Here Mr. Trilling's covert passage between two very different levels of experience becomes apparent. Whatever one may say about the feelings depicted in the lines from *Tintern Abbey*, it is obvious that they have little to do with the routine trivialities of modern middle-class life. Wordsworth himself, as Mr. Trilling is surely aware, felt his sentiment of being in opposition to the life of the common routine, or at least to the routine of the urban middle class of his time (and we can be sure he would have felt the same about our time). He turns to images of nature that revive his sentiment of being " 'mid the din of towns and cities" and "In darkness and amid the many shapes/ Of joyless daylight; when the fretful stir/ Unprofitable and the fever of the world/ Have hung upon the beatings of my heart."

In other words, by lumping Wordsworth's "beatitude" with Eliot's "the common routine," Mr. Trilling is being false to the spirit of Wordsworth; but even more, he is trying to make us believe that a passive acceptance of social convention is on the same level of spiritual dignity as the quasi-mystic experience of Wordsworth. The only element the two have in common is that of passivity, the suspension of the will. And while the sentiment of being of Wordsworth or Keats may truly be called a projection of the experience of art as the ideal form of the moral life, it is difficult to see how the same may be said of a simple acquiescence in the common urban routine.

The same type of illegitimate identification between two quite different kinds of being—to use Mr. Trilling's own criterion—comes out even more sharply at the conclusion of the Wordsworth essay. At this point Mr. Trilling is maintaining that "again and again in our literature, at its most apocalyptic and intense, we find the impulse to create figures who are intended to suggest that life is justified in its elemental biological simplicity." And he then goes on to give a list of such creations—D. H. Lawrence's primitives, Dreiser's Jennie Gerhardt and Mrs. Griffiths, Hemingway's waiters, Faulkner's Negroes and idiot boys. According to Mr. Trilling, all these figures show the tendency of our literature to "depict the will seeking its own negation—or, rather, seeking its own affirmation by its rejection of the aims which the world sets before it and by turning its energies upon itself in self-realization."

But what, one cannot help asking, has the biological *justification* of life to do with the will seeking its own negation? And what have these examples to do with anything that can remotely be called self-realization? The transcendence of the will by the artist (or by the ascetic and the saint) is self-realization; but this idea carries with it the implication of conscious purpose, self-dedication, discipline, struggle—it implies, in short, having a will to surrender. From Mr. Trilling's examples it is clear that he makes no distinction between such self-realization and a blind and dumb submission to destiny—a condition of being that never reaches a level on which the will may properly be spoken of. Here, too, Mr. Trilling is assigning the ideal values of the aesthetic attitude to a condition of being with which it has in common only an absence of will.

This tendency of Mr. Trilling's thought, working with another set of categories, may also be observed in his provocative essay on "William Dean Howells and the Roots of Modern Taste." The announced intention of this piece is the laudable one of removing Howells from the history of American culture and giving him a place in literature. All too many writers belong in the first category, and Mr. Trilling thinks that Howells deserves a better fate. No modern critic excels Mr. Trilling in giving fresh and perceptive readings of novels; and one would have expected him to do for Howells what he did for *The Princess Cassamassima* and the novels of E. M. Forster. But, instead of concerning himself at length with Howells's creations, Mr. Trilling adopts the same oblique tactic as in his Wordsworth essay. He argues that our modern apocalyptic and charismatic culture, addicted to power-worship and the deification of evil, is incapable of justly evaluating the sunlit merits of Howells.[4] And Mr. Trilling goes on to talk not about Howells but about the roots of modern taste, using some remarks made by Henry James as indices to what disqualifies us from appreciating Howells.

Modern taste is dominated by an antipathy to what Mr. Trilling calls "the conditioned" and favors what he calls "pure spirit" (whose agent and instrument is the will). The conditions to which we moderns respond, he says, "are the ones which we ourselves make, or over which we have control, which is to say conditions as they are virtually spirit, as they deny the idea of the conditioned. Somewhere in our mental constitution is the demand for life as pure spirit." Now Mr. Trilling contends, roughly, that our longing for pure spirit has made us blind to such aspects of the conditioned as the family and our class status, and has caused us to deprecate such necessary matters as those which Howells listed among possible subjects for a novelist—"the family budget, nagging wives, daughters who want to marry fools, and the difficulties of deciding whom to invite to dinner."

Our dislike of the conditioned also accounts for our passion for form and artifice in literature, since the triumph of form is primarily that of spirit imposing its own conditions. And then, after having identified the conditioned in Howells with the most commonplace concerns of civil life ("for Howells the center of reality was the family life of the middle class"), Mr. Trilling clinches his argument in the following startling fashion: "The knowledge of the antagonism between spirit and the conditioned—it is Donne's, it is Pascal's, it is Tolstoi's—may in literature be a cause of great delight because it is so rare and difficult; beside it the knowledge of pure spirit is comparatively easy."

In the light of what Mr. Trilling has told us about

Howells's sense of "the conditioned," this invocation of Donne, Pascal, and Tolstoy is unexpected to say the least. What has Howells to do with Donne's conflict between a skeptical sensuality and a passionate religiosity? With Pascal's conflict between the impasses of reason and the eternal silence of the infinite spaces? With Tolstoy's titanic search for the meaning of history, and his anguished struggle to reconcile the abundance of life with the gnawing awareness of physical death?

It is Mr. Trilling himself who has called our attention to the importance of qualities of being; and his own attempt to wipe out the differences between the social trivia of Howells and the tragic sense of the conditioned in Donne, Pascal, and Tolstoy is thus all the more disturbing and disconcerting. Once again Mr. Trilling's antagonism to the will has led him to assign the same spiritual significance to totally diverse levels on which "the conditioned" may enter into a relationship with "pure spirit." And the result is that the will, instead of transcending the social world and its particular aims, now finds itself enjoined to treat the most casual conventions of the family life of the middle class as the sacrosanct conditions of life itself.

IV

The remaining essays in *The Opposing Self* are dominated either by the idea of transcendence and negation of the will in a quasi-religious sense (Dickens, Flaubert), or by the dialectic of pure spirit and the conditioned turning up in an explicit or implicit form (James, Tolstoy, Orwell, Jane Austen). Mr. Trilling shows remarkable skill in working these diverse subjects around to conform to his ideas. And while one may feel that he too often and too readily finds what he is looking for, with the aid of the convenient ambiguities of such words as "culture" and "self," all these studies are nonetheless valuable and suggestive contributions. Taken as a whole, however, the total impression they create serves to reinforce Mr. Trilling's preference for stability and stasis over the restless agitations of pure spirit. In his brilliant interpretation of *Mansfield Park,* which one does not have to agree with to admire, Mr. Trilling speaks of the antivital element in the novel, the self-mockery of spirit, the choice of the sanctions of principle over the exigencies of consciousness. And it is this facet of the novel, lovingly caricatured in the somnolent and almost inanimate figure of Lady Bertram, that he says "speaks to our secret inexpressible hopes." It speaks, at any rate, to the hopes of Mr. Trilling; and in a language considerably different from the one we had heard in *The Liberal Imagination.*

In his earlier book Mr. Trilling had attacked the tyranny of the will in wishing to impose its aims on other modes of apprehending reality. Naturally, in the course of doing so, Mr. Trilling stressed art's tragic sense of the conditioned nature of life and of the ultimate insolubility of most human dilemmas. But this was still done in the name of freedom—in the name of the artist's freedom to transcend the concerns of the will and in the name of what Mr. Trilling called "the lively sense of contingency and possibility, and of those exceptions to the rule which may be the beginning of the end of the rule." On the literary level this concern for freedom appeared also in Mr. Trilling's defense of plot, fable, and form in the novel against the realistic prejudices of liberal critics. Authorial minds playing with reality, Mr. Trilling wrote, were for him "the great and strangely effective symbols of liberty operating in a world of necessity."

Mr. Trilling, however, is no longer concerned to defend this authorial freedom from the hampering clogs of realism; he now feels that his urgent task is to defend not freedom but the virtues of acknowledging necessity. For he seems to have acquired an uneasy sense that the spirit of man is ready to fly off at any moment to some distant goal "pinnacled dim in the intense inane"; and for man's own protection Mr. Trilling keeps recalling him to his earthbound condition. Writing of Howells's preference for the "smiling aspects of life," Mr. Trilling concedes that these latter may not be very exciting; but at least, he adds, they will serve "to bind us to the earth, to prevent our being seduced by the godhead of disintegration."

No doubt this anxiety about disintegration is linked to Mr. Trilling's puzzling inability to conceive of the will (pure spirit) except in terms of an apocalypse. Even in *The Liberal Imagination* he had already defined the modern idea of "progress" as being in reality the extinction of history; and in his intellectual world no alternative now seems left but total acceptance or total disintegration. It is one of the paradoxes of his position that his aversion to the apocalyptic and charismatic, instead of causing him to reprobate extremism in any form, should simply have driven him to adopt the alternative extreme himself.

From a critic of the liberal imagination, then, Mr. Trilling has evolved into one of the least belligerent and most persuasive spokesmen of the conservative imagination. For, on the plane of the imagination, the distinction between liberal and conservative—as Karl Mannheim has explained in his *Ideology and Utopia*—pivots precisely on this feeling for the conditioned. "The deepest driving force of the liberal ideas of the Enlightenment," Mannheim writes, "lay in the fact that it appealed to the free will and kept alive the feeling of being indeterminate and unconditioned. . . . And if one wishes to formulate the central achievement of conservatism in a single sentence, it could be said that in conscious contrast to the liberal outlook, it gave positive emphasis to the notion of the determinateness of our outlook and behavior." [5] However he may have misread Hegel, Mr. Trilling's flair did not betray him when he thought to find sustenance in Hegel's work. For Hegel is the philosopher who, to quote Mannheim again, "set up against the liberal idea a conservative counterpart"; in Hegel, "reality, the 'here and now,' is no longer experienced as an 'evil' reality but as the embodiment of the highest value and meanings." [6]

Some light on this evolution, which hardly seems to have been noticed, may perhaps be cast by a quick look at Mr. Trilling's brochure on *Freud and the Crisis of Our Culture*. Freud has generally been considered a radical and disintegrating influence, but it is striking to see how Mr. Trilling singles out for special praise one of the few Freudian ideas which have been called "reactionary." Man, Freud contended, is biologically determined; he is not simply a creature of cultural conditioning; and Mr. Trilling praises this notion because, if we refuse to accept it, then "there is no revision of the nature of man that we cannot hope to bring about." Far from being reactionary, Mr. Trilling considers Freud's position "liberating" because "it suggests that there is a residue of human quality beyond the reach of cultural control, and that this residue of human quality, elemental as it may be, serves to bring culture itself under criticism and keeps it from being absolute."

One can sympathize with Mr. Trilling's revulsion against the idea of man as infinitely malleable and helplessly exposed to the "conditioning" imposed by the brave new world of 1984; but this is no reason to locate the ideas of freedom and liberation in stasis, immutability, and barely conscious biological existence. For the problem still remains of understanding how immutable biological determination can be a root of *freedom,* and how purely biological attributes can "criticize" culture and exhibit "human quality" without the intervention of some more positively human spiritual force. The curious concatenation of stasis and freedom in Mr. Trilling's thought thus very probably has a Freudian source; and one suspects that Freud's sympathy for socialism, his battle against sexual obscurantism, and his general aura of radicalism, may well have enabled Mr. Trilling to adopt an essentially conservative position under Freud's aegis without feeling it as self-betrayal.

The weakness of the liberal imagination, as Mr. Trilling shows in his book of that title, is that it views the realm of the ultimate, the eternal, and the immitigable in the perspective of the will. But we may now retort that the weakness of the conservative imagination lies in imposing its sense of the ultimate conditioned nature of life on areas where the will may fruitfully intervene. One of the great merits of *The Liberal Imagination* was that it criticized the illegitimate ravages of the will without openly impugning its efficacy or necessity in its proper realm; but in adopting the positive standpoint of the conservative imagination, Mr. Trilling has taken over its weakness as well as its strength. And it is to bring out this weakness that we have emphasized so strongly those passages in which Mr. Trilling seems to have yielded too easily to this congenital conservative temptation. For it would be a great pity indeed if Mr. Trilling were to use his scrupulous sensitivity, his lucid and ingratiating style, and his considerable moral authority to encourage this all-too-prevalent failing of the conservative imagination. And one cannot help but feel that, if he continues to do so, he will unwittingly promote what he himself characterizes, in the Howells essay, as "a debilitation of the American psychic tone, the diminution of moral tension."

Howells had already noticed, at the end of the nineteenth century, "the displacement of doctrine and moral strenuousness by a concern with 'social adjustment' and the amelioration of boredom"; and Mr. Trilling refers to David Riesman's *The Lonely Crowd* as proof that this process has by no means slackened in our own time. The society of *The Lonely Crowd,* however, is hardly threatened by the godhead of disintegration—at any rate, not so far as that godhead takes the form of pure, free, and independent spirit striving to impose its own conditions on life. The real danger to such a society surely does not arise from an excess of pure spirit; it is far more likely to stem from a submissive acceptance of the conditioned in the form of social pressure and convention.

When Mr. Trilling defended art and the tragic sense of the conditioned in *The Liberal Imagination,* he performed a distinct service to American culture. These values always need defenders against the overwhelming predominance in American life of a shortsighted optimism and utilitarianism. But in defending the conditioned on the level of middle-class values, and in endowing the torpid acceptance of these values with the dignity of aesthetic transcendence, Mr. Trilling is merely augmenting the already frightening momentum making for conformism and the debilitation of moral tension. The presence of spirit and will has always carried with it the danger of disintegration; but the absence of these qualities inevitably carries with it the far more immediate danger of moral and cultural stultification.

Indeed, if we are to judge from a little essay on Edith

Wharton called "The Morality of Inertia," which appears in Mr. Trilling's most recent volume, *A Gathering of Fugitives,* it may well be that he is becoming uneasily aware of this danger in his position. It would be wrong to say that such a morality of inertia was explicitly advocated all through *The Opposing Self*—or at least, if such an assertion were not literally mistaken, it would yet be unforgivably heavyhanded. Still, Lady Bertram comes uncomfortably close to symbolizing such a morality; and Mr. Trilling, as we have tried to show, did not pay sufficient attention to the moral and qualitative difference between inertia and tragic acceptance. It is thus only fair to cite what he now has to say.

"The morality of inertia," he writes, "of the dull, unthinking round of duties, may, and often does, yield the immorality of inertia; the example that will most readily occur is that of the good simple people, so true to their family responsibilities, who gave no thought to the concentration camps in whose shadow they lived. No: the morality of inertia is not to be praised, but it must be recognized." To which one can only say "Amen!"—with the reminder that more than biological determination has always been needed for the immorality of inertia to be conquered and surpassed.

NOTES

9. LIONEL TRILLING AND THE CONSERVATIVE IMAGINATION

1. R. P. Blackmur, *The Lion and the Honeycomb* (New York: Harcourt, Brace, 1955), p. 41.

2. Mr. Trilling cites no evidence for his contention about Hegel except a reference to a passage in the fourth part of the *Philosophy of History*. This passage turns out to deal with the German barbarians who invaded the Roman Empire and to whom Hegel attributes a quality that he calls *Gemüth*. This latter is a common German word meaning, roughly, the emotional temper of a man or a group. Hegel, however, gives it a special definition. "Character is a particular form of the will," he writes, "and of the interests that manifest themselves through the will. *Gemüthlichkeit*, however, has no particular aims, such as riches, honors, and the like; in fact, it does not concern itself with any worldly conditions of wealth, prestige, etc., but with the entire condition of the soul—a general sense of enjoyment."

Mr. Trilling is quite captivated with this idea of *Gemüth*—no doubt because it seemed to furnish a term for expressing the condition of the will that he had tried to define in "Art and Fortune." But this should not have led him to pretend that Hegel's remarks about the German barbarians refer to the relation of the modern self to culture since the French Revolution.

Hegel clearly is not talking about the "modern self" in Mr. Trilling's sense—unless we assume that nothing significant happened to culture between the *Völkerwanderung* and the French Revolution. Moreover, even if we overlook this anachronism, Hegel's text does not bear out Mr. Trilling's interpretation. "*Gemüth*," Hegel also writes, in a passage that Mr. Trilling fails to cite, "in the abstract is stupidity, and so we see in the original condition of the Germans a barbaric stupidity, confusion and in-determinacy." Far from making *Gemüth* the basis of a new cate-gory of cultural judgment, Hegel regards it as an empty form of infantile self-enjoyment and self-preoccupation. In his view, it only became valuable after having assimilated the objective content of Greco-Roman culture preserved by the Catholic Church. G. W. F. Hegel, *Werke,* Jubilaumsausgabe, ed. by H. Glockner (Stuttgart, 1927–1930), Vol. II, pp. 447–449.

3. *Ibid.,* Vol. XII, pp. 100–105.

4. In this connection, it may be apposite to cite a critic writing in the halcyon days of 1912, and by no means unfriendly to Howells.

"Instead of demonstrating that life was interesting," John Macy says, "that the commonplace is uncommonly interesting if you get under it and understand it, *A Modern Instance* demon-strates with fine precision that life is not interesting to the people that live it and that the commonplace is just as commonplace as the romantic had always supposed it to be." John Macy, *The Spirit of American Literature* (New York: Modern Library, n.d.), p. 284.

It would seem that times have not changed as much as Mr. Trilling would have us believe!

5. Karl Mannheim, *Ideology and Utopia* (New York: Harvest, Har-court, Brace, n.d.), p. 229.

6. *Ibid.,* p. 232.

Index